HOUSING ISSUES, LAWS AND PROGRAM

AMERICA'S FORECLOSURE CRISIS

CAUSES AND RESPONSES

Housing Issues, Laws and Program

Additional books in this series can be found on Nova's website
under the Series tab.

Additional E-books in this series can be found on Nova's website
under the E-book tab.

Economic Issues, Problems and Perspectives

Additional books in this series can be found on Nova's website
under the Series tab.

Additional E-books in this series can be found on Nova's website
under the E-book tab.

HOUSING ISSUES, LAWS AND PROGRAM

AMERICA'S FORECLOSURE CRISIS

CAUSES AND RESPONSES

RUSSELL BURNS
AND
ROY A. FOSTER
EDITORS

Nova Science Publishers, Inc.
New York

For permission to use material from this book please contact us:
Telephone 631-231-7269; Fax 631-231-8175
Web Site: http://www.novapublishers.com

Library of Congress Cataloging-in-Publication Data

America's foreclosure crisis : causes and responses / editors, Russell Burns and Roy A. Foster.
p. cm.
Includes index.
ISBN 978-1-61942-271-1 (hardcover)
1. Foreclosure--United States. 2. Mortgages--United States. I. Burns, Russell. II. Foster, Roy A.
KF697.F6A945 2011
346.7304'364--dc23
2011045800

Published by Nova Science Publishers, Inc. † New York

CONTENTS

PREFACE

The problems in the mortgage market are routinely referred to as a "foreclosure crisis" because the level of defaults and foreclosures greatly exceed previous peak levels in the post-war era and, as a result, have drawn comparisons to the levels of distress experienced in the Great Depression. This book contains a review of the academic literature and industry press on the root causes of the current foreclosure crisis, data and analysis of trends in the market, and policy responses and recommended actions to mitigate the current crisis and help prevent similar crises from occurring in the future.

Chapter 1 - This study of the root causes of the current extremely high levels of defaults and foreclosures among residential mortgages represents the final report to Congress by the Secretary of the Department of Housing and Urban Development (HUD) pursuant to Section 1517 of the Housing and Economic Recovery Act (HERA) of 2008 (P.L. 110-289). The problems in the mortgage market are routinely referred to as a "foreclosure crisis" because the level of defaults and foreclosures greatly exceed previous peak levels in the post-war era and, as a result, have drawn comparisons to the levels of distress experienced in the Great Depression. This report contains a review of the academic literature and industry press on the root causes of the current foreclosure crisis, data and analysis of trends in the market, and policy responses and recommended actions to mitigate the current crisis and help prevent similar crises from occurring in the future.

Chapter 2 - Mortgage servicers—entities that manage home mortgage loans—halted foreclosures throughout the country in September 2010, finding that documents required to be provided to courts in some states may have been improperly signed or notarized. In addition, academics and court cases are raising questions over whether foreclosures are being brought properly because of concerns over how loans were transferred into mortgage-backed securities (MBS). GAO was asked to examine (1) the extent to which federal laws address mortgage servicers' foreclosure procedures and federal agencies' past oversight, (2) federal agencies' current oversight and future oversight plans, and (3) the potential impact of these issues on involved parties. GAO reviewed federal laws, regulations, exam guidance, agency documents, and studies, and conducted interviews with federal agencies, mortgage industry associations, investor groups, consumer advocacy groups, and legal academics.

Chapter 3 - Borrowers who used alternative mortgages to finance homes during the housing boom have experienced rising foreclosure rates as housing markets have declined. Some types of alternative mortgages may have exacerbated price declines and damaged the finances of consumers and lenders. The use of mortgages with adjustable rates, zero down payment, interest-only, or negative amortization features raise economic risk compared to traditional mortgages. Because some borrowers and lenders did not adequately evaluate these risks, housing finance markets have been hit with significant losses and financial markets have been in turmoil. Policymakers have responded with a housing rescue package (H.R. 3221/P.L. 110-289). They have also authorized the Department of Treasury to institute a Troubles Asset Relief Program (TARP) to buy bad debts from banks (H.R. 1424 / P.L. 110-343).

Chapter 4 - The introduction of legislation such as H.R. 1106, the Helping Families Save Their Homes Act of 2009 (Representative John Conyers Jr. et. al.) serve as evidence of the concern in the 111th Congress over recent foreclosure activity. This report describes and analyzes foreclosure and related issues generated by the behavior of U.S. housing and mortgage markets.

Specifically, this report explains the foreclosure process, both from the point of view of a traditional financial lending institution, and from the viewpoint of securitization when loans are sold in secondary markets. The decision by the servicer to foreclose is also discussed, as are foreclosure data sources and recent foreclosure trends. Finally, this report examines estimates of average foreclosure costs and relevant computational issues.

In: America's Foreclosure Crisis
Editors: Russell Burns and Roy A. Foster

ISBN: 978-161942- 271-1

Chapter 1

REPORT TO CONGRESS ON THE ROOT CAUSES OF THE FORECLOSURE CRISIS*

United States Department of Housing and Urban Development

FOREWORD

Section 1517 of the Housing and Economic Recovery Act of 2008 (P.L. 110-289) mandated preliminary and final reports to Congress on the root causes of the foreclosure crisis. This final report responds to that mandate by analyzing data and trends in the residential housing market and reviewing the academic literature and industry press on the root causes of the current foreclosure crisis. The report also provides a review of policy responses and recommended actions to mitigate the crisis and help prevent similar crises from occurring in the future.

As we move forward, better understanding of the root causes of this crisis will support informed choices among the many policy options available to address the laws and institutions that will govern the origination of residential mortgages in the future. As we have seen from the current crisis, successful outcomes from these policy debates are critical to the health of the overall economy and to the well-being of American families.

Raphael W. Bostic, Ph.D.
Assistant Secretary for Policy
Development and Research

* This is an edited, reformatted and augmented version of the United States Department of Housing and Urban Development, Office of Policy Development and Research Publication, dated January 2010.
Based on a draft report prepared by Christopher E. Herbert and William C. Apgar, Jr., of Abt Associates Inc. under contract with the Office of Policy Development and Research of the U.S. Department of Housing and Urban Development.

EXECUTIVE SUMMARY

This study of the root causes of the current extremely high levels of defaults and foreclosures among residential mortgages represents the final report to Congress by the Secretary of the Department of Housing and Urban Development (HUD) pursuant to Section 1517 of the Housing and Economic Recovery Act (HERA) of 2008 (P.L. 110-289). The problems in the mortgage market are routinely referred to as a "foreclosure crisis" because the level of defaults and foreclosures greatly exceed previous peak levels in the post-war era and, as a result, have drawn comparisons to the levels of distress experienced in the Great Depression. This report contains a review of the academic literature and industry press on the root causes of the current foreclosure crisis, data and analysis of trends in the market, and policy responses and recommended actions to mitigate the current crisis and help prevent similar crises from occurring in the future.

Trends in Delinquencies and Foreclosures

To help define the nature of the foreclosure crisis, the report begins by presenting basic information on trends in mortgage delinquencies and foreclosure starts, relying largely on data from the Mortgage Bankers Association *National Delinquency Survey*. According to this survey, between late 2006 and mid-2007, the share of loans that were seriously delinquent or beginning the foreclosure process reached their highest levels since the survey was begun in the late 1970s. Since then, these rates have continued to rise sharply, and, by mid-2008, had more than doubled the previous record highs. Most of the initial increase in foreclosures was driven by subprime loans, both due to the fact that these inherently risky loans had come to account for a much larger share of the mortgage market in recent years and because the foreclosure rates among these loans were rising rapidly. In addition, "Alt-A" loans, another fast-growing segment of the market, began experiencing higher delinquency and foreclosure rates.[1] In both the subprime and Alt-A market segments, foreclosures have grown most rapidly among adjustable-rate loans. But, as the economy deteriorated in 2008 and into 2009, the level of foreclosures among prime fixed-rate loans also rose, further exacerbating the crisis.

Given the magnitude of this crisis, it is perhaps not surprising that the increase in foreclosures is evident across the country, affecting most areas. Nonetheless, there are significant differences in the extent of the foreclosure crisis across market areas. The report analyzes the regional patterns comparing the most recent year's foreclosure start rates and increases in foreclosure start rates since the start of the crisis by state.

Consistent with popular press accounts, one group of states stands out as having been most severely impacted by the crisis—these states not only had the highest rates of foreclosure starts in 2008, they also experienced the highest increase in foreclosure starts since 2005. This group has been referred to in the press as the "sand states" as it includes Arizona, California, Florida, and Nevada. The sand states all had a high incidence of high-cost (subprime) lending in 2006, coupled with a much larger run-up in home prices before the crisis hit. Perhaps because of this robust house price growth, these states enjoyed some of the lowest foreclosure start rates in the nation in 2005. However, the fall in house prices from

2005 to 2008 was most dramatic in the sand states. Further exacerbating problems in these four states has been a sharp rise in unemployment since 2005, with unemployment rates rising from below the national average to among the highest rates in the country.

It is noteworthy to contrast the experience of the sand states with a second group of states that were also severely impacted by the crisis, but in a different way. This second grouping comprises states that had relatively high foreclosure rates even before the crisis began due to weaknesses in local economies, although the gain in foreclosure rates was less dramatic than in the sand states. Prominent among these states are the industrial states from the Midwest, including Illinois, Indiana, Michigan, and Ohio. House prices fell in these states after 2005, but not by as much as in states that experienced higher price increases prior to the crisis. In 2005, the industrial states had much higher unemployment rates than other states. Since 2005, economic conditions have deteriorated further, with falling housing prices and rising unemployment contributing to foreclosure rates in 2008 and 2009 nearly as high as those in the sand states.

Literature Review

The literature review begins by assessing the factors that have most commonly been associated with rising delinquencies and foreclosures in the past. There is a rich economics literature examining the cause of mortgage foreclosures, generally referred to as "default" in the literature.[2] Since the 1980s, this literature has been dominated by an option-based theory of mortgage default, where the mortgage contract is viewed as giving homeowners an option to "put" the home back to lenders by defaulting on their mortgage.[3] In an option-theoretic view, the primary factor driving defaults is the value of the home relative to the value of the outstanding mortgage; when the home value falls substantially below the mortgage debt, owners are better off by ceding the home to the lender (a so-called "ruthless" default). However, while a lack of equity in a home is strongly associated with foreclosures, most borrowers become delinquent due to a change in their financial circumstances that makes them no longer able to meet their monthly mortgage obligations. These so called "trigger events" commonly include job loss or other income curtailment, health problems, or divorce. As a result, foreclosures are most accurately thought of as being driven by a two-stage process: first a trigger event reduces the borrower's financial liquidity, and then a lack of home equity makes it impossible for the borrower to either sell their home to meet their mortgage obligation or refinance into a mortgage that is affordable given their change in financial circumstances. In this view, a lack of home equity is an important determinant of foreclosures as it precludes other means that borrowers can take to resolve an inability to meet their mortgage obligations, but defaults are most commonly triggered by some other event that makes borrowers financially illiquid.

But, while softening housing prices were clearly an important precipitating factor in the present crisis, it seems clear from the literature that the sharp rise in mortgage delinquencies and foreclosures is fundamentally the result of rapid growth in loans with a high risk of default—due both to the terms of these loans and to loosening underwriting controls and standards.[4] Mortgage industry participants appear to have been drawn to encourage borrowers to take on these riskier loans due to the high profits associated with originating these loans and packaging them for sale to investors. While systematic information on borrowers' motivations in obtaining these loans is not available, existing evidence suggests that some borrowers did not understand the true costs and risks of these loans while others were willing to take on these risks to tap accumulated home equity or to obtain larger homes.

The current crisis is unusual in that general economic weakness did not play a significant role in producing delinquencies and foreclosures in most market areas—at least not initially. Instead, it was a slowdown in house price growth that removed the primary safety valve for the high volume of unaffordable mortgages that had been made. These loans had allowed borrowers to take advantage of robust house price growth to avoid foreclosure by refinancing into a new loan or selling the property for a profit. In fact, several studies have found an association between increases in high-cost lending that enabled borrowers to obtain larger mortgages than they could otherwise afford and more rapid house price growth than would be predicted by other fundamental measures of housing demand. Thus, the slowdown and then decline in house price growth that precipitated the foreclosure crisis is itself a product of the inevitable end of the ability of lenders to keep extending more credit to borrowers.

Given the significant role that an increase in risky lending appears to have played in causing this crisis, a key question is what were the factors that made it possible for the mortgage market to make so many risky loans in recent years? McCoy and Renuart (2008) outline a variety of developments in the mortgage markets during the 1980s and 1990s that helped set the stage for the rapid growth of subprime lending after 2003. These include legislative changes that removed interest rate ceilings on mortgages and allowed lenders to offer loans with variable interest rates, balloon terms, and negative amortization. The authors suggest that, when used in appropriate circumstances, these nontraditional loan terms can be useful for both lenders and borrowers to provide loans that address borrower needs or market circumstances. But, as recent experience has shown, when used inappropriately, these loan terms can significantly raise the risk of borrower default.

While these legislative changes enabled the risk-based pricing that lies at the heart of subprime lending, this type of lending was given a substantial spur by technological developments in the 1990s that allowed lenders to use statistical models and credit scores to create more fine-grained estimates of borrower risk. Another important development over this period was the growth of the asset-backed securities market, which shifted the primary source of mortgage finance from federally regulated institutions to mortgage banking institutions that acquired funds through the broader capital markets and were subject to much less regulatory oversight.

Numerous authors have argued that the regulatory structure may not have changed rapidly enough to keep up with the pace of fundamental change that was transforming the mortgage market.[5] Borrowers' protections largely consisted of disclosure rules, which proved to be insufficient protection against consumers making poor choices given the new market's much greater variation both in loan costs and in loan terms.[6] The Home Ownership and Equity Protection Act (HOEPA) of 1994 was intended to provide greater consumer protection against predatory loan terms, but, in practice, applied to less than 1 percent of all loans and so protected very few borrowers. In the absence of more stringent federal regulations, a large majority of states passed their own versions of HOEPA. But the Office of Thrift Supervision and the Office of the Comptroller of the Currency, the primary regulators of federal depository institutions, issued regulations preempting these state laws from applying to the institutions these agencies regulated. Importantly, this preemption also applied to the mortgage banking operating subsidiaries of these institutions, which greatly reduced the number of lenders covered by these state laws. While federal regulators' concern with the safety and soundness of banking institutions provides a check against risky lending activities by these institutions, an increasing number of mortgage loans were made by independent mortgage banking institutions subject to less federal oversight than depository institutions and their mortgage banking subsidiaries.

Another important hole in the regulatory framework was the lack of significant federal oversight of the rating agencies.[7] These agencies played a key role in opening the markets for mortgage-backed securities and collateralized debt obligations to a wide range of institutional investors and regulated financial firms seeking AA- or AAA-rated investments. In hindsight, it is clear that the rating agencies were excessively optimistic in their assessment of the risks associated with subprime mortgages and the securities built on these loans. The ratings compensation structure—under which the agencies were paid by the very firms that sold the securities to investors—likely played an important role in the agencies' failure to more soundly assess these securities.

The factors cited previously helped set the stage for the mortgage market problems that developed in recent years, but several other factors precipitated the rapid growth of subprime and Alt-A lending and the substantial deterioration in underwriting controls that began around 2003. One commonly cited factor is the increasing demand for high-yield, investment-grade securities from both domestic and foreign investors.[8] The strong demand for these securities was evident in the shrinking risk premiums demanded by investors in asset-backed securities through 2006. In part, the willingness of investors to purchase risky mortgages with relatively little risk premium also reflects the belief that innovations in financial market instruments were shielding them from default risk.

The surge in subprime lending was also driven by the high profits participants earned at each stage of the process from loan origination through bond issuance. As housing affordability worsened after 2003, lenders began offering new mortgage products intended to stretch borrowers' ability to afford ever more expensive homes as a means of keeping loan origination volumes high. Efforts to keep origination volumes high also appear to have contributed to loosened underwriting standards during this period.

The final—and perhaps most important—ingredient that fostered the surge in risky lending was the rapid increase in housing prices in large swaths of the country through 2006. The quickening pace of house price appreciation papered over the increasing risks of mortgage origination in the years leading up to the emergence of the foreclosure crisis in 2007. In fact, the growth in risky lending seems likely to have fueled the dramatic rise in house prices. In short, market developments since 2000 helped create a self-perpetuating cycle. In pursuit of high profits, lenders and investors poured capital into ever riskier loans, particularly after 2003. This flood of capital helped to spur rising home prices that masked the riskiness of the loans being made, leading to continued loosening of underwriting standards. When house price growth finally slowed in late 2006, the true nature of these risky loans was exposed and the "house of cards" came tumbling down.

There is a general recognition that fraud on the part of mortgage brokers and borrowers may have made a significant contribution to the foreclosure crisis.[9] Ultimately, examinations of the growing incidence of fraud conclude that the fundamental cause can be traced back to the lack of adequate underwriting controls by lenders to oversee brokers' activities. The most commonly cited information on trends in mortgage fraud is derived from Suspicious Activity Reports (SARs), which are filed by financial institutions, including federally insured depository institutions, and are utilized by several federal agencies, including the Federal Bureau of Investigation (FBI), the Financial Crimes Enforcement Network, and HUD, amongst others, in their efforts against mortgage fraud. Importantly, with significant shares of loans made by institutions not regulated or insured by the federal government, this reporting system leaves out a significant portion of the mortgage industry. Even with a large segment of the market excluded from this system and with strong housing price growth potentially masking many cases of fraud, the number of SARs grew sharply beginning in 2004. In 2003 a total of 6,939 SARs were filed; by 2007, this number had increased nearly sevenfold to 46,717. Nonetheless, the number of SARs was still fairly small relative to the number of loans originated annually. However, the low share undoubtedly reflects both the difficulty of identifying fraud as well as the limited scope of institutions reporting SARS. BasePoint Analytics, a private firm specializing in detecting mortgage fraud, has estimated that 9 percent of loan delinquencies are associated with some form of fraud. Thus, while mortgage fraud is certainly not a trivial issue, it is estimated to account for only about 1 in 10 delinquencies.

In terms of the nature of fraud, the FBI distinguishes between two types of fraud: (1) "for profit," mostly perpetrated by brokers and others to generate profits, and (2) "for housing," perpetrated by homebuyers with the goal of purchasing or retaining a home. The FBI estimates that roughly 80 percent of fraud is "for profit" and conducted by brokers and other professional parties to the transaction. Consistent with this conclusion, BasePoint Analytics has concluded that most fraud is driven by mortgage brokers in their efforts to earn profits by originating loans. Existing information further suggests that the vast majority of fraud involves the misrepresentation of information on loan applications related to income, employment, or occupancy of the home by the borrower. The growth in no- and low-documentation loans appears to be highly related to the growth in fraud. Another significant share of cases of fraud involve appraisal misrepresentations, where property conditions are materially different than presented in the appraisal or information that is typically outside of accepted parameters is used to derive the property value.

Another common factor alleged in the popular press to have contributed to the foreclosure crisis is the Community Reinvestment Act (CRA).[10] CRA was passed by Congress in 1977 with the goal of encouraging banks to meet the credit needs of the communities in which they have branches, with a specific emphasis on low- and moderate-income neighborhoods. Some critics of CRA claim that the wave of risky lending was generated in no small part by banks having been pushed into making these loans to meet their CRA requirements. However, a variety of empirical evidence supports the view that CRA's requirements played little or no role in producing the foreclosure crisis. To begin with, only a very small share of the high-priced loans that have been a key driver of the crisis can be linked to efforts to meet CRA's lending requirements. Furthermore, while CRA lending requirements have been in force for over three decades, the foreclosure crisis is a recent phenomenon. In fact, the rise of the foreclosure crisis came after a period of sustained decline in the share of mortgage lending activity covered under the CRA. Finally, there is also some evidence that loans made to low- and moderate- income homebuyers as part of banks' efforts to meet their CRA obligations have actually performed better than subprime loans. CRA loans were about half as likely to go into foreclosure as loans made by independent mortgage companies not covered by CRA, suggesting that CRA may have helped to ensure responsible lending even during a period of overall declines in underwriting standards.

Many of the same voices raising questions about CRA' s role in producing the foreclosure crisis have also argued that federal regulations requiring the government-sponsored enterprises (Fannie Mae and Freddie Mac, or the GSEs) to devote a sizeable share of their lending to low- and moderate-income homeowners also played a significant role in fostering the growth of risky lending. The serious financial troubles of the GSEs that led to their being placed into conservatorship by the federal government provides strong testament to the fact that the GSEs were indeed overexposed to unduly risky mortgage investments. However, the evidence suggests that the GSEs' decisions to purchase or guarantee nonprime loans was motivated more by efforts to chase market share and profits than by the need to satisfy federal regulators. Another argument is that the GSEs helped fuel the growth of subprime lending by purchasing a significant share of subprime mortgage-backed securities to meet their low- and moderate-income housing goals. While the GSEs did purchase just under one-half of all subprime securities in 2004, and were allowed by federal regulators to count qualifying loans in these securities toward their goals, their purchases of these securities dropped sharply in subsequent years even as the growth in the subprime market took off. In short, while the GSEs certainly contributed to the growth of the subprime market, there was clearly substantial demand for these securities from a wide variety of investors.

Potential Policy Changes for Addressing Rising Foreclosures

One important category of policy options are those options designed to address problems associated with rising foreclosure. Rising mortgage delinquency and foreclosure rates exact a tremendous toll on individual borrowers and their communities. Foreclosures also exert downward pressure on home prices, further exacerbating problems in the housing market and the broader economy. Concerns about the impacts of rising foreclosures have led to a variety of efforts aimed at helping owners to remain in their homes, including substantial support for foreclosure prevention counseling and expanded loan modification and refinancing options.

One prominent early effort launched in late 2007 by HUD's Federal Housing Administration (FHA) was the FHASecure program, which was intended to use FHA insurance to replace risky subprime and high-cost loans, including those that became delinquent due to a payment reset, with fixed-rate, long-term financing. However, there was limited use of this program in part due to eligibility criteria that prevented participation for many borrowers. In July 2008, Congress authorized FHA, under the Housing and Economic Recovery Act of 2008, to insure up to $300 billion in loans via a new program: HOPE for Homeowners. Although some lenders have expressed interest in the program, as of July 2009 the program had insured only one loan. Amendments have been made to increase program participation, including a reduction in the amount of principal lenders are required to write down in order to place a borrower in the program. Additional legislative changes that were enacted in May 2009 further modify HOPE for Homeowners with the goal of helping additional families.

Another prominent effort is the HOPE NOW Alliance, formed in 2007 to help keep borrowers in their homes by increasing their access to counseling and information and creating a unified private industry plan to facilitate loan workouts. Initially, the majority of these workouts consisted of repayment plans, accounting for more than two-thirds of all workouts in the first year of operations. While workouts can help some households meet their mortgage payment obligations, for many subprime borrowers repayment plans offer limited relief as they place additional debt repayment obligations on households already struggling to make mortgage payments. Given continued increases in foreclosures and deepening economic distress, public pressure has been rising on investors and servicers to engage in more aggressive loan modifications through interest rate and principal reductions in order to keep more borrowers in their homes. Since mid-2008, HOPE NOW has reported an increasing number of loan modifications by its participating servicers. From July through December 2008, nearly one-half of the loan workouts reported were loan modifications rather than repayment plans.

Even as the number of modifications increases, larger numbers of recently modified loans are now redefaulting. In large part, this performance reflects the fact that most loan modifications to date do not reduce monthly payments. White (2008) found that voluntary loan modifications of subprime borrowers completed through August 2008 typically increased a borrower's principal debt and virtually none involved a reduction in principal owed. While servicers did seem willing to lower mortgage interest rates, a recent assessment of the HOPE NOW Alliance program by the Center for Responsible Lending estimated that only one in five of all subprime workout plans actually lowered monthly mortgage payments for financially distressed borrowers.

Most recently, the federal government announced a new effort to encourage loan modifications as part of its Making Home Affordable plan on February 18, 2009.[11] This plan is designed to offer assistance to 7 to 9 million homeowners making good-faith efforts to stay current on their mortgage payments. It provides access to low-cost refinancing that will reduce monthly payments for homeowners who owe more than 80 percent of their home value and whose mortgages are owned or guaranteed by Fannie Mae or Freddie Mac. The plan also commits $75 billion through the Treasury Department, working with the GSEs, FHA, the Federal Deposit Insurance Corporation, and other agencies, to undertake a comprehensive multipart strategy to achieve loan modifications for 3 to 4 million at-risk homeowners to help them stay in their homes.

This homeowner stability initiative aims to reduce mortgage payments to 31 percent of income to help those borrowers in imminent danger of default. The Home Affordable Modification Program aims to achieve this goal primarily through subsidizing interest rate reductions, although the program does provide servicers and investors with the option of reducing outstanding principal balance as a means of achieving the 31-percent payment-to-income target. To date, many servicers have been reluctant to offer interest rate and principal write-downs even when such modifications could avoid lengthy and costly foreclosure costs. In part this reflects concerns that existing pooling and servicing agreements (PSAs, or the legal agreements that govern the servicer's authority to engage in loan modifications on behalf of the collection of investors with interests in any single mortgage-backed security pool) may limit ability of servicers to engage in loan modification activities. Yet, at the same time, many of these agreements contain inconsistent, and arguably not enforceable, language as to what actions are permissible under the contract. The expectation is that the Home Affordable Modification Program will encourage wider use of loan modification tools because it offers substantial interest rate subsidies, offers bonus success payments to borrowers and servicers, and creates clear industrywide standards on how best to interpret these PSAs.

Some question whether the Home Affordable Modification Program approach is sufficient to address all situations. For some borrowers, the subsidies provided through the program will not be sufficient to allow them to stay in their homes. Some of these borrowers may be helped through the improved HOPE for Homeowners Program. But many have argued that bankruptcy reform is needed to allow bankruptcy judges to modify mortgages for families who have run out of other options.

Potential Policy Changes to Reduce the Risk of Future Foreclosure Crises

A fundamental cause of the foreclosure crisis was the substantial increase in loans made to borrowers with insufficient willingness or ability to meet their payment obligations. As a result, there is a growing consensus regarding the need for policy changes to improve the functioning of both the primary and secondary mortgage markets to help reduce the number of foreclosure-prone loans before they are made. A June 2009 report by the Treasury Department presenting a comprehensive plan for reform of regulatory oversight of the financial system has identified a series of detailed proposals that has provided a framework for this ongoing policy debate (U.S. Department of the Treasury, 2009).

To begin with, there is a clear need to enhance the ability of consumers to make appropriate choices in the mortgage market. Recent research on consumer behavior provides growing evidence that many consumers took out mortgages that they did not understand or that were not suitable for their needs. In particular, there is ample evidence that consumers are often overwhelmed by aggressive mortgage sales and marketing efforts that exploit various consumer decision making weaknesses.

One potential approach to aide consumers is to expand consumer awareness campaigns to warn against abusive lending practices. Unfortunately, even the best-designed education and outreach efforts can be easily swamped in a marketplace characterized by aggressive marketing by lenders. In the face of this marketing onslaught, many community groups and counseling organizations are expanding their capacity to act as a "buyer's broker" to help clients search for the best mortgages while earning a small fee for offering this service like any other mortgage broker. Building on this concept, there have been calls for the government to help establish a national network of "trusted advisors," independent of mortgage providers who are available on demand to review loan documents, educate borrowers, and advise them of the suitability of their loan to their circumstances.

Another potential approach to help consumers make better choices is to apply the "opt-in/opt-out" principle identified in the consumer behavior literature to structure more effective mortgage marketing of "good loans"; that is, loans that are fairly priced and that consumers understand and can afford to repay over the life of the loan.[12] For example, many programs first offer a prospective consumer a "safe," level-payment fixed-rate mortgage priced in an affordable manner. By starting with the default option of offering a simple and safe product, this approach builds on the observation that consumers often latch onto the first option for which they qualify.

While expanding the range of consumer counseling and assistance efforts is likely to be helpful, it may also be important to more forcefully counteract aggressive marketing practices and to consider banning inherently deceptive loan features. Moreover, since the mortgage market will continue to create new products, efforts to ban specific loan terms or mortgage products may not keep pace with these innovations. A number of initiatives have been enacted or proposed to enhance existing consumer protections, including recently released protections for subprime borrowers under the Truth in Lending Act, which requires lenders to evaluate both a borrower's income and ability to repay prior to originating a subprime loan, and 2008 HUD revisions to the Real Estate Settlement Procedures Act regulations.

But even while applauding these initial efforts, many consumer advocates argue that additional reform is needed. They recommend limiting or banning yield spread premiums, which provide brokers and loan officers with incentives to sell borrowers higher priced loans, and prepayment penalties, which lock borrowers into high-priced loans and expose them to high fees if they need to refinance or sell their homes. A proposed revision to Regulation Z, the regulation which implements the Truth In Lending Act, would ban yield spread premiums and lender loan officer compensation related to loan terms. There are also proposals to develop new standards for truth in lending so that mortgage brokers and lenders do not have incentives to get around disclosure rules. Under this approach, federal regulators would evaluate whether a creditor's disclosure was objectively unreasonable, in that the disclosure would fail to communicate effectively the key terms and risks of the mortgage to the typical borrower.

Finally, the recent mortgage crisis has exposed a range of shortcomings with the approaches that have been used in the past by many mortgage servicers, including the tendency to push less costly (to the servicer) repayment plans and short-term modifications rather than aggressively pursue options that may benefit both borrowers (by helping them stay in their homes with an affordable monthly payment) and investors (by finding resolutions that have a higher expected return than a foreclosure). This has led to proposals, such as the federal government's Making Home Affordable plan, that seek to better align mortgage servicer incentives with those of both consumers and investors and set standards for loan modifications. Some have also called for imposing a duty to engage in loss mitigation efforts before initiating foreclosure actions.

A key aspect of the Treasury Department's proposals with regard to consumer protections include the establishment of a new Consumer Financial Protection Agency, which would have broad jurisdiction to protect consumers across the financial sector from unfair, deceptive or abusive practices. In addition, the Treasury Department recommends that this new agency develop stronger regulations governing consumer disclosures to ensure that they are transparent, simple, and fair.

In addition to greater consumer protections, many also argue that improvements are needed in the general regulatory structure overseeing the origination and financing of mortgages. The failure of federal regulation to adapt to the rapid changes in both the primary and secondary market was a key element in the explosion of high-risk lending and resulting surge in mortgage delinquency and default.

In the primary market, federal oversight has largely focused on federally insured depository institutions. But since the boom and bust of the subprime market was led by nonbank institutions and less fully regulated affiliates and subsidiaries of banks, in large measure, the nation's regulatory mechanisms have been focused on the wrong parts of the system. To realign regulation with today's organization of financial services, uniformity of regulation is needed across the lending practices of all segments of the mortgage industry and its regulators.[13] Reforms could reduce the incidence of nonbanks or affiliates and subsidiaries of banks playing by different rules, and they could encourage hands-on oversight to improve fair lending enforcement and improve compliance monitoring. An example of harmonizing the rules for all loan originators could be reform of the CRA. Such reform applied to CRA would involve expanding the current onsite reviews and detailed file checks now performed on assessment area lending of CRA-regulated entities to all mortgage lending activities. Most importantly, CRA could be expanded to cover independent mortgage banking operations and other newly emerging nonbank lenders.

The Treasury Department's recommendations address these concerns by calling for the Federal Reserve to oversee and set stronger capital requirements for all financial firms even if they do not own banks. In addition, these recommendations also call for the creation of a single National Bank Supervisor to oversee all federally chartered banks as well as the elimination of loopholes that allow some depositories to avoid bank holding company regulation by the Federal Reserve.

Lack of uniformity is also a problem in the regulation of secondary market participants. The two housing GSEs, Fannie Mae and Freddie Mac, are subject to extensive federal oversight; however, most of the funds flowing into the subprime market come through the lightly regulated private-label mortgage-backed securities markets. Although the U.S. Securities and Exchange Commission is charged with the responsibility of monitoring the wide range of security transactions linked to the subprime sector, the degree of due diligence in this sector falls short of the oversight review of the GSEs. The development of a new and comprehensive regulatory structure for the non-GSE segment of the market will represent a critical piece of the coming mortgage market reforms. With regard to the secondary markets, the Treasury Department's recommendations call for enhanced regulation of securitization markets, including greater oversight of credit rating agencies and a requirement that originators and security issuers retain a financial interest in securitized loans.

In considering how best to regulate the GSEs or other secondary market participants, it is important to place these issues in the broader context of how the capital markets channel investment dollars into the subprime mortgage market. Just as is the case in the primary market, the development of detailed secondary market regulations that apply to only one segment of the marketplace can be both counterproductive and unfair. Considering how best to reduce the tendency for capital used to fund higher priced mortgages to flow through less-regulated capital market channels is a worthy addition to the current debate on GSE reform in particular, and capital markets in general.

INTRODUCTION

This study of the root causes of the current extremely high levels of defaults and foreclosures among residential mortgages represents the final report to Congress by the Secretary of the Department of Housing and Urban Development (HUD) pursuant to Section 1517 of the Housing and Economic Recovery Act (HERA) of 2008 (P.L. 110-289). The problems in the mortgage market are routinely referred to as a "foreclosure crisis" because the level of defaults and foreclosures greatly exceed previous peak levels in the post-war era and, as a result, have drawn comparisons to the levels of distress experienced in the Great Depression. This report contains a review of the academic literature and popular and industry press on the root causes of the current foreclosure crisis and a discussion of initial federal policy responses to the crisis. The report expands upon the earlier interim report submitted to Congress on this subject with additional data and analysis of trends in the market as well as an updated review of policy responses and recommended actions to mitigate the current crisis and help prevent similar crises from occurring in the future.

Since HERA was passed in July 2008, the problems in the mortgage market have triggered a more general crisis in global financial markets as first the securitization market for broad classes of assets seized up and then a broader credit crunch ensued as a shortage of capital held by banks and other lenders cut off lending generally (Gorton, 2008). Although the broader financial crisis has roots in the mortgage market turmoil, there are many aspects of the financial market problems that go beyond issues in the mortgage markets. Thus, while this report will touch on some of the causes of problems in the broader financial markets, much of this broader topic is beyond the scope of this report.

To help define the nature of the foreclosure crisis, section 1 presents basic information on trends in mortgage delinquencies and foreclosure starts based on the Mortgage Bankers Association's (MBA's) *National Delinquency Survey.*

Section 2 then presents a detailed review of the literature on the causes of the foreclosure crisis. This section is divided into three parts. First, it reviews the general academic literature over the last two decades analyzing the general causes of mortgage delinquencies and foreclosures. Second, it reviews studies that have specifically examined the causes of the recent spike in delinquencies and foreclosures to levels not seen since the Great Depression. Finally, section 2 concludes by reviewing both the academic literature and articles in the popular press that shed light on factors that fostered significant growth in the origination of the highly risky loans that were the root cause of the current crisis.

Section 3 then focuses on potential policy responses to the crisis. This section draws upon articles and reports by academics and advocacy groups. There are three main parts to this section. The first part discusses potential efforts to remedy the high levels of delinquencies and foreclosures among current homeowners. The second part then presents policy options to help reduce the risk of high foreclosure rates in the future. The last part outlines potential approaches for more comprehensive reform of regulation of the primary and secondary mortgage markets.

1. Trends in Delinquencies and Foreclosures

Arguably, the first tremors of the national mortgage crisis were felt in early December 2006 when two sizeable subprime lenders, Ownit Mortgage Solutions and Sebring Capital, failed. *The Wall Street Journal* described the closing of these firms as "sending shock waves" through the mortgage-bond market. [14] The failure of these firms was triggered by high levels of early payment defaults—newly originated loans on which borrowers quickly miss several payments. Under the terms of sales agreements with investors, lenders can be forced to buy back loans with early payment defaults. Since mortgage banking firms are not highly capitalized, a significant number of forced mortgage buybacks can quickly lead to insolvency. By late 2006, the volume of early payment defaults was rising rapidly, spurring a spike in the volume of mortgage buybacks and pushing more and more subprime lenders into untenable financial positions.[15]

Yet, when the MBA released the results of its *National Delinquency Survey* for the third quarter of 2006 on December 14, 2006, there was not yet a sense of panic (see Exhibit 1). While the survey showed that delinquency and foreclosure start rates were rising, particularly among subprime borrowers, the tone surrounding this news was still cautiously optimistic, with the MBA predicting that there would only be a "modest increase" in delinquencies over the next several quarters as the housing market bottomed.[16] At the same time, a very different assessment was presented in a report released on December 19 by the Center for Responsible Lending (CRL), which estimated that more than 1 million subprime loans originated in recent years would end in foreclosure, producing the worse foreclosure crisis in the modern mortgage era (Schloemer et al., 2006). CRL's foreclosure outlook was based on forecasts by Moody's Economy.com showing that house prices were likely to fall in many market areas in the wake of recent record levels of housing price growth.

By late February 2007, when the number of subprime lenders shuttering their doors had reached 22, one of the first headlines announcing the onset of a "mortgage crisis" appeared in *The Daily Telegrap*h of London. [17] By March, it was clear that a mortgage crisis had begun and was worsening.[18] When the MBA released the results of its delinquency survey for the fourth quarter of 2006 in March 2007, the foreclosure start rate was found to have hit a record level. [19]

Exhibit 1 presents trends in two key measures of mortgage distress from the MBA's *National Delinquency Survey*: the share of mortgages that were 90 or more days behind in their payments and the share that started the foreclosure process. As shown, the foreclosure start rate for all mortgages exhibited a fairly sizeable increase of 0.08 percentage points in the fourth quarter of 2006, pushing the rate to the new record high of 0.54 percent. While the 90-day delinquency rate was also trending strongly upward at this point, it would not reach a new record high until two quarters later, in mid-2007. The fact that the rate of foreclosure starts was already at record levels 6 months ahead of when the 90-day delinquency rate would set a new record is an indication of the importance of early payment defaults in the early stages of the crisis, with many loans going straight from delinquency to the start of foreclosure proceedings.

In hindsight, the increases in delinquency and foreclosure rates experienced in early 2007 were still somewhat mild compared to what was to come. Both of these measures of distress experienced large and steady increases into 2008, shattering previous records for both. Prior to 2006, the highest rate of foreclosure starts had been 0.50 percent, reached in the aftermath of the economic recession that started the decade. By the second quarter of 2008, this rate was more than twice as high, at 1.08 percent. Similarly, the 90-day delinquency rate, which had reached a new record of 1.00 percent in 2005, had more than doubled to 2.09 percent by the third quarter of 2008. Most recently, foreclosure starts declined in the third quarter of 2008, but the MBA speculated that this reflected some lenders' temporary moratoria on foreclosures and increased efforts by lenders to increase the volume of workouts with borrowers short of foreclosure.[20] But, with serious delinquencies continuing to surge into new records each quarter, there does not appear to be any sense that the growth in the magnitude of the crisis is slowing. Indeed, foreclosure starts increased sharply in the first quarter of 2009 to reach yet a new high.

The MBA data provide a number of useful insights into the nature of the mortgage crisis. As is well known, subprime loans have accounted for a significant share of troubled loans during the current crisis. Exhibit 2 shows trends in foreclosure starts by major market segment as categorized in the MBA data—prime, subprime, and Federal Housing Administration (FHA)-insured loans. Since 1998, when the MBA first began reporting separately on the prime and subprime sectors, foreclosures rates in the subprime sector had been many multiples the rate of foreclosure starts in other market segments—roughly nine times the rate of prime loans and two-and-ahalf times the rate in the FHA-insured sector. As shown in Exhibit 2, since 2006, when the foreclosure start rate began to rise sharply, the increase in the rate in the subprime sector has been particularly dramatic.

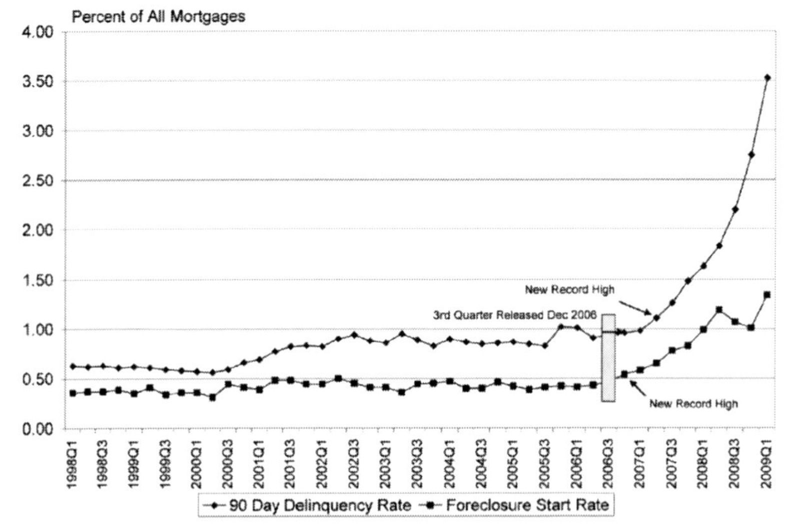

Source: Mortgage Bankers Association, National Delinquency Survey

Exhibit 1. 90-Day Delinquency and Foreclosure Start Rates.

Source: Mortgage Bankers Association, National Delinquency Survey
Note: Annual figures are average of quarterly data.

Exhibit 2. Foreclosure Start Rate by Mortgage Market Segment.

The much higher risk of foreclosure among subprime loans is also made evident when 90-day delinquency rates are compared across market segments (Exhibit 3). While subprime loans have always had a much higher foreclosure start rate than other segments, there was little difference in the 90-day delinquency rates between subprime and FHA-insured loans—until these trends diverged drastically in 2007. The much larger difference in foreclosure start rates among subprime loans relative to differences in 90-day delinquency rates reflects the fact that once subprime loans became delinquent, they were much more likely to enter foreclosure than other market segments.

The high foreclosure risk among subprime loans was no secret even before 2006. As early as 1998, the National Training and Information Center (NTIC) in Chicago highlighted a sharp rise in foreclosures in minority neighborhoods in Chicago and linked these increases to the growth of subprime lending in these areas (NTIC, 1998). In the wake of NTIC's work, a number of other studies revealed similar trends in other market areas around the country (Bunce et al., 2000). As will be discussed in more detail at the end of this section, historically high foreclosure rates were evident among 20 states in 2002 in the wake of the 2001 recession.

But, while the subprime foreclosure risk was well documented, the overall market share of subprime loans was still low enough that the high rates of foreclosure starts were not pushing up overall foreclosure rates to record levels. As shown in Exhibit 3, the foreclosure start rate among subprime loans was higher in 2001 at the time of the last recession than it was in 2006, when the current foreclosure crisis began. But whereas subprime loans only accounted for 2.6 percent of all loans in MBA's survey in 2001, by 2006 this share had increased more than fivefold to 13.5 percent (see Exhibit 4).[21]

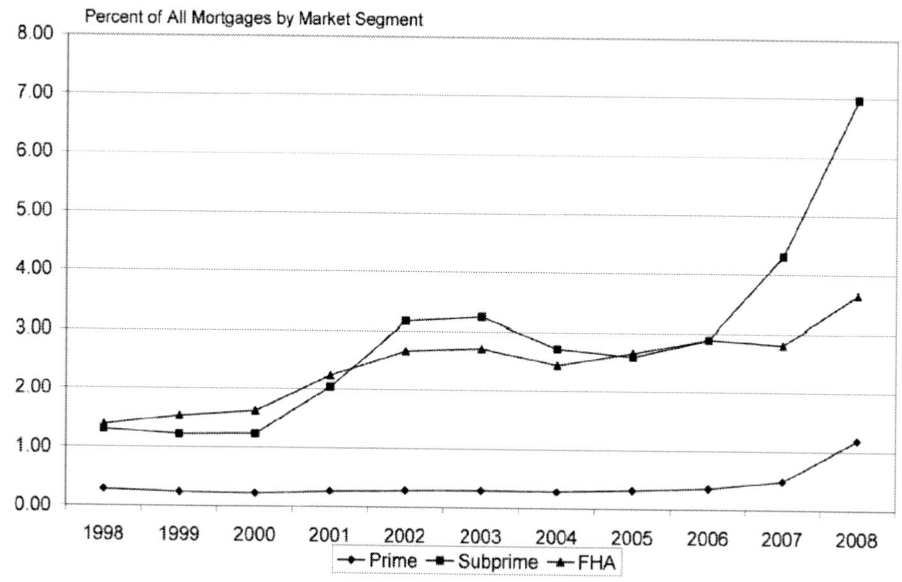

Source: Mortgage Bankers Association, National Delinquency Survey
Note: Annual figures are average of quarterly data.

Exhibit 3. 90-Day Delinquency Rate by Mortgage Market Segment.

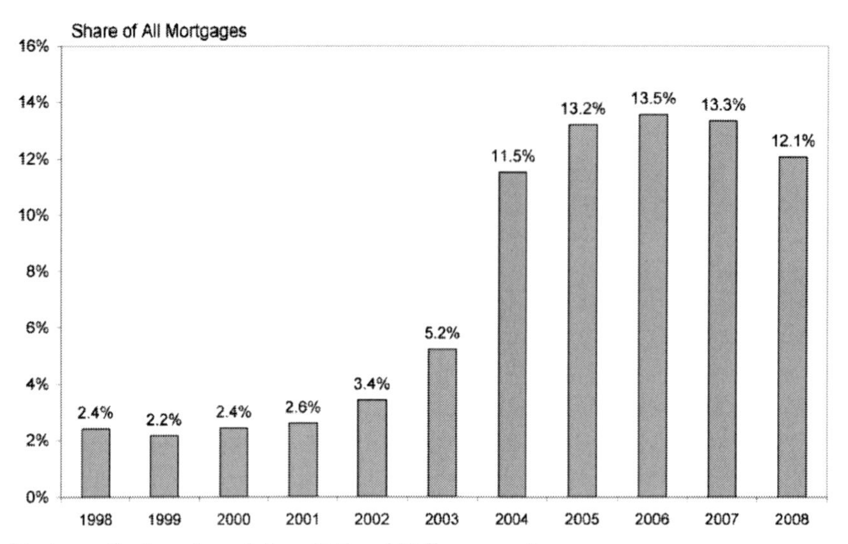

Source: Mortgage Bankers Association, National Delinquency Survey
Note: Annual figures are average of quarterly data.

Exhibit 4. Subprime Share of Mortgages in Mortgage Bankers Association National Delinquency.

In fact, because the MBA data show the share of all *outstanding* mortgages by market segment, these data do not adequately illustrate the growing importance of subprime and other riskier loan segments among loans *originated* during this period. Using data from *Inside Mortgage Finance*, Exhibit 5 shows the share of mortgage originations in dollars accounted for by subprime, Alt-A, and home equity loans from 2001 through 2006. The Alt-A market segment consists of loans made to borrowers with prime credit histories, but incorporates other loan terms that make these loans riskier than standard prime mortgages—most commonly entailing the use of limited or no documentation requirements for borrowers' income and/or assets as well as interest-only or optional monthly payment levels.[22] Home equity loans are second mortgages, most commonly originated during this period in tandem with a first mortgage for 80 percent of the home's value. These simultaneous home equity loans, known as "piggy-back" loans, would be for up to 20 percent of the home value, allowing the borrower to obtain a prime first mortgage without mortgage insurance while paying much higher interest rates on the home equity loan. Between 2001 and 2003, these three segments together accounted for about 15 percent of all mortgage originations. Beginning in 2004, all three of these market segments grew rapidly, achieving a combined market share of 48 percent in 2006. In reviewing data from the MBA's *National Delinquency Survey,* it is important to bear in mind that the Alt-A segment is likely to be reported in the prime market segment while home equity loans are not covered by the MBA survey.

With subprime mortgages accounting for such a large share of outstanding loans, the relatively modest rise in the foreclosure starts rate among subprime loans in 2006 had a much larger impact on the market than the spike in foreclosure rates in 2001. Exhibit 6 shows the trends in the number of loans starting foreclosure by market segment from 1998 through 2008. In 2006, as the foreclosure crisis first became evident, the volume of subprime foreclosures increased by more than 100,000, accounting for much of the increase of about 120,000 in foreclosure starts in the overall market. This sharp increase in the volume of foreclosure starts occurred even though the subprime foreclosure start rate was still below peak levels from 2001 (see Exhibit 2). In 2007, the volume of subprime foreclosure starts increased by nearly 300,000, accounting for more than one-half of the overall increase—even though subprime loans only accounted for about one in eight of all outstanding mortgages. In part, the sharp increase in 2007 reflects the much higher foreclosure start rate—up more than a full percentage point from 2006—as well as the fact that the number of subprime loans reported in the MBA survey was nearly seven times the volume reported in 2001.

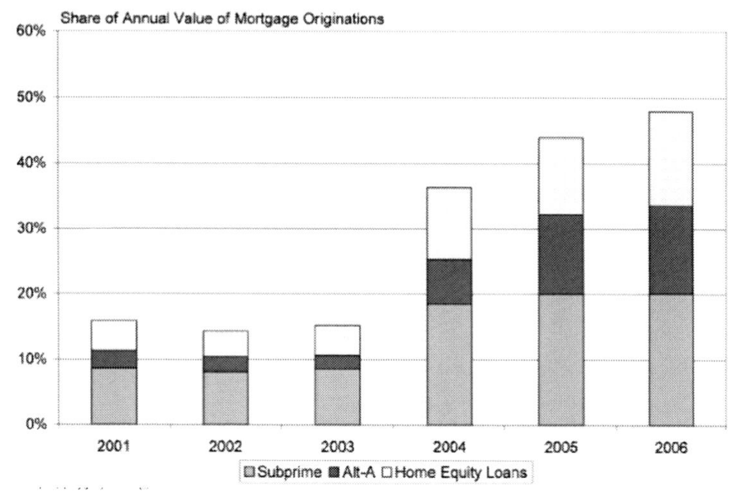

Source: Inside Mortgage Finance

Exhibit 5. Subprime, Alt-A, and Home Equity Loan Share of All Mortgage Originations.

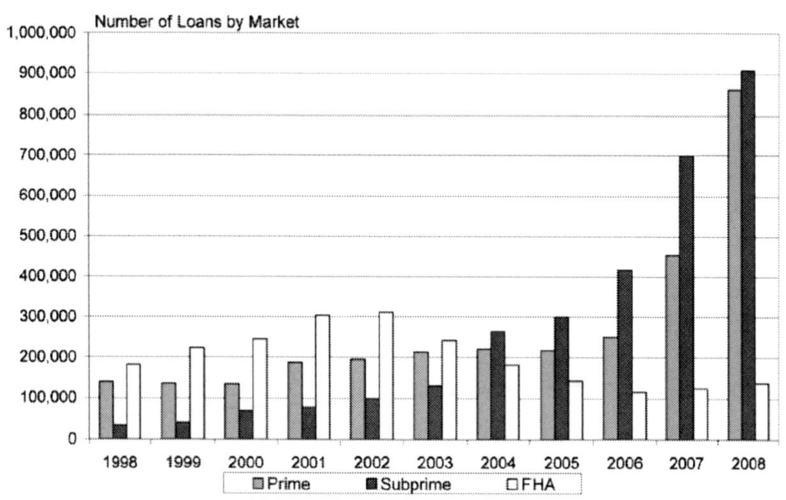

Source: Mortgage Bankers Association, National Delinquency Survey
Note: Annual figures are average of quarterly data.

Exhibit 6. Numbers of Loans Starting Foreclosure by Market Segment.

However, in 2007 and 2008, the volume of prime foreclosure starts also increased sharply. In 2007, the number of prime loans entering foreclosure nearly doubled to about 500,000. The increase in prime foreclosure starts was even larger in 2008, reaching more than 850,000 loans. While still less than the roughly 900,000 foreclosure starts among subprime loans, in 2008 the prime market has come to account for an increasingly large share of all foreclosures. Across all market segments, foreclosure starts reached nearly 2 million loans in 2008—greatly exceeding the levels predicted by CRL in 2006 as representing the worst mortgage crisis in the modern era.[23]

While the MBA data do not identify subsegments of the prime market, based on information from other sources, much of the increase in prime market foreclosures is occurring among "Alt-A" loans.[24] The MBA data also highlight the fact that much of the foreclosure crisis can be linked to adjustable-rate mortgages (ARMs) in both the prime and subprime sectors. Exhibit 7 shows annual trends in the number of prime and subprime mortgages starting foreclosure by whether the loan has a fixed or adjustable rate. At the start of the mortgage crisis in 2006, the rise in foreclosure starts occurred only among adjustable-rate prime and subprime mortgages. There have continued to be sharp increases in foreclosures among both subprime and prime ARMs; in 2008, these two categories of loans accounted for a large majority of all foreclosure starts. However, foreclosure starts have also increased substantially among fixed-rate loans, particularly in 2008 as economic conditions have deteriorated.

The high percentage of prime foreclosures accounted for by ARMs is out of proportion to the share of all prime loans that are ARMs. While ARMs only accounted for 18 percent of prime loans reported in the MBA data in 2008, these loans accounted for 52 percent of all prime foreclosure starts. The disparity is also evident among subprime loans, although it is not as large. ARMs accounted for 48 percent of subprime loans in the MBA data but 73 percent of subprime foreclosure starts.

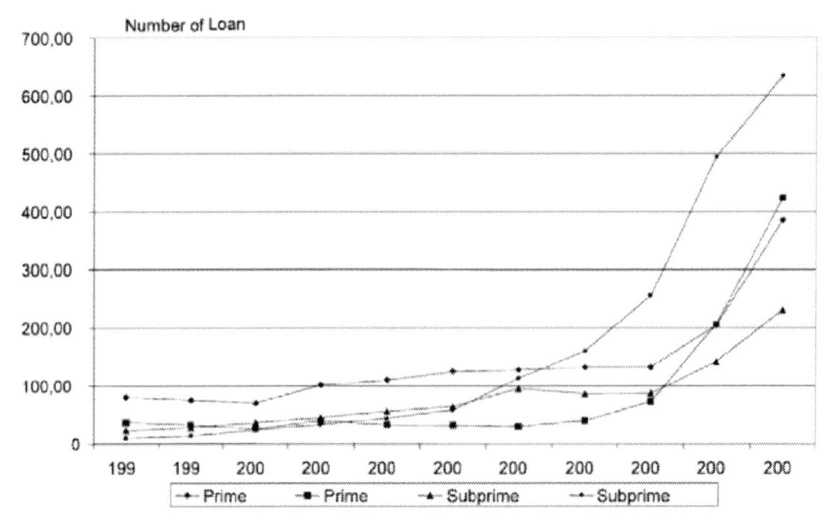

Source: Mortgage Bankers Association, National Delinquency Survey
Note: Annual figures are sums of quarterly

Exhibit 7. Number of Loans Starting Foreclosure by Loan Type and Market Segment.

In part, the high foreclosure rates among ARMs may reflect the potential for payment shock for borrowers when the interest rates on these loans first reset. However, as will be discussed further later in this report, the incidence of early payment defaults among these loans suggests that much of their poor performance may be related to lax underwriting that allowed borrowers to take on monthly payments that were unaffordable even before interest rate resets occurred.

In sum, data from the MBA *National Delinquency Survey* highlight a few key features of the foreclosure crisis. First, a substantial portion of the crisis can be traced to both the growing volume of and rising foreclosure rates among subprime loans—particularly in the initial phases of the crisis. Second, foreclosure starts have been much higher among adjustable-rate loans in both the subprime and prime sectors, with much of the problem among prime loans concentrated in the Alt-A segment of the market. However, as the crisis continues into its third year and the nation's economic recession worsens, foreclosure starts are also rising sharply among prime fixed-rate loans as well.

Regional Trends in Foreclosures

As shown earlier, data from the MBA find that foreclosure rates are now nearly three times higher than previous peak levels from any time over the past 30 years. Where new records for foreclosure starts rates used to be measured in hundredths of a percent, it has not been uncommon for this measure to increase by tenths of a percent in a single quarter. Given the magnitude of this crisis, it is perhaps not surprising that the increase in foreclosures is evident in most areas of the country. Nonetheless, there are significant differences in the extent of the foreclosure crisis across market areas.

Exhibit 8 shows the number of states with a foreclosure start rate exceeding 0.50 percent in a given year beginning in 1979, when the MBA first conducted the *National Delinquency Survey*. A foreclosure start rate of 0.50 percent is taken as an indicator of severe distress in the mortgage market as this was the national record level prior to 2007. As shown in Exhibit 8, there were widespread problems evident at the state level as early as 2000. During the 1980s, the severe economic recession in the oil patch states led to significant foreclosure start rates in seven to nine states each year from 1986 through 1990. This period has been viewed as one of the most serious mortgage foreclosure episodes in the post-war era. More specifically, foreclosure rates in Texas and surrounding states from this time were used as the basis for the stress test of the government-sponsored enterprises' capital requirements by its regulator. But by 2000, the number of states with foreclosure start rates exceeding 0.50 percent was already at nine. By 2002, at the height of foreclosures in the wake of the previous economic recession, the number of states exceeding this rate reached 20, more than double the number achieved in the 1 980s. Most of these states were in the Midwest and the South in areas with high shares of subprime loans. While the number of states exceeding a foreclosure start rate of 0.50 percent declined through 2006, there were several states that saw the situation deteriorate even further, experiencing very high rates of starts (in excess of 0.80 percent). These states included Indiana, Ohio, and Michigan. With the start of the national foreclosure crisis in 2007, the number of states with foreclosure start rates above 0.50 percent exploded, reaching 35 in 2007 and 46 in 2008. The number of states with very high rates of foreclosure starts also reached unprecedented levels, with 18 states in this category in 2008. Clearly, the foreclosure crisis is not limited to a small number of states.

Table 1 in the appendix provides summary information for all 50 states and the District of Columbia on changes in foreclosure starts rates from 2005, before the national foreclosure crisis began, to 2008. The table also provides selected information for each state on high-cost loan shares, changes in house prices, and unemployment rates to provide some indication of the factors that may help explain variations across states in foreclosure levels.[25] States have been divided into six groups in this exhibit based on changes in the foreclosure start rate between 2005 and 2008 as well as the level of foreclosure starts in 2008.

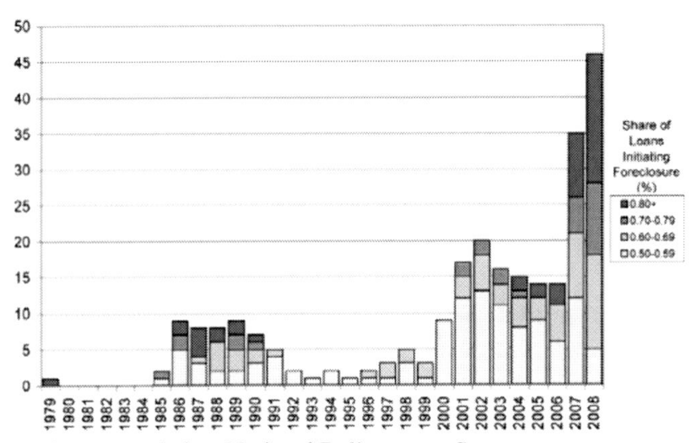

Source: Mortgage Bankers Association, National Delinquency Survey
Note: Annual rates of foreclosures started are average of the quarterly rates.

Exhibit 8. Number of States With Foreclosure Start Rates Above 0.50 Percent.

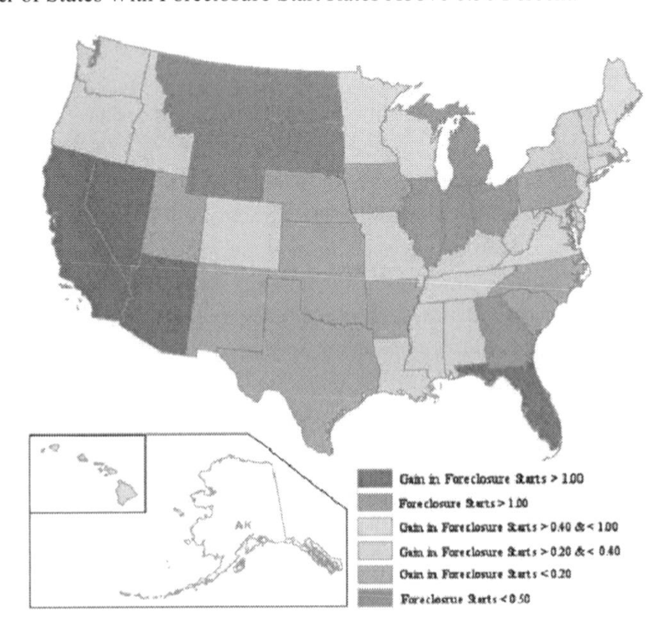

Exhibit 9. State-Level Trends in Foreclosure Starts.

Exhibit 9 maps the six categories identified in Table 1. The first group, shown in red, consists of the four states that have experienced the sharpest rise in foreclosures from 2005 to 2008, with an increase of more than 1.00 percentage points. The average foreclosure start rate among this group is 1.76 percent—more than twice the national average. This group has been referred to as the "sand states" as it includes Arizona, California, Florida, and Nevada. There are several characteristics of this group that stand out from the data in Table 1 in the appendix. Specifically, these sand states all had high incidence of subprime lending based on their high shares of high-cost loans in 2006. While the average high-cost loan share across states was 27.2 percent, high-cost loans averaged 33.6 percent across the sand states. The high-cost lending in theses states was also coupled with a much larger run-up in home prices before the crisis hit, as indicated in Table 1 by an average gain in home prices of 24.2 percent in 2005 compared to a national average across states of 10.3 percent. Perhaps because of this robust house price growth, these states also had the lowest foreclosure start rate in 2005 of any the groups, averaging just 0.20 percent. However, the fall in house prices has also been most dramatic among the sand states, declining by an average of 20.9 percent in 2008 alone. Further exacerbating problems in these markets has been a sharp rise in unemployment since 2005, with unemployment rates rising from below the national average to among the highest rates in the country.

It is noteworthy to contrast the experience of the sand states with the "Group 2 states," which are defined as those states for which the level of foreclosures starts in 2008 was high (above 1.00 percent), but the gain in foreclosure starts from the inception of the crisis was not as high as the gain exhibited by the sand states in Group 1. Group 2, shaded in orange in Exhibit 9, comprises states that had high foreclosure rates even before the crisis began due to weaknesses in local economies. Prominent among these states are the industrial states from the Midwest, including Illinois, Indiana, Michigan, and Ohio. As of 2005, this group of states had the highest average foreclosure rates in the country at 0.62 percent compared to an average across all states of 0.39 percent. As of 2005, the housing problems in these areas appear related to a combination of high shares of high-cost lending (30.5 percent of all loans in 2006) and the weakest house price growth of any group of states (5.2 percent in 2005). This group also had much higher unemployment rates in 2005 than other states. Since 2005, economic conditions have deteriorated even further, with falling housing prices and rising unemployment contributing to increases in foreclosure rates of more than 0.50 percent on average. With high foreclosure starts rates in 2005 and worsening conditions since then, this group of states has the second highest average foreclosure starts rate in 2008 after the sand states.

The third group in Exhibit 9 consists of states that had increases in foreclosure starts rates since 2005 of more than 0.40 but less than 1.00 percentage points. This increase is actually similar in magnitude to that of the second group of states, but because the third group had below-average foreclosure rates in 2005, the 2008 rates are lower than those of the second group, averaging 0.79 percent. States in this group, shaded in yellow, are mostly located along the eastern seaboard from Virginia to Maine but also include Wisconsin and Minnesota in the Midwest and Hawaii in the West. The most prominent characteristics of this group that seem related to rising foreclosure rates are above-average house price growth in 2005 (13.4 percent) followed by slightly higher than average price declines in 2008 (-4.8 percent). The share of high-cost loans in 2006 was close to the national average. Overall, the experience of this group of states has been closest to the national average.

The fourth group of states is marked by an increase in foreclosure starts since 2005 of between 0.20 and 0.40 percentage points. Foreclosure starts were close to the national average in 2005 but are now below average, having had smaller than average increases since then. Still, the average foreclosure start rate among these states is 0.69 percent, well above previous national highs. This group, shaded in light green, includes a number of states in the south-central region, the Pacific Northwest, and the Northeast. Like the third group, these states had an average share of high-cost loans in 2006, but they were also marked by somewhat less volatility in house prices, having slightly below-average gains in 2005 and smaller declines in 2008.

The fifth group of states is marked by having foreclosure starts rates of less than 0.20 percentage points; this group is among the states with the most modest increases in foreclosures since 2005. This group is distinguished from the sixth group, however, by having foreclosure starts rates of above 0.40 percent in 2005. These states were among those with the highest foreclosure rates in 2005, averaging 0.51 percentage points, and second only to the states in the industrial Midwest at that time. This group, shaded in green, is concentrated in the central and southern plains states from Nebraska down through Texas and also includes the Carolinas, Pennsylvania, and Utah. Like Groups 3 and 4, these states also had average levels of high-cost lending in 2006 but had below-average house price increases in 2005, which may have contributed to the higher foreclosure rates at that time. In 2008, house price declines were relatively small, averaging just 0.9 percent, which may explain why foreclosure rates have risen less sharply in these areas. Like the fourth group, the average foreclosure starts rate of 0.65 percent is somewhat below the current national average but well above previous national highs.

The sixth group of states are the only states where it can be said that a foreclosure crisis has not been evident, as foreclosure starts rates have remained well below 0.50 percent. These states, shaded in dark green, include the northern plains states of the Dakotas, Montana, and Wyoming as well as Alaska. One prominent characteristic of these states is a very low share of high-cost loans, averaging only 21.7 percent in 2006. These areas also had average house price growth in 2005 and generally have not experienced house price declines.

In general, there are two factors that stand out in differentiating the six groups of states. The first is the share of high-cost loans originated in 2006. States with the greatest increase and highest levels of foreclosures in 2008 all had above-average shares of high-cost loans in 2006, while the states that have avoided the foreclosure crisis all had very low shares of these loans. The second key factor is trends in house price increases since 2004. Many states with the sharpest increases in foreclosures were marked by sharp increases in house prices through 2005, followed by the sharpest declines through 2008.

To illustrate how the foreclosure crisis has played out in different areas of the country, Exhibit 10 shows trends in foreclosure starts rates from 2004 through the beginning of 2009 for a sample of states from Groups 1, 2, 5, and 6. At the beginning of the period, states from the industrial Midwest stand out as having foreclosure rates that are well in excess of other parts of the country. States in the central and southern plains also had foreclosure rates that were consistently in excess of the national rate and close to the 0.50-percent level. In contrast, the sand states and upper plains states both had foreclosure rates that were well below the national average. By the end of 2006, the national foreclosure crisis begins to be evident with foreclosure starts increasing most dramatically in the sand states. These states had a clear influence on the national foreclosure rate, which also moved up markedly over this same period. Foreclosures also increased in the industrial Midwest, although the increases were much less dramatic than in the sand states. Foreclosure rates in the central and southern plains states, which were consistently above the national average prior to 2006, increased relatively modestly until the end of 2008 and so are now well below the national average despite being higher than the nation prior to the crisis. Finally, states in the upper plains have had only a mild increase in foreclosure starts, with most of the gains occurring since the beginning of 2008 when the nation entered a severe recession.

To illustrate the role that house price trends appear to have played in regional variations in the crisis, Exhibit 11 presents trends in housing prices for these same groups of states since 2004. In general, the order of the lines for the four state groups is in inverse order from Exhibit 10. The sand states had house price increases that were well in excess of the national level through the end of 2005. In 2006, these increases slowed substantially and by 2007 were declining. The sharp rise in foreclosure starts in Exhibit 10 for these states mirrors this dramatic fall in house prices. In contrast, the industrial Midwest states had the lowest rates of housing price appreciation prior to 2006 and have also experienced fairly significant declines in house prices since 2006. The central and southern plains states had house price increases prior to 2006 that were only slightly higher than in the industrial Midwest, but the declines since 2006 have been fairly modest. Finally, the upper plains states had house price increases that were about the national average through 2005 but have maintained positive growth rates for much longer than other regions.

While the data presented in this section is only illustrative, it does suggest the likely importance of both subprime lending shares and house price trends in contributing to the foreclosure crisis. The next section of the report presents a detailed review of the literature that examines with more rigor the relative importance of various factors in producing the crisis.

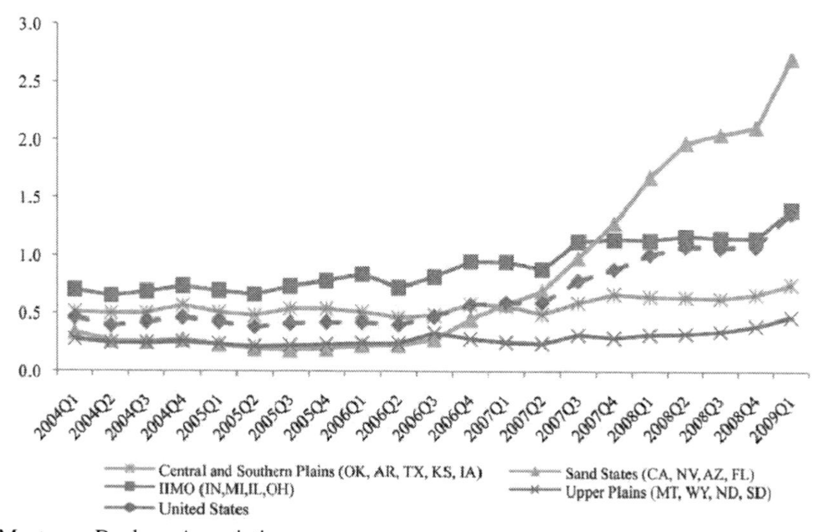

Source: Mortgage Bankers Association

Exhibit 10. Foreclosure Starts for Selected States.

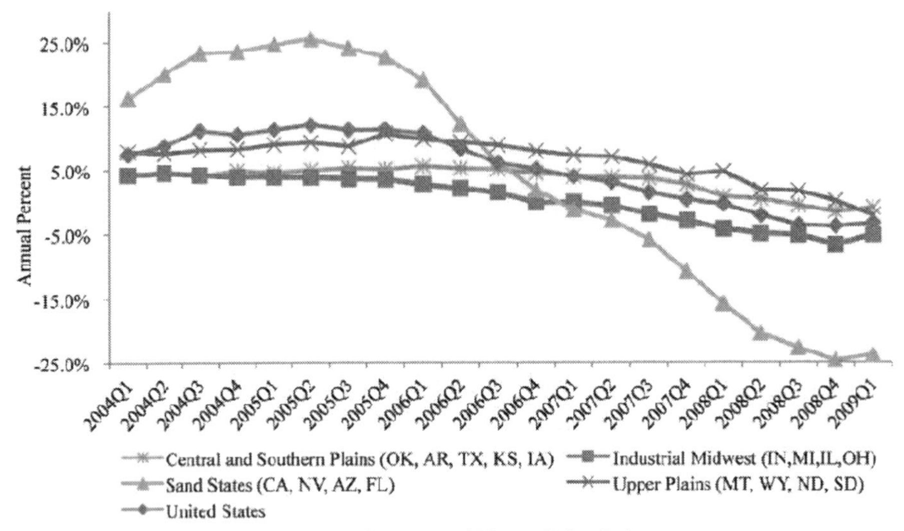

Source: Federal Housing Finance Agency, State-Level House Price Index

Exhibit 11. Annual Changes in House Prices for Selected States.

2. LITERATURE REVIEW

2.1. General Literature on Causes of Foreclosures and Delinquencies

There is a rich economics literature examining the cause of mortgage foreclosures, generally referred to as "default" in the literature.[26] As noted in detailed reviews of this literature by Quercia and Stegman (1992) and Vandell (1995), since the 1980s, this literature has been dominated by an option-based theory of mortgage default, where the mortgage contract is viewed as giving homeowners an option to "put" the home back to lenders by defaulting on their mortgage. In an option-theoretic view, the primary factor driving defaults is the value of the home relative to the value of the outstanding mortgage; when the home value falls substantially below the mortgage debt, owners are better off by ceding the home to the lender.[27] This type of situation has been characterized in the literature as a "ruthless default," where borrowers simply walk away from their mortgage obligations when it is in their financial interest to do so.

However, as argued most prominently by Vandell (1995) and Elmer and Seelig (1999), a lack of housing equity by itself generally does a poor job of predicting mortgage delinquencies, which are a necessary precursor to foreclosures. As these papers point out, it is generally understood that most borrowers become delinquent due to a change in their financial circumstances that make them no longer able to meet their monthly mortgage obligations. These so called "trigger events" commonly include job loss or other income curtailment, health problems, or divorce. Both Vandell and Elmer and Seelig argue that foreclosures are most accurately thought of as being driven by a two-stage process: a first trigger event that produces financial illiquidity among borrowers which is then coupled with a lack of home equity that makes it impossible for the borrower to either sell their home to meet their mortgage obligation or refinance into a mortgage that is affordable given their change in financial circumstances. In this view, a lack of home equity is an important determinant of foreclosures as it precludes other means that borrowers can take to resolve an inability to meet their mortgage obligations, but foreclosures are most commonly triggered by some other event that makes borrowers financially insolvent.

For the most part, the literature provides numerous examples to support the view that most defaults are not ruthlessly driven by falling house prices. One of the first articles to put forth an option-theoretic view of mortgage default was Foster and Van Order (1984, 1985). However, the data on Federal Housing Administration (FHA) borrowers used in their analysis show that only 4.2 percent of borrowers with estimated loan-tovalue ratios of 110 percent or higher actually defaulted on their mortgage. Ambrose and Capone (1998), again examining data on FHA borrowers, find that loans with negative equity accounted for a small share of all loans that became seriously delinquent and also a minority of loans that ended in foreclosure. More recently, Foote, Girardi, and Willen (2008) examine data on all homeowners in Massachusetts over a 20-year period and found that in the early 1990s only 6.4 percent of homeowners whose house values dropped below their mortgage amounts ended in foreclosure.

Of course, while it may be that most defaults are not strictly ruthless, this does not preclude ruthless defaults from occurring. The magnitude of house price declines occurring now in many markets around the country as well as the number of markets simultaneously experiencing house price declines are unprecedented in the post-war era. Some owners are property investors who are purely motivated by financial concerns and may be more likely to pursue a ruthless default if it is in their financial interest. Some owner-occupants who have the ability to meet their monthly payments may decide to default when house values are substantially below their mortgage debt either because of a desire to move to a new home or because they see limited financial benefit from continuing to pay the mortgage given the level of prevailing rents relative to their mortgage costs and the degree to which home prices would have to recover to make them whole.[28] But, given the high cost of foreclosure to borrowers, these ruthless defaults are unlikely to be widespread.

While borrower illiquidity is largely believed to be a root cause of foreclosures, the literature has found only an inconsistent relationship with measures of trigger events such as unemployment or divorce rates. On the other hand, there is always a strong association between negative home equity and the likelihood of foreclosure. As both Quercia and Stegman and Vandell note, in part this reflects the fact that there is little systematic information available on the incidence of trigger events among individual borrowers. Instead, the literature has relied on aggregate measures of these events at the metropolitan area or state level. The finding of a strong association between foreclosures and declines in house prices is also consistent with the view that while delinquencies are brought on by a trigger event, a delinquency is only likely to end in a foreclosure in cases where homeowners do not have sufficient equity to be able to sell their home or refinance into a more affordable mortgage. To the extent that the literature has largely focused on estimating the causes of foreclosures and not delinquencies, it is not altogether surprising that measures of declining housing prices are found to be much more significant predictors of these outcomes than measures of trigger events. Foote, Girardi, and Willen (2008) note that while Massachusetts experienced a record-high level of mortgage delinquencies at the time of the last economic recession in 2001, this period was also marked by a record *low* level of foreclosures as steep increases in house prices offered delinquent borrowers options for resolving the delinquency short of foreclosure.

While the importance of house prices as a determinant of foreclosures has continued to be evident in the literature since the mid-1990s, there has also been a growing emphasis on the importance of borrowers' credit history and specific loan terms in contributing to foreclosure risk. During the 1 990s, as automated underwriting became more common in the prime mortgage market and as the subprime market developed, there was greatly expanded use of credit scores in evaluating borrowers' risk of default (Gramlich, 2007). A variety of studies have confirmed the importance of credit scores in predicting the likelihood that an individual borrower will default (see, for example, Pennington-Cross, 2003 and Demyanyk and Van Hemert, 2008). Pennington-Cross finds that, all else being equal, borrowers with low credit scores (less than 600) were two to three times more likely to default than borrowers with high credit scores (700 or higher). Demyanyk and Van Hemert find that even among subprime borrowers, credit scores were one of the strongest predictors of default along with starting loan-to-value ratios, initial interest rates, and changes in house prices.

A number of studies have found that a variety of loan terms common in the subprime market are associated with higher risk of default. While adjustable-rate mortgages (ARMs) have long been known to be associated with higher risk (see, for example, Cunningham and Capone, 1990), recent work has shown that hybrid ARMs, which are particularly common in the subprime market, exhibit a spike in default and prepayment risk at the time when interest rates first adjust from initially lower rates.[29] In examining a group of hybrid loan originated in 1995–96 and tracked through mid-2000, Ambrose, LaCour-Little, and Huszar (2005) find that hybrid ARMs exhibited a sharp spike in the risk of both default and prepayment in the month when the interest rate first adjusted. Similarly, in examining the performance of hybrid ARMs originated between 1998 and 2005, Pennington-Cross and Ho (2006) find that these loans exhibited a strong spike in prepayment rates in the month when interest rates first adjusted along with a mild increase in default rates. While these authors do not find as strong a spike in defaults as Ambrose, LaCour-Little and Huszar do, the time period studied by Pennington-Cross and Ho was marked by significant increases in house prices which may have contributed to the predominance of prepayment over default at the time of interest rate resets.[30]

In addition to adjustable-rate features, other characteristics of subprime and Alt-A loans that have been found to have an independent association with higher default risk include the following:

- Prepayment penalties (Quercia, Stegman, and Davis, 2005; Danis and Pennington-Cross, 2005a; Demyanyk and Van Hemert, 2008).
- Low or no documentation of income or savings (Danis and Pennington-Cross, 2005 a; Pennington-Cross and Ho, 2006; Demyanyk and Van Hemert, 2008).
- Balloon terms (Quercia, Stegman, and Davis, 2005; Danis and Pennington-Cross, 2005a; Demyanyk and Van Hemert, 2008).

In short, subprime mortgages have been found to be inherently associated with much higher foreclosure risk than prime mortgages both because they are made to riskier borrowers and because they frequently contain a range of loan terms that are associated with higher foreclosure risk. While Alt-A loans are generally made to borrowers with higher credit scores, these loans also exhibit higher risk than prime loans because of the risks associated with lower documentation of income and assets as well as the higher risk of payment shock associated with various loan terms.

But even prime mortgages may also have been of higher risk during recent years as underwriting standards allowed higher loan-to-value ratios, which has been an important predictor of foreclosure risk in the past. The surging volume of piggy-back loans noted earlier may also have masked the degree to which prime mortgages were becoming riskier as relatively low loan-to-value ratio first mortgages were often teamed with second mortgages that brought the combined loan-to-value ratio to 100 percent. In 2006, it is estimated that nearly one-quarter of all home purchase loans reported in the Home Mortgage Disclosure Act (HMDA) involved a piggy-back loan, suggesting that the share of prime loans where borrowers had essentially no equity investment was very high in recent years (Avery, Brevoort, and Canner, 2007).

2.2. Literature Assessing Causes of the Current Foreclosure Crisis

There have been a number of reviews of the fundamental causes of the sharp rise in mortgage delinquencies and foreclosures since 2006. Prominent among these are reviews by the Chairman of the Federal Reserve Board (Bernanke, 2008), the Government Accountability Office (GAO) (GAO 2007), the Majority Staff of the Joint Economic Committee of the U.S. Senate (2007), the Fitch Rating Agency (Costello, Mistretta, and He, 2007), and Mayer, Pence, and Sherlund (2009). In general, each of these sources point to three prominent factors underlying the current crisis: (1) the widespread slowdown in house price growth followed by actual declines in prices in most areas of the country, (2) weak economic conditions in selected market areas, and (3) substantial growth in the volume of risky loans originated—made even riskier by loosening underwriting and lender quality control in the years leading up to the crisis. This section presents a review of the literature that has supported these conclusions.

The literature provides fairly strong evidence that slowing growth and then decline in house prices played a significant role in precipitating the foreclosure crisis in many market areas. On the other hand, weak economic conditions have been a much less important factor than in previous times of high foreclosure rates. Taken as a whole, the literature suggests that the more fundamental cause of the foreclosure crisis was the surge beginning in 2003 in the origination of loans that were at high risk of foreclosure due to a combination of unaffordable initial payment levels relative to borrower incomes coupled with loan terms that would make these loans even more unaffordable over time. The riskiness of these mortgages was masked by rapid house price appreciation through 2006 that allowed many—but certainly not all—borrowers to avoid foreclosure by either refinancing into a new mortgage or selling their home for more then they had originally financed. In fact, as described in the following text, there is evidence that the surge in risky lending itself fed the rapid house price growth that occurred since 2003. Once the limit of extending risky mortgage credit was reached in 2006, house price growth slowed.

House price declines were further exacerbated by an oversupply of new homes, particularly in markets where rapid house price growth had spurred significant housing demand by investors and borrowers that were aided by the ready availability of mortgage financing. As house prices softened, demand by both investors and owner-occupants dropped sharply, leaving an excess supply of new housing that further added to downward pressure on prices (Joint Center for Housing Studies, 2008). Foreclosures themselves also undoubtedly add to this downward pressure.

As a result, declining house prices can be viewed as an inevitable *result* of the surge in risky lending rather than a cause of the resulting foreclosure crisis. As the crisis matures, however, a downward spiral can take hold as declining house prices could exert their own influence to increase foreclosures, which, in turn, depress prices further.

2.2.1. Contribution of House Price Declines

Given the central role that has long been assigned to home price declines in explaining foreclosure trends, it is perhaps not surprising that most reviews of the current crisis begin by pointing to the slowdown in house price growth that began in 2006 as the main factor precipitating the sharp rise in delinquencies and foreclosures. There have been several studies by researchers in the Federal Reserve System that are commonly cited as evidence of the importance of house price trends in the current crisis.

The most prominent of these studies is an analysis of foreclosure rates in Massachusetts from 1989 through mid-2007 by researchers from the Federal Reserve Bank of Boston (Gerardi, Shapiro, and Willen, 2008).[31] A key conclusion of the study is that the decline in house price appreciation that began in Massachusetts in 2005 accounts for much of the dramatic rise in foreclosures in the state in 2006 and 2007. Specifically, they find that a one standard deviation decrease in house price appreciation is associated with a doubling of foreclosure risk. However, the study also finds that homeownership spells that begin with a mortgage originated by a subprime lender are six times more likely to end in foreclosure than homeownership spells that begin with a prime mortgage.[32]

In fact, a related study by Gerardi and Willen (2009) suggests that a significant portion of the current foreclosure surge in Massachusetts is related to changes in mortgage underwriting associated with the growth of subprime lending. This paper compares actual foreclosure levels among multifamily properties during both the early 1 990s and the late 2000s with foreclosure levels estimated by applying housing price trends during these two time periods. The simulation finds that while price declines were much more substantial during the early 1990s, the level of foreclosures was much lower than current levels. The authors conclude that the growth in subprime lending is the most likely explanation why foreclosure levels are higher in the 2000s despite less- precipitous house price declines.

Another commonly cited source of evidence of the importance of house price declines is a study by researchers from the Federal Reserve Bank of San Francisco (Doms, Furlong, and Krainer, 2007), which points to changes in house price appreciation rates as the single most important factor in explaining variation in serious delinquency rates in subprime mortgages across 309 metropolitan areas in 2005 and 2006. This study finds that variations in house price appreciation rates explain about two-thirds of the variation in serious delinquency rates. While the study does find some association between delinquency rates and measures of borrower risk (proxied by high-cost loan shares and the median interest on high-cost loans as reported in HMDA) and economic conditions (measured both by employment growth and unemployment rates), these factors are largely insignificant when house price appreciation rates are taken into account.

A number of studies using data from Loan Performance on subprime and Alt-A loans originated since 2000 have concluded that declines in house prices were the single most important factor associated with the sharp rise in delinquencies and foreclosures after 2005 (see, for example, Sherlund, 2008; Haughwout, Peach, and Tracy, 2008). Perhaps the most prominent of these is a study by Yuliya Demyanyk of the Federal Reserve Bank of St. Louis and Otto Van Hemert of New York University. They find that declines in metropolitan-area house price appreciation rates were the single most important factor contributing to very high rates of early delinquency (60 days or more late within 12 months of origination) among subprime loans originated nationally in 2006 and 2007 (Demyanyk and Van Hemert, 2008). This study pools loans originated from 2001 through 2007 and predicts early delinquency as a function of loan characteristics and house price appreciation rates over the 12-month period after origination. For the entire pool of loans, the study finds that borrower FICO score, the combined loan-to-value ratio of all loans, the original mortgage interest rate, and the rate of house price appreciation all have similarly large associations with early default rates. However, when they further examine deviations in underlying explanatory factors across cohorts of loans by the year of origination, they find that the very high rates of early payment default among loans originated in 2006 and 2007 are almost entirely due to lower rates of house price appreciation and not due to higher incidence of any specific loan terms or borrower credit scores.

Yet, while there is significant evidence that softening house prices played a prominent role in precipitating the crisis, it is also remarkable that the rise in mortgage delinquencies and foreclosure starts began as the *growth* in house prices slowed—and generally before house prices actually began to *drop*. Between the second quarter of 2006 and the second quarter of 2007, 47 states experienced an increase in the foreclosure start rate in the Mortgage Bankers Association's (MBA's) *National Delinquency Survey*, with an average increase of 47 percent. Over this same period, the Federal Housing Finance Agency's house price index indicates that 44 states experienced declines in the rate of house price *growth*, but only 5 states had actual price *declines* over this period. In many states the rise in foreclosures appears to have been brought on by slowing house price growth as much as outright declines.[33]

2.2.2. Contribution of Weak Economic Conditions

While reviews of the foreclosure crisis generally point to weak economic conditions in some regions of the country as a contributing factor, most studies actually find only a weak association between variations in economic conditions and subprime delinquency rates. Gerardi, Shapiro, and Willen (2008) do find a statistically significant association between town-level unemployment rates and foreclosure rates in Massachusetts over a period from 1989 through mid-2007, but the association is much weaker than that for either house price appreciation or the use of a subprime lender. While they find that a one standard deviation increase in unemployment rates raises foreclosure risk by 10 percent, the same change in house price appreciation rates is associated with a 200-percent change in foreclosure risk. However, given this study's focus on foreclosure incidence rather than delinquency, it would be expected that house price changes would play a much more important role than employment trends.

Doms, Furlong, and Krainer (2007) find that variations in employment growth and unemployment rates by themselves explain about one-third of the variation in subprime delinquency rates in 2005 and 2006, but this association is either statistically insignificant or much smaller in magnitude once variations in house price appreciation are taken into account. The GAO review (2007) cites work by researchers from Moody's, noting that weaker employment growth accounts for about 20 to 32 percent of elevated delinquency rates in selected Midwest markets, but the Moody's study is also reported to have found that employment growth trends had little impact on delinquencies nationally. In keeping with this conclusion, Demyanyk and Van Hemert (2008) indicate that they dropped the unemployment rate from their model due to statistical insignificance.

In fact, what may be most unique about the current crisis in mortgage delinquencies and foreclosures is that weak economic conditions were not a significant factor in precipitating these events, although, after the crisis began, they have contributed to worsening the crisis. This view is aptly summarized in a review of the drivers of high delinquencies among subprime loans originated in 2006 by Fitch Ratings Agency which concludes that "the 2006 subprime vintage performance is remarkable for the magnitude of early mortgage defaults given a benign economic environment apart from home prices." As an indication of the lack of importance of weak economic conditions in producing the mortgage crisis, it is notable that 48 states had an increase in the foreclosure start rate between 2006 and 2007 in the MBA's *National Delinquency Survey*, but, over this period, only 16 states had an increase in the unemployment rate, and in 10 of these states the increase was 0.2 percentage points or less.

2.2.3. Contribution of Growth in Risky Loans

Investor Loans

One reason why there may have been such a significant rise in mortgage delinquencies and foreclosures in the wake of merely softening home prices in 2006 is that there was much greater potential for "ruthless" default among home buyers given trends in the housing market. Using data reported by lenders under the HMDA, Avery, Brevoort, and Canner (2008) document the significant growth in home purchase loans made to investors from the late 1 990s through the mid-2000s. From 1993 to 2001, the share of purchase loans made to investors grew steadily from 5.1 percent to 8.6 percent. But, between 2001 and 2005, this share doubled to 17.3 percent. So by 2005, more than one in six of all home purchase mortgages were made to investors. The investor share declined after 2005, but these buyers still accounted for 14.9 percent of home purchase loans in 2007. In states experiencing very rapid house price growth, including California, Arizona, Nevada, and Florida, investors accounted for roughly one-quarter or more of all purchase loans in 2005 and 2006 (Bernanke, 2008).

These figures also appear likely to understate the true share of home purchases by investors, as a common form of mortgage fraud during this period was for lenders and/or borrowers to falsely claim that the investor buyers intended to occupy purchased homes as their principal residence. In reviewing a small sample of early payment defaults from 2006, Fitch Rating Agency (2007b) found that two-thirds of these properties were never occupied by the purchaser.

To the extent that investors were motivated to purchase properties to realize gains from house price appreciation, a mere slowdown in house price growth would be sufficient to induce a ruthless default. Given that real estate agent commissions are on the order of 5 to 10 percent of the sales price (not to mention costs incurred during the period when a home is on the market), if house prices are growing by less than this rate, investors will begin to incur losses. Thus, the high share of purchase loans made to investors is likely to have made a significant contribution to the high level of early payment defaults among loans originated in 2006. However, while the analysis by Demyanyk and Van Hemert (2008) did find that investor loans were more likely to experience early payment defaults, they also found that the much worse performance of loans made in 2006 and 2007 was not related to there being a higher share of investor loans in these years. It may be that the increase in investor loans was masked by fraudulent applications indicating the properties would be owner occupied. As will be discussed further later, a rise in mortgage fraud was evident in recent years, with misrepresentations about owner-occupancy a common form of fraud.

Unaffordability of Subprime Loans Generally

Beyond the growth of investor loans, there is strong evidence that the slowdown and subsequent decline in house prices played such a prominent role in producing the mortgage crisis fundamentally because the rapid growth in the volume of risky mortgages meant that many loans were made to borrowers who were struggling to make monthly payments even at the time loans were originated. In part, the unaffordability of these loans reflects situations where borrowers did not adequately understand the terms of their loans (see, for example, Bucks and Pence, 2006). However, in other cases, borrowers likely understood the risks they were taking but chose to obtain these loans either to tap accumulated home equity or to purchase larger homes than they could otherwise afford. In either case, the originators of these loans ultimately determined that overall these loans were expected to be profitable even if the risk of default were high.

In fact, the early termination rate of subprime loans was extraordinarily high throughout the first half of the decade, but rapid increases in housing prices meant that a large majority of borrowers were able to avoid or resolve a delinquency by prepaying their mortgage—either by selling their homes or by refinancing into a new mortgage. Thus, when house price growth slowed, subprime borrowers' inability to afford their mortgage payments could no longer be masked through refinancing or selling the home.

The strongest indications of the importance of prepayment as a means of avoiding delinquencies and foreclosures are the findings by Ambrose, LaCour-Little, and Huszar (2005) and Pennington-Cross and Ho (2006) that subprime hybrid loans experience a sharp rise in prepayment rates when interest rates on ARMs first adjust. Recent work by Foote et al. (2009) also find a sharp spike in subprime prepayments at both 12 and 24 months after origination. As noted earlier, Ambrose, LaCour-Little, and Huszar also find that foreclosures spike at the time of interest rate resets, while Pennington-Cross and Ho find only a slight rise in foreclosure rates at reset. But this may well reflect the fact that the first study examined loan performance through mid-2000 while the second study examined a period that extended into 2005, when house price growth was exceptionally strong in most areas of the country. Finally, Danis and Pennington-Cross (2005b) further find that the likelihood that a subprime loan will prepay rises substantially after a delinquency occurs, leading them to conclude that there is strong evidence that delinquent subprime loans are more likely to prepay than default.

Whether distressed or not, the prepayment rates on subprime mortgages have consistently been very high. Foote et al. (2008) plot prepayment rates through mid-2007 for subprime hybrid loans originated in Massachusetts, Connecticut, and Rhode Island between 2001 and 2006. They find that these subprime loans begin to prepay at a high rate almost immediately after origination. For loans originated from 2001 to 2004, roughly 60 percent had prepaid by the time they reached the first interest rate reset. By 36 months after origination, more than 70 percent of these loans had prepaid.

In part, the high prepayment rates might be expected in an environment where interest rates are declining so that refinancing would provide lower payments. However, several factors argue against this being an appropriate explanation for subprime loans. First, the vast majority of subprime loans had prepayment penalties requiring borrowers to pay roughly 6 months of interest on the outstanding balance if the loan is paid off within 3 years of origination (Quercia, Stegman, and Davis, 2005). Demyanyk and Van Hemert (2008) present data indicating these penalties were included in 70 to 75 percent of subprime loans originated from 2001 through 2007. Given the stiff penalty from prepayment, it seems unlikely that borrowers would be motivated to prepay with the goal of reducing mortgage costs. In addition, since the London Interbank Offered Rate (LIBOR) index used to set interest rates on most subprime loans began rising steadily after mid-2004, for loans originated in 2004 there would have been little incentive to refinance in the first 2 years of the loan in order to obtain a lower interest rate. Yet, these loans are shown to have prepaid at nearly the same rate as loans originated in 2001—which experienced declining market interest rates in the 2 years after origination. Finally, Pennington-Cross and Ho (2006) also find that the prepayment rates on fixed-rate subprime mortgages originated from 1998 to 2005 were also fairly high, with 60 percent having prepaid or foreclosed within 36 months of origination. In short, the high prepayment rates among subprime loans are consistent with the argument that borrowers used prepayment as a means of managing unaffordable payments.

However, Foote et al. (2009) argue that there is only weak evidence that the unaffordability of subprime loans at origination is an important predictor of defaults. The study finds that variations in the debt-to-income ratio at origination are not associated with large changes in the probability of default. They argue that these defaults are likely due to changes in income after origination. However, the study shows that default risk rose sharply among subprime loans only a few months after origination and remained high for the first 2 and one-half years of the loan's life. If changes in income account for these high default rates, it must be the case that these changes occur almost immediately after origination. The study's conclusions may also be tempered by the fact that the data used do not include any information on second liens and so may understate the true debt-toincome ratio faced by borrowers. Nonetheless, a large share of borrowers had debt-to-income ratios in excess of 40 percent. Furthermore, the debt-to-income measure is missing for about one-half of all subprime loans, greatly limiting the sample of loans that could be included in their analysis.

Rapid House Price Growth—Cause and Consequence of the Crisis

The data presented by Foote et al. (2008) provide evidence for the importance of rapid house price growth in fueling prepayments. They find that the prepayment rate for subprime loans originated in 2005 and 2006 began to slow substantially compared to earlier cohorts. For loans originated in 2005, only 50 percent had prepaid 24 months after origination compared to 60 percent of earlier cohorts. For loans originated in 2006, prepayment rates were roughly another 10 percentage points below the rates experienced by the 2005 cohort. The authors speculate that the lower prepayment rates of these later cohorts are due to declining housing prices, leaving borrowers without any equity in their homes and thus an inability to refinance their existing mortgages.

There is also some empirical evidence that high house price growth spurred lenders into originating riskier loans. An analysis of denial rates reported in HMDA by Dell'ARiccia, Igan, and Laeven (2008) find evidence that metropolitan areas with more rapid house price growth had larger declines in mortgage denial rates even after controlling for variations in income and employment. The impact of house price appreciation rates on denial rates was also much larger for subprime lenders than for prime lenders.

Rapid house price growth may also have been a result of the surge in the use of nontraditional mortgages and looser underwriting. Greater inflation in house prices might be expected to the extent that new loan products gave borrowers the ability to make higher bids for homes than would have been possible using more traditional mortgage products and more conservative underwriting standards. Several recent studies described in the following text provide empirical support for this view. Appraisal fraud may also have contributed to rapid house price growth. As discussed further in the following text, misrepresentation of property characteristics, or the use of disallowed parameters in arriving at property valuations, has been identified as a common type of mortgage fraud. Bitner (2008) describes how subprime lenders worked with appraisers to manipulate valuations to support higher loan amounts. He further describes how these transactions then become comparable sales that are used to justify other excessive appraisals in the same neighborhood, creating a self-reinforcing cycle of house price inflation.

Mian and Sufi (2008) find that ZIP Codes where denial rates declined by more than would be expected given changes in underlying factors related to borrower quality (and so, areas where lenders' underwriting is thought to have loosened) experienced more rapid increases in house prices than expected given changes in borrower incomes. In essence, they find that looser underwriting was associated with faster house price growth than predicted by basic demand factors.

Wheaton and Nechayev (2008) develop time-series models of house price trends in 59 metropolitan areas for the period from 1998 through 2005. They find that fundamental measures of housing demand predict much lower levels of house price appreciation than actually occurred. They further find that prediction errors are larger in markets with higher shares of subprime mortgages and where second home and investor buying was more prevalent.

Pavlov and Wachter (2008) develop a theoretical model to support the view that aggressive lending instruments will fuel more volatile house price cycles by allowing greater borrowing than would occur in the absence of these loan products. Using several data sets, they also find empirical evidence of a link between greater use of riskier loan products and more volatile house price cycles. Specifically, they find evidence of an association between greater use of ARMs and more volatile housing price cycles loans in Los Angeles County during the period 1990 to 1995 as well as nationally from 1996 through 2002. They also find an association between greater house price volatility and higher levels of subprime lending based on HMDA data at the metropolitan area level from 2001 through 2007.

Finally, Shiller (2007) examines long-run changes in housing prices at the national level through mid-2007 and finds that the increase in house price growth experienced since the start of the current decade cannot be explained by economic fundamentals. Instead, he argues that the house boom was a classic bubble, fueled by self-fulfilling expectations by consumers of continued robust price growth. However, at some point consumer expectations should be choked off by their inability to bid housing prices up beyond levels they can afford. With the advent of nontraditional mortgages and a decline in underwriting standards, this constraint may have effectively been removed.

Rapid Growth of Risky Loan Volumes

One way in which overall mortgage market risk increased in recent years was by the rapid growth in the market share of loans that by their very nature were riskier. Exhibit 12 shows trends from 2001 through 2006 in the market shares of all mortgage originations by dollar volume that were accounted for by subprime, Alt-A, and home equity loans (HELs).

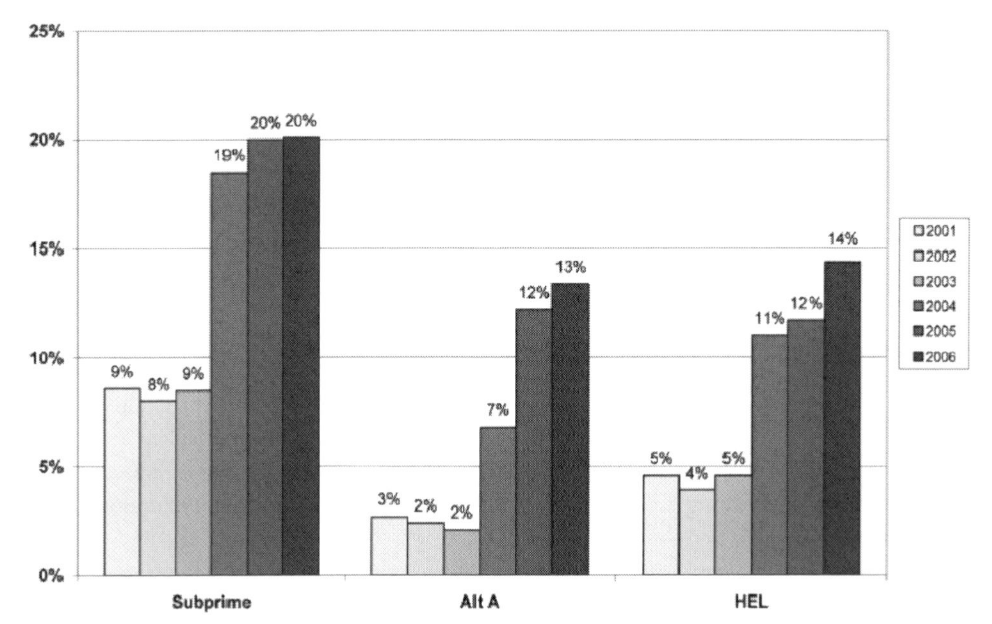

Source: Inside Mortgage Finance Publications, Inc.

Exhibit 12. Market Share of Subprime, Alt-A and Home Equity Loans (HELs) 2001–2006.

Exhibit 13. Nontraditional Mortgage Volumes and Market Share

	Interest Only	Option ARM	40-Year Balloon	Total Nontraditional	Total Mortgage Market
Dollar Volume (in Billions)					
2004	60	145	0	205	2,920
2005	481	280	10	771	3,120
2006	520	255	90	865	2,980
Market Share					
2004	2.1%	5.0%	0.0%	7.0%	100%
2005	15.4%	9.0%	0.3%	24.7%	100%
2006	17.4%	8.6%	3.0%	29.0%	100%

ARM = adjustable-rate mortgage.

Source: Inside Mortgage Finance Publications, Inc.

In 2003, subprime loans accounted for 9 percent of the total dollar volume of originations; by 2006, this share had risen to 20 percent. The growth in Alt-A loans was even more spectacular, increasing from 2 percent in 2003 to 13 percent by 2006. There was also substantial growth over this period in HELs, primarily so-called piggyback loans, which allowed borrowers to take out a first mortgage for 80 percent of the purchase price to avoid mortgage insurance premiums and then finance the remaining 20 percent of the price with a HEL. These loans increased from just 5 percent of the market in 2003 to 14 percent by 2006. In all, these three segments went from a combined market share of just 16 percent in 2003 to 48 percent in 2006—essentially one-half of all mortgages originated.

The rapid growth in these broad market segments does not reveal the full extent to which lenders were increasing the volume of risky loans. In the *State of the Nation's Housing Report* from 2006, researchers from the Joint Center for Housing Studies noted that the combination of rapidly rising home prices and interest rates had eroded the affordability of homeownership. With borrowers eager to buy into rapidly appreciating home markets and lenders motivated to maintain high origination volumes, lenders began to offer a variety of nontraditional mortgage products designed to lower monthly payments and allow borrowers to buy ever more expensive homes. The most common of these loans were interest-only mortgages, where monthly payments did not include any payment toward reducing the principal but also included payment-option loans, where borrowers could choose to make payments that were less than the monthly interest owed, and 40-year amortization mortgages due and payable after 30 years. As shown in Exhibit 13, prior to 2003, Inside Mortgage Finance did not even track the volumes of these types of loans. In 2004, they were found to account for 7 percent of the entire mortgage market, but, by 2006, they totaled 29 percent of all mortgages.

When used in appropriate circumstances, these nontraditional loan terms can be useful for both lenders and borrowers to provide loans that address borrower needs or market circumstances. But, as recent experience has shown, when used inappropriately, these loan terms can raise the risk of borrower default to unacceptable levels.

Weakening of Underwriting and Lender Quality Controls

In addition to the fact that there was substantial growth in risky loans made to risky borrowers, there is also significant evidence that underwriting and lender quality control mechanisms deteriorated in the years leading up to the mortgage crisis. Certainly, underwriting standards were loosened in terms of such factors as income qualification standards, allowable debt-to-income ratios, loan-to-value ratios, and borrower credit quality. For example, Reeder and Comeau (2008) use HMDA data to observe a substantial weakening of income qualification standards particularly in the private-label lending sector but also at Fannie Mae and Freddie Mac. This weakening permitted a significant shift to higher leverage mortgage lending in terms of mortgage loan-toincome ratios between 2004 and 2006 that could only be achieved by qualifying borrowers at higher paymentto-income ratios or very low introductory interest rates with an implied future payment shock. Although the increase in high leverage lending was more pronounced among high-cost loans, borrowers were disproportionately much more likely to use high-leverage loans in both the high- and low-cost sectors to refinance rather than purchase their homes.

In addition, quality control standards to ensure the validity of borrower and property characteristics also appear to have deteriorated. Perhaps the strongest evidence for the deteriorating credit quality of originated loans is provided by Demyanyk and Van Hemert (2008), who estimate the likelihood that subprime loans originated from 2001 through 2007 experienced a serious delinquency 12 months after origination. The authors conclude "... during the growth of the subprime (securitized) mortgage market, the quality of the market deteriorated dramatically." The authors explain that they measure loan quality as the performance of loans statistically adjusted for differences in borrower and loan characteristics and macroeconomic conditions, such as house price appreciation, neighborhood income, and change in unemployment. "In many respects, the subprime market experienced a classic lending boom-bust scenario with rapid market growth, loosening underwriting standards, deteriorating loan performance and decreasing risk premiums. ...Rapid appreciation in housing prices masked the deterioration in the subprime mortgage market and thus the true riskiness of subprime mortgage loans."[34]

Haughwout, Peach, and Tracy (2008) also decompose the rise in early defaults among loans originated in 2005 through 2006 into components related to changes in loan terms, deteriorating economic conditions, and an unexplained portion. They find that deteriorating economic conditions accounted for most of the rise in foreclosures that was explainable, but that a majority of the rise was unexplained. "Observable changes in standard underwriting standards and key economic measures appear to be unable to explain the majority of the run-up in early defaults."[35]

Anderson, Capozza, and Van Order (2009) employ a somewhat different methodology to decompose the increase in foreclosure starts into components due to poor economic conditions and to deterioration in loan quality due to changes in underwriting. They estimate a model predicting the MBA foreclosure start rate across states and over time as a function of year fixed effects and an economic default risk index based on projections of house prices and local economic conditions. The index is derived from a proprietary model of mortgage loan performance over time. The study concludes that roughly one-half of the increase in foreclosure starts after 2005 is attributable to worsening economic conditions captured by their index, with the remainder captured by the time fixed effects which they attribute to deterioration in loan underwriting.

Keys et al. (2008) investigate whether the increased use of securitization to fund loans weakened screening of borrowers as financial intermediaries had less incentive to worry about subsequent loan performance. Their approach is to compare early default rates among subprime and Alt-A loans originated from 2001 through 2006 with FICO scores just above and below 620. They argue that this FICO score was commonly used as a cutoff for loans eligible for pooling into securities, which is supported by the fact that in the data set they analyzed loans with FICO scores of 620 or higher were twice as likely to be securitized. Their analysis finds that, in fact, loans with FICO scores just above 620 had early default rates that were 10 to 25 percent higher than among loans just *below* this cutoff. This effect was much more pronounced for loans with low documentation, which, they argue, is consistent with the view that entities reviewing loan pools for securitization over-relied on FICO scores as an indicator of default risk.

Rajan, Seru, and Vig (2008) also present evidence that increased reliance on securitization as a means of funding loans was associated with poorer assessment of credit risk. Their primary analysis consisted of estimating a model of default based primarily on borrowers' FICO scores and loan-to-value ratio. The model is estimated for loans originated in 1997 through 2000 and then applied to loans originated in later years. They find that the model underpredicts default probabilities for later loan cohorts, and that this underprediction increases as the share of loans securitized increases. The underprediction was most evident among loans with low documentation, while fully documented loans had much smaller underpredictions of default rates. This underprediction for low-documentation loans remains even when they include forward-looking measures of house prices to account for the substantial decline in house prices that occurred after 2005. They conclude that the securitization process relied too extensively on readily observable measures of credit risk and failed to account for "soft" measures of risk that provided valuable information about default risk.

Further evidence on loosening underwriting is provided by two studies examining trends in HMDA loan denial rates. Dell'Ariccia, Igan, and Laeven (2008) find evidence that metropolitan-area level denial rates declined over time from 2000 through 2006 for reasons not related to their measures of borrower risk (primarily income and employment measures). Mian and Sufi (2008) undertake a very similar analysis of HMDA denial rates, but at the ZIP Code rather than metropolitan-area level. They identify ZIP Codes that had high denial rates in 1996 and test to see how much of declines in denial rates could be related to improvements in borrower risk measures—captured by trends in income, employment, and establishments—and how much is related to simply lenders extending more credit in areas previously deemed too risky. They find evidence the denial rates declined more sharply in areas with previously high denial rates—despite the fact that these areas actually had relatively worse trends in their measures of underlying borrower risk.

Payment Shock from ARM Resets

Another factor that is often identified as making a significant contribution to rising delinquencies and foreclosures is the payment shock associated with adjustable-rate loans, either due to initial "teaser" rates that were substantially below the fully indexed rate or simply because of increases in underlying interest rate indexes that produced large increases in payments upon reset. An important part of the evidence for the contribution of ARMs to the current crisis is the high delinquency and foreclosure rates among these loans in MBA's *National Delinquency Survey*. However, there are several studies that suggest that the importance in the crisis of resetting interest rates on ARMs may be overstated for a number of reasons.

First, Demyanyk and Van Hemert (2008) find that all types of subprime loans—fixed and adjustable rate— experienced consistent increases in early delinquencies over time. But they note that because fixed-rate loans accounted for lower shares of loans in more recent years, the rise in delinquency rates of fixed-rate subprime loans was masked by the fact that the overall portfolio of subprime fixed-rate loans tended to include a higher share of older loans than ARMs. The overall fixed-rate portfolio therefore was more seasoned than the overall ARM portfolio and, for this reason, appeared not to suffer as much from increased delinquency rates as more seasoned loans will in general perform better.

Second, Foote et al. plot trends in default probabilities for subprime ARMs originated in 2002, 2005, and 2006 and find that there is no evidence of an uptick in default rates at the time that loans reset. They cite average measures of initial interest rates compared to fully indexed rates to suggest that the number of loans with initial steep discounts on teaser rates that would experience very large increases in interest rates was fairly small.

Finally, a number of market observers have noted that the underlying index used by many subprime ARMs (the LIBOR) declined sharply from September 2007 into the first part of 2008, which would reduce the likelihood of a payment shock (see, for example, Berry, 2008). Payment shocks simply have not been as evident as they would have been in a less favorable interest rate environment. Based on an example of a subprime loan pool from 2006 drawn from the study by Ashcraft and Schuermann (2008), Berry notes that had LIBOR rates remained near the level from when these loans were originated, the average borrower in this loan pool would have experienced a payment increase of about 28 percent by 31 months after origination. Assuming borrowers were paying roughly 40 percent of their income on mortgage payments, the increase would have meant they would be paying more than 50 percent of their income for mortgage payments after the adjustment. However, with LIBOR rates down sharply, loans in this pool were not expected to experience much change in monthly payments when their rates adjusted.

However, the fact that a substantial number of loans face a potentially large payment shock is beyond dispute. One of the most comprehensive reviews of this issue is Cagan (2007), who examined more than 8 million ARMs originated between 2004 and 2006 and found that given interest rate levels prevailing as of the time of his analysis in 2007, 39 percent would face a payment increase of between 25 and 50 percent upon initial reset, 10 percent would face a payment increase of 51 to 99 percent, and 15 percent would face a payment increase of 100 percent or more. When it is considered that a typical subprime borrower had a housing-payment-togross-income ratio of 40 percent, increases in payments of 25 percent are fairly substantial. Cagan's analysis was based on interest rates prevailing in 2007 and so did not take into account the decline in the LIBOR rate that subsequently occurred. But his analysis does put into perspective the number of loans that are at risk of payment shock should rates rise again.

It may also be that the issue of payment shock triggering delinquencies and foreclosures has not been evident mainly because many subprime loans are unaffordable even before payments adjust, as described previously. In support of the argument that payment resets do make loans unaffordable, more rigorous studies of subprime loan performance have found a very significant impact of interest rate adjustments on the probability of prepayment (Ambrose, LaCour-Little, and Huszar, 2005; Pennington-Cross and Ho, 2006). Ambrose, LaCour-Little, and Huszar, also found a significant impact of payment resets on the probability of default in their sample that spanned the period from 1995 to 2000, although Pennington-Cross and Ho did not find such an effect during the period of more robust housing price growth from 1998 through 2005. Finally, tabulations of serious delinquency rates among subprime ARMs originated in 2005 by Fitch Ratings Agency do show an upward inflection in these rates in the few months leading up to the initial rate reset, suggesting that for recent loan cohorts payment shock is at least a contributing factor.

2.2.4. Overall Conclusions on Precipitating Causes of Crisis

While softening housing prices were clearly an important precipitating factor in the present crisis, it seems clear from the literature that the sharp rise in mortgage delinquencies and foreclosures is fundamentally the result of rapid growth in loans with a high risk of default—due both to the terms of these loans and to loosening underwriting controls and standards. The current crisis is actually unusual in that general economic weakness did not play a significant role in producing delinquencies and foreclosures in most market areas—at least not initially. Instead, it was a slowdown in house price growth that removed the primary safety valve for the high volume of unaffordable mortgages that had been made, which was for borrowers to take advantage of robust house price growth to avoid foreclosure by refinancing into a new loan or selling the property for a profit. As Demyanyk and Van Hemert (2008) concluded: "...the seeds for the crisis were sown long before 2007, but detecting them was complicated by high house price appreciation between 2003 and 2005—appreciation that masked the true riskiness of subprime mortgages." Or, as Mark Zandi of Moody's Economy.com more prosaically put it, "Skyrocketing house prices fed many dreams and papered over many ills" (Zandi, 2008).

In fact, several studies have found an association between increases in high-cost lending that enabled borrowers to obtain larger mortgages than they could otherwise afford and more rapid house price growth than would be predicted by other fundamental measures of housing demand. Thus, the slowdown and then decline in house price growth that precipitated the foreclosure crisis is itself a product of the inevitable end to the ability of lenders to keep extending more credit to borrowers. Once the downturn began, both an oversupply of new homes and a rising tide of foreclosures added to downward pressure on prices, exacerbating the crisis. But, given that a significant increase in risky lending lies at the heart of the current crisis, the key question becomes, what were the factors that made it possible for the mortgage market to make so many ill-advised loans? The next section addresses this question.

2.3. Factors Enabling Expanded Risky Lending

In this section we examine the factors that have contributed to the growth in risky lending since 2000. The first part of the section outlines key market developments in the 1980s and 1990s that were important antecedents of the trends that emerged since 2000. The second part examines issues related to regulation of the mortgage market and how the regulatory structure may not have changed quickly enough to keep up with developments in the market. The third section reviews key developments since 2000 that fostered the growth in risky mortgage lending. Finally, the last part of this section examines evidence for several specific factors that have commonly been cited as important contributing factors to the crisis, including an increase in fraud among market participants and the role of the Community Reinvestment Act (CRA) and the government-sponsored enterprises (GSEs) in spurring risky lending.

2.3.1. Key Market Developments in the 1980s and 1990s

As described by McCoy and Renaurt (2008), the seeds for the growth of the subprime market were planted in the early 1980s by two congressional acts that were intended to mitigate the challenges posed by doubled-digit mortgage interest rates. The first of these was the Depository Institutions Deregulation and Monetary Control Act (DIDMCA) of 1980, which abolished interest rate ceilings on first mortgages for residences (with "interest" defined to include all costs included in estimating annual percentage rates on mortgages). Two years later, Congress passed the Alternative Mortgage Transaction Parity Act (AMTPA), which preempted state laws to enable the national use of variable-rate terms, balloon payments, and negative amortization of both first and subordinate lien loans. While McCoy and Renaurt acknowledge that these laws were aimed at alleviating a crisis in mortgage lending brought about by high interest rates, they conclude, "Ultimately, however, both statutes had far reaching structural effects. By liberalizing the permissible features of loan products and facilitating differential pricing according to risk, the DIDMCA and AMTPA set the legal stage for the emergence of the subprime market a decade later."

While these legislative changes enabled the use of risk-based pricing, the actual development of lending practices that offered different interest rates to different classes of borrowers based on risk was aided by technological advancements allowing lenders to statistically analyze credit risk and to incorporate this analysis into automated underwriting systems. A key innovation in the development of automated underwriting was the application of credit scores to assess the credit risk of mortgage applicants. FICO™ (formerly known as Fair Isaac Corporation) pioneered the summary of credit history information in credit scores beginning in the 1950s and introduced the FICO score for general use in 1989. In 1992, Freddie Mac researchers evaluated the ability to predict mortgage default using these general credit scores and found them to be a strong, statistically significant predictor (Straka, 2000). This led both to greater use of credit scores in manual underwriting as well as the incorporation of scores in the development of automated underwriting systems used by the GSEs in the 1 990s. The subprime market was slower to develop automated underwriting systems, but, by the late 1 990s, large subprime lenders began to adopt this technology as well (Browning, 2007). A number of studies have pointed to the growth of automated underwriting systems as facilitating the rapid growth of subprime lending over the past decade (see, for example, Apgar, Calder, and Fauth, 2004; Gramlich, 2007; and Belsky and Essene, 2008).

Another key factor fueling the growth of the subprime market was the development of the asset-backed securities (ABS) market, where the revenue stream from financial assets—including mortgages—is used to back the issuance of a security sold to investors. As described by Belsky and Essene (2008), in 1985 the total value of all ABS was $1.2 billion. By 1991, the market had increased to $50.6 billion—a large increase, but still small compared to the size of the residential mortgage market, which was nearly $600 billion that year. But the ABS market continued to grow extremely rapidly through the 1990s, reaching $1.9 trillion in 2005.

The development of the ABS market as a source of capital for mortgage lending opened the door to the rapid growth of mortgage lending by nondepository institutions. Apgar, Calder, and Fauth (2004) describe the significant evolution of the mortgage market over the 1980s and 1990s from one where depository institutions originated most mortgages and either held them in portfolio or sold them into the secondary market with guarantees by the federal government or by the GSEs to one where nondepository institutions originated large shares of mortgages using financing provided through the sale of mortgage-backed securities (MBS).

Trends in the primary sources of mortgage financing illustrate this story. As of the early 1990s, a majority of mortgages were originated through depository institutions. The U.S. Department of Housing and Urban Development's (HUD's) *Survey of Mortgage Lending Activity* found that nearly two-thirds of the total dollar volume of mortgages in 1990 was originated by depositories (see Table 18 in HUD (1999). At the same time, the secondary market for residential mortgages was dominated by the GSEs and Ginnie Mae. Based on data from Inside Mortgage Finance, in 1990, a total of $259 billion in mortgage-backed securities were issued, with 66 percent guaranteed by the GSEs, 25 percent guaranteed by Ginnie Mae, and only 9 percent issued by other sources.

The heavy reliance on either portfolio lending by depositories or sale of mortgages on the secondary market with guarantees by the GSEs or Ginnie Mae helped keep standard mortgage underwriting fairly conservative into the mid-1990s. In fact, in developing a strategy to help increase homeownership among low-income and minority families, HUD characterized the inability to qualify for mortgage financing as a "very serious barrier to homeownership" and, in response, made it a priority to foster more "flexible underwriting" and to promote availability of "alternative financing products" (HUD, 1995).

The growth of the nonagency mortgage-backed security market during the 1990s helped to expand the sources of mortgage financing beyond the GSEs and government-insured sectors. By 1997, the share of MBS issued by nonagency sources had increased to 24 percent. Along with increased access to nonagency sources of capital to finance mortgages, the share of loan volume accounted for by depositories fell rapidly. By 1997, these lenders only accounted for 42 percent of mortgage originations, down from 64 percent in 1990. By 2005, the share of MBS from nonagency sources had increased to 55 percent. HUD's *Survey of Mortgage Lending Activity* was discontinued in 1998, but undoubtedly the share of loans originated by depository institutions fell further in the years leading up to 2005. One indication of the growing importance of nondepository institutions in originating mortgages is that the number of mortgage brokerage firms increased more than sixfold, from 7,000 in 1987 to 53,000 in 2007 (Essene and Apgar, 2007).

As described by Belsky and Essene (2008), the greater access to broader capital markets brought by securitization not only expanded the amount of funding available for mortgages but also brought investors with a broader range of risk preferences and tolerances and so helped expand the range of mortgage products available. The growth of securitization was also associated with the vertical disintegration of the mortgage market. Previously, the process of originating, servicing, and investing in mortgages involved either a single institution (in the case of loans held in portfolio by depository institutions) or a couple of institutions (in cases where loans were sold into the secondary market through the GSEs or federally insured programs). With the growth of securitization, there was a significant unbundling of the various steps in this process, with brokers processing mortgage applications, wholesale lenders originating loans, large mortgage banking organizations purchasing loans and aggregating them into pools, Wall Street investment banking firms issuing securities based on these pools, and investors from around the world purchasing these securities. Since the actors in this process are compensated by transaction fees at each step and have little capital at risk, this system is rife with principal-agent problems— where the principals acquiring loans cannot be sure that the agents supplying these loans have acted in their best interests in insuring the quality of the loans produced. As will be described in the following text, in hindsight it seems clear that the regulatory system did not adequately evolve to adjust to this new mortgage market.

2.3.2. Failure of the Regulatory Environment to Adapt to Market Changes

In contrast to the fairly dramatic changes occurring in the structure of the mortgage market during the 1990s, there was little change in the regulatory regime overseeing mortgage lending activity. Various authors have identified that one way in which the regulatory structure failed to adequately adapt to changes in the market was through its continued reliance on consumer disclosure rules as the principal means of ensuring that borrowers made appropriate choices with regard to mortgage financing—even in the face of much greater variation in mortgage interest rates and fees as well as growing complexity of mortgage terms (see, for example, Gramlich, 2007; Essene and Apgar, 2007; McCoy and Renaurt, 2008; and

Barr, 2008). Two key federal laws governing mortgage transactions are the Truth in Lending Act (TILA) and the Real Estate Settlement Procedures Act (RESPA), both of which are intended to ensure that consumers are provided timely and accurate information about mortgage pricing and terms before closing a loan. These commentators have argued, however, that the existing system of disclosures was no longer sufficient to protect consumers from making poor choices given the increased complexity of choices. The inadequacy of the disclosure system was perhaps most succinctly described by the Government Accountability Office in its review of federal efforts to combat predatory lending:

> "Although improving loan disclosures would undoubtedly have benefits, once again the inherent complexity of loan transactions may limit any impact on the incidence of predatory lending practices. Moreover, even a relatively clear and transparent system of disclosures may be of limited use to borrowers who lack sophistication about financial matters, are not highly educated, or suffer physical or mental infirmities" (GAO, 2004).

Essene and Apgar (2007) provide a thorough review of the challenges facing consumers in choosing the best mortgage for them even given the information made available as a result of TILA and RESPA. Among the factors hampering consumers are the challenges inherent in accurately assessing risk and in evaluating the total cost of a stream of payments over time. In addition, consumers often have little awareness of mortgage prices and struggle with shopping for a mortgage due to the effort involved in obtaining multiple offers and then in comparing these offers across the many factors that affect mortgage pricing (HUD, 2008).

Another way in which the subprime mortgage market presents challenges for consumers is that these loans are often aggressively sold to consumers by profit-seeking lenders rather than sought out by consumers. Essene and Apgar (2007) provide a number of examples of the ways in which common marketing approaches by subprime lenders are designed to sell loans to borrowers that are not in their best interests. A study by the GAO (2006) similarly documented concerns by both federal regulators and mortgage industry groups that advertising by subprime lenders generally emphasized the benefits of nontraditional mortgage products without explaining the risks. However, there is little systematic information on the extent of these practices. Renuart (2004) argues that a significant volume of court decisions and government enforcement actions suggest that overly aggressive lending practices are widespread. One significant example of such legal actions is described in congressional testimony by the Iowa Attorney General, Thomas J. Miller (2003). In his testimony, Miller described a consent judgment against a large subprime lender for a variety of misleading sales practices that involved a settlement providing injunctive relief of nearly $500 billion. One study that does provide some more systematic evidence of the extent to which mortgage brokers are involved in selling subprime loans to borrowers is Kim-Sung and Hermanson (2003). These researchers found that among a random sample of roughly 1,000 elderly homeowners who refinanced their loan between 1999 and 2000, more than one-half of those with broker-originated loans reported that brokers initiated contact with them about the loan, while only one-quarter of borrowers with lender-originated loans were first contacted by their lender.

Subprime lenders also have strong incentives to get borrowers to agree to higher priced loans than they might otherwise qualify for as they earn yield spread premiums for loans with rates above prevailing levels (Jackson and Berry, 2002; Woodward, 2003). Subprime lenders have also revealed that subprime loans in general were much more profitable to originate than other types of loans. One lender reported that subprime loans were three to five times more profitable than any other type of loan his firm offered, and he saw "no logical reason to sell something that made less money." Similarly, the chief executive officer (CEO) of Ownit Mortgage Solutions was quoted as saying, "The market is paying me more to do a no-income verification loan than it is paying me to do the full documentation loans. What would you do?"

While difficult to prove, there is evidence that many subprime borrowers took on mortgages that were more costly than warranted given their level of credit risk. Lax et al. (2000) compared interest rates on a group of A-minus loans purchased by Freddie Mac with a similar group of loans originated by a subprime lender. They found that the subprime loans had average interest rates that were more than 2 percentage points higher. Even after factoring in differences in default risk and servicing costs, Lax et al. concluded that roughly one-half of the interest rate differentials could not be accounted for by higher risk. Furthermore, they note that the interest rate difference does not even account for the fact that the subprime loans were also likely to have paid higher points and fees.

Gruenstein, Ernst, and Li (2006) examined differences in interest rates on a large number of subprime loans, taking into account a variety of risk measures (including credit scores), and found that African-American and Latino borrowers were more likely to receive higher priced loans than Whites did. Woodward (2003) examined a small sample of loans from a single lender originated through mortgage brokers and found that borrowers with less than a college degree paid $1,500 more in fees, all else being equal, than other borrowers. In addition, African-American borrowers paid $500 more, and Latinos paid $275 more than otherwise similar Whites did.

Taken as a whole, these studies support the view that at least some subprime borrowers faced higher rates and fees than necessary given their level of credit risk and provide an indication that the reliance on a system of disclosures failed to help consumers successfully navigate the increasing complex mortgage market. Of course, other borrowers also knowingly took on loans that were unaffordable as a means of tapping more home equity or purchasing larger homes than they might otherwise have been able to.

The one relevant exception to federal reliance on consumer disclosures was the Home Ownership and Equity Protection Act (HOEPA), which was enacted in 1994 in response to concerns about the emergence of subprime lending (McCoy and Renaurt, 2008).[36] HOEPA prohibits certain loan terms and practices on "high-cost" refinance loans, with high cost defined as loans with interest rates more than 8 percentage points above the rate on Treasury securities of a comparable term or where total points and fees exceed the greater of 8 percent of the loan balance or $400. For loans exceeding these thresholds, HOEPA restricts or bans balloon clauses, negative amortization, increased interest rates after default, prepayment penalties, and loans made without regard to the borrower's ability to make payments. However, in practice, HOEPA has had little influence on mortgage lending as the definition of "high cost" was set at such elevated levels that only a tiny fraction of mortgages have been covered by the law—less than 0.1 percent of refinancing and home improvement loans in 2006 (Avery, Brevoort, and Canner, 2007). While the Federal Reserve Board was given authority to implement HOEPA and to adopt regulations to achieve the act's purposes, it largely refrained from exercising this authority until July 2008.

Over the course of the past decade, many states became concerned about the growth of lending practices that were deemed to be predatory. In the absence of stronger federal protections, starting in 1999 states passed HOEPA-like legislation to ban or restrict specific loan terms or practices on loans defined as high cost. By 2007, only seven states had no mini-HOEPA statutes or other laws or regulations in effect restricting prepayment penalties, balloon clauses, or mandatory arbitration clauses in residential mortgages (Bostic et al., 2007). In their analysis of the effect of state laws on subprime lending activity, Bostic et al. generally find that the passage of these laws is associated with an *increase* in subprime originations and a *decrease* in loan rejection rates. They speculate that the laws may actually increase consumer confidence in the subprime lending market. The study does not address whether entities subject to state predatory lending laws have had lower foreclosure rates than entities not subject to such laws.

One significant factor that may have limited the impact of these laws is that federal depository institutions and affiliated mortgage banking operations were largely exempt from these state laws. As described by McCoy and Renaurt (2008), the Office of Thrift Supervision (OTS) issued a series of opinion letters and regulations over the course of the 1 990s asserting federal preemption of state laws restricting mortgage lending for federal savings institutions, culminating in a sweeping preemption regulation issued in 1996. With the growing wave of state antipredatory lending laws after 1999, national banks pushed for their regulator, the Office of the Comptroller of the Currency (OCC) to provide them with the same relief as federal thrifts. In response, in 2004 the OCC issued a preemption regulation virtually identical to that of the OTS. McCoy and Renaurt and others (see, for example, Wilmarth, 2004 and Renuart et al., 2005) also argue that since the OTS and OCC pay for their operations through fees earned from chartering and examining their member institutions, they have a strong incentive to offer member institutions the favorable regulatory regimes to help build their membership base.

Importantly, both agencies extended these preemption privileges to mortgage banking operating subsidiaries as well. McCoy and Renaurt assert that the appeal of being able to claim federal preemption gave impetus to mortgage banking operations being acquired by depository institutions. McCoy and Renaurt further claim that while the mortgage banking affiliates are granted the same preemption authority over state laws, they are not subject to nearly the same level of examination and review as their affiliated depository institution. As a result, McCoy and Renaurt state that these mortgage banking affiliates are subject to little oversight by these federal regulators—even though mortgage banking organizations have been playing a larger role in the market.

There are no studies in the literature that make a rigorous comparison of foreclosure rates between entities subject to state predatory lending laws and those not subject to these laws. It is also not clear, however, that there were a sufficient number of active market participants subject to the preempted state laws to accurately measure differences in performance.

The high volume of mortgages being bundled into securities revealed another hole in the regulatory fabric. Under the holder in due course doctrine of the Uniform Commercial Code, purchasers of securities are generally not liable for the illegal activities of lenders who made these loans (McCoy and Renaurt, 2008). So, even if borrowers were the victims of illegal, unfair, or deceptive practices in the origination of their loans, they often do not have recourse against the current owners of the loans. Engel and McCoy (2004) identify several ways that borrowers can overcome the holder in due course restrictions on bringing claims as well as ways in which security holders may be at risk of litigation under other federal regulations. Nonetheless, Engel and McCoy conclude that borrowers face significant obstacles in bringing claims against holders of securities so that the litigation risk to investors is not substantial. Thus, the securitization process itself provides another layer of protection for predatory lending practices.

McCoy and Renuart (2008) argue that the failure of the OTS, the OCC, and the Federal Reserve Board to impose greater protections for borrowers in part reflects the fact that these agencies are principally charged with overseeing the safety and soundness of depository institutions and not with consumer protection.[37] In fact, there are a variety of ways in which the regulatory structure failed to adequately protect the safety and soundness of the finance industry given changes in the market over time. As already noted, more mortgage lending was being conducted through mortgage banking organizations, both affiliated and unaffiliated with depository institutions. In the case of those affiliated with depositories, federal bank regulators have responsibility for examining these institutions. But since regulators are largely concerned with depository failures, the failure of a subsidiary is not nearly as important, and so subsidiaries are subject to less rigorous review (McCoy and Renuart, 2008; Gramlich, 2007). Meanwhile, mortgage banking organizations unaffiliated with a depository fall under the purview of various state financial agencies, but the resources states have for this function are small compared with those of the federal government (Gramlich, 2007).

Perhaps a larger hole in the regulatory fabric was the lack of meaningful oversight of nationally recognized statistical rating agencies—who themselves were the de facto regulators of the securities market through their role in assigning ratings to issued securities.[38] By assigning AAA and AA ratings to large portions of mortgage pools, the rating agencies not only gave investors confidence in the safety and soundness of these investments but in many cases actually made it legally feasible for financial institutions to invest in these securities. A key impetus for the role of the rating agencies in the mortgage-backed securities market was the Secondary Mortgage Market Enhancement Act of 1984, which not only made it easier for private entities to issue mortgage-backed securities but also enabled banks, thrifts, state-chartered financial institutions, pension funds, and insurance companies to invest in the two top-rated tranches of these securities (McCoy and Renaurt, 2008).

Yet, the activities of rating agencies have been subject to very limited federal oversight. It was not until September 2007 that the rating agencies were made to register with the U.S. Securities and Exchange Commission (SEC) under the Credit Agency Reform Act of 2006 (SEC, 2008). In the wake of the subprime crisis, it has become apparent that the rating agencies were subject to a substantial conflict of interest in that their fees were paid for by security issuers and not investors in these securities. With competition among the rating agencies for business, there was substantial pressure on rating agencies to meet the needs of their clients in providing favorable ratings.

A recent formal review by the SEC (2008) of rating agencies' role in the subprime securities market found that the agencies did not appropriately manage the conflict of interest between their role in providing investors with ratings while being compensated by the firms structuring and marketing the securities. Accounts in the literature and popular press provide a variety of anecdotes about how the process of chasing profits led rating agencies to downplay the increasing risk of subprime mortgage pools (see, for example, Calomiris, 2008 and Lewis, 2008). Beyond conflicts of interest in their compensation structure, the SEC also found a number of other deficiencies in rating agency performance, such as not adequately disclosing significant aspects of the rating process (including rationales for deviations from their models), not having as robust a surveillance process for lenders as was evident prior to 2003, and not having consistent internal audit processes. The SEC has also argued that the rating agencies may have struggled to handle the increased volume and complexity of deals after 2002. Jaffee (2008) argues that rating agencies greatly underestimated the importance of house price trends in subprime loan performance as the only relatively large-scale historical experience with these loans during an economic downturn occurred around the recession of 2001, which was unusual in having weak employment growth coupled with robust house price increases.

Calomiris (2008) finds that the failure of the rating agencies' statistical models to account for the potential shock of falling house prices resulted in very high proportions of subprime loan pools being rated as AAA. In addition to underestimating the default risk of individual loans, Coval, Jurek and Stafford (2009) also argue that the rating agency models underestimated the risk of structured securities by failing to account for the correlation of default both among loans in individual securities and across securities in collateralized debt obligations of pooled securities. Given rules requiring many institutional investors to only purchase securities with the highest ratings as well as capital requirements that greatly favored investments in these same securities by banks and other regulated financial firms, achieving a high rating opens up a much larger market for these securities. A number of reviewers have argued that rating agencies' supposedly sophisticated methods for assessing risk helped sell institutional investors on the "alchemy of securitization," in which pools of risky mortgages were transformed into safe investments (President's Working Group on Financial Markets, 2008; Coval, Jurek, and Stafford, 2009). In this view, given the agencies' ratings, investors and regulators alike felt confident that the market could appropriately price this risk. In a widely cited speech from April 2005, Federal Reserve Chairman Alan Greenspan touted the benefits of technological advancements in helping to achieve "significant efficiencies in collecting and assembling the data necessary to evaluate risk and make corresponding decisions about credit pricing."

However, Calomiris (2008) argued that the underestimate of default risk due to falling house prices in rating agency models was clearly observable by investors. By this view, the overly optimistic assessment of risk by the rating agencies was driven by investors who were demanding high volumes of AAA-rated MBS in which to invest. In support of this view, Calomiris cites an anecdote told to him by a ratings agency executive that when a large institutional investor was warned about an upcoming security issuance rated by a competitor using overly optimistic assumptions, the investor responded by saying "we have to put our money to work." Calomiris argues that the low default rate experienced during the 2001 recession gave asset managers the excuse of "plausible deniability"—that when house prices inevitably fell and led to high losses among subprime loans, the asset managers could explain that the experience with subprime loans during the 2001 recession had misled them.

His argument is that asset managers were compensated on the basis of fees earned on transactions and thus had incentives to place large risky investments for institutional investors since they would not share in the losses.

In contrast to this view, the President's Working Group on Financial Markets (2008) argued that a lack of transparency in the rating agency process made it difficult for investors to understand what was used to determine the ratings. Coval, Jurek, and Stafford (2009) have also argued that investors were generally unprepared to play a role of questioning the rating agencies' methods. In either case, with little oversight of rating agencies by federal regulators, it is clear that investors were left on their own to question the ratings process. Whether investors were unable or unwilling to play this role, clearly very few questioned the rating agencies' methods for rating subprime securities.

2.3.3. Factors Fostering the Surge in Risky Lending in the 2000s

For the most part, the antecedents to the foreclosure crisis—changes in federal laws, evolution in the mortgage market, and a lack of regulatory reform to keep pace with these changes—were largely in place in the 1990s. So another important question is, what factors have come together since 2000 to foster the high volume of risky lending that led to the foreclosure crisis?

One commonly cited ingredient was the high demand for asset-backed securities by investors from around the world. As described by Zandi (2008), U.S. trade deficits had left international investors with a flood of dollars to invest. With global investors seeking dollar-denominated investments, there was a surge in demand for U.S. securities markets. Between 2002 and 2006, there was a threefold increase in U.S. credit market instruments held by foreigners, from $2 trillion to more than $6 trillion. By 2006, international investors owned nearly one-third of all U.S. mortgages. The growth of hedge funds also contributed to rising demand, with the value of assets under management by these funds more than tripling from $490 billion in 2000 to $1.7 trillion in 2007 (DiMartino, Duca, and Rosenblum, 2007). The sharp rise in investor demand for securities was evident in trends in the spread between Treasury securities and junk bond and emerging-market interest rates, with risk premiums in these markets all but vanishing by 2006 (DiMartino, Duca, and Rosenblum, 2007).

In part, the willingness of investors to purchase risky mortgages with relatively little risk premium also reflects the belief that innovations in financial market instruments were shielding them from default risk (DiMartino, Duca, and Rosenblum, 2007). In addition to the security provided by the carving up of loan pools into distinct tranches with different priorities for repayment, the development of collateralized debt obligations (CDOs) and credit default swaps (CDS) were designed to provide further layers of protection against credit losses. CDOs are essentially pools of securities, which are intended to further diversify investor risk. CDS transfers default risk from security holders to CDS sellers. CDS sellers are essentially selling insurance against defaults to holders of the actual security. If a default occurs, the CDS seller either takes delivery of the defaulted security at par value or pays the security holder the difference between par and recovery value. With the availability of CDS, security investors felt they had the ability to fully hedge default risk. From 2000 to 2007, the volume of CDS rose dramatically from $631 billion to over $45 trillion (DiMartino, Duca, and Rosenblum, 2007). The rapid growth in both of these financial instruments also played a significant role in fostering the broader financial crisis that ensued from the meltdown in the residential mortgage market.

But in addition to demand by investors, the surge in subprime lending was also driven by the high profits earned by participants at each stage of the process, from origination through the selling of securities derived from these loans. Between 2001 and 2003, the volume of mortgages originated surged as efforts by the Federal Reserve to stimulate the economy led to very low mortgage interest rates and spurred both a refinancing boom and strong demand for new housing. According to Inside Mortgage Finance, in 2000 slightly more than $1 trillion in mortgages were originated; by 2003, the volume had nearly quadrupled to just under $4 trillion. A combination of interest rate increases and rapidly appreciating house prices dampened demand for new mortgages, with originations declining to about $3 trillion in 2004.

In order to keep origination volumes high, lenders began offering new mortgage products intended to stretch borrowers' ability to afford ever more expensive homes (Joint Center for Housing Studies, 2006). Efforts to keep origination volumes high also appear to have contributed to loosened underwriting standards. Fishbein and Woodall (2006) cite a variety of evidence that lenders were relaxing underwriting standards in pursuit of higher loan volumes, including information gathered by regulators about loosening credit standards by lenders as well as accounts in the popular press about lenders pushing the envelope on underwriting to maintain loan volumes. An analysis of HMDA data by Reeder and Comeau (2008) also documented a substantial increase in the share of loans with high mortgage payment-to-income ratios during the 2004-to-2006 period, particularly among high-cost and refinance loans. In addition, as noted earlier, several studies by Federal Reserve economists have found evidence that mortgage denial rates declined during this period more than would have been expected given trends in underlying borrower risk factors (Demyanyk and Van Hemert, 2008; Dell'Ariccia, Igan, and Laeven, 2008; Mian and Sufi, 2008).

Further fueling loosening underwriting standards was increased competition among lenders (Apgar, Calder, and Fauth, 2004). The growing use of technology at all stages of mortgage origination and servicing led to greater economies of scale in operation. As a result, the mortgage industry experienced tremendous consolidation, with the top 25 lenders accounting for more than three-quarters of loan originations. The loosening underwriting standards since 2000 appear to have been driven in part by lenders seeking to maintain market share. Belsky and Essene (2008) describe this as a "classic collective action problem" where lenders might have been better served by enforcing more restrained underwriting but to do so would result in a loss of market share and so few lenders were willing to unilaterally tighten lending standards. Recent congressional hearings into the federal takeover of the GSEs identified a potentially similar phenomenon among these institutions, as efforts to maintain their market share led the GSEs to purchase risky Alt-A loans over the objections of their own risk managers. A review of company documents found presentations indicating that a failure to enter this market segment would mean they would lose relevance with their largest lender partners and thus relegate the GSEs to a "niche" role in the industry. In essence, efforts to maintain market share and profits led most participants in the mortgage market to engage in a race to the bottom in making risky loans.

The final—and perhaps most important—ingredient that fostered the surge in risky lending was the rapid increase in housing prices in large swaths of the country through 2006. As summarized earlier, a number of commentators have observed that the rapid pace of house price appreciation papered over the increasing risks of mortgages originating in the years leading up to the emergence of the foreclosure crisis in 2007. In fact, as also noted earlier, the growth in risky lending seems likely to have fueled the dramatic rise in house prices. In short, market developments since 2000 helped create a self-perpetuating cycle. In pursuit of high profits, lenders and investors poured capital into ever riskier loans particularly after 2003. This flood of capital helped to spur rising home prices that masked the riskiness of the loans being made, leading to continued loosening of underwriting standards. Unrealistic expectations of continued high price appreciation by both borrowers and lenders prevented the use of prudent risk management by both parties and created an upward spiral of easy capital availability and demand for housing even with inflated prices. When house price growth finally slowed in late 2006, the true nature of these risky loans was revealed, bringing down the "house of cards" (Stiglitz, 2007).

2.3.4. Contribution of Mortgage Fraud, the CRA, and the GSEs

Mortgage Fraud

There is a general conception that fraud on the part of mortgage brokers and borrowers may have made a significant contribution to the foreclosure crisis. Technically, mortgage fraud is defined as "the intentional misstatement, misrepresentation, or omission by an applicant or other interested parties, relied on by a lender or underwriter to provide funding for, to purchase, or to insure a mortgage loan" (Federal Bureau of Investigation, 2008). There are significant challenges with quantifying the degree of mortgage fraud. One challenge is that there can be a blurry distinction between outright fraud and "creative" methods used by brokers to help borrowers qualify for a mortgage. One subprime lender has recounted a variety of ways that brokers could manipulate a borrower's profile—in ways that may not have constituted fraud—to help meet underwriting requirements, such as employing quick fixes to increase credit scores, omitting co-borrowers with poor credit histories, or reporting only recent temporarily increased income levels (Bitner, 2008). Fraud is also hard to detect because it generally does not become evident until a borrower defaults on their mortgage, revealing the misinformation that was used to originate the loan. During periods of robust housing price growth, such as was experienced through 2006, many cases of fraud would be hidden by the ability of borrowers to refinance or sell their property to satisfy their outstanding mortgage (Mortgage Assessment Research Institute, 2008).

The most commonly cited information on trends in mortgage fraud are derived from Suspicious Activity Reports (SARs), which are filed by financial institutions, including federally insured depository institutions, and are utilized by several federal agencies, including the Federal Bureau of Investigation (FBI), the Financial Crimes Enforcement Network, and HUD, amongst others, in their efforts against mortgage fraud. Importantly, with significant shares of loans made by nonfederally insured institutions, this reporting system leaves out a significant portion of the mortgage industry. But, even with a large segment of the market excluded from this system and with strong housing price growth potentially masking many cases of fraud, the number of SARs grew sharply beginning in 2004 (Exhibit 14). In 2003 a total of 6,939 SARs were filed; by 2007, this number had increased nearly sevenfold to 46,717.

Nonetheless, the number of SARs was still fairly small relative to the number of loans originated annually. However, the low share undoubtedly reflects both the difficulty of identifying fraud as well as the limited scope of institutions reporting SARs. BasePoint Analytics, a private firm specializing in detecting mortgage fraud, has estimated that 9 percent of loan delinquencies are associated with some form of fraud (BasePoint Analytics, 2006). Thus, while mortgage fraud is certainly not a trivial issue, it is estimated to only account for about 1 in 10 delinquencies.

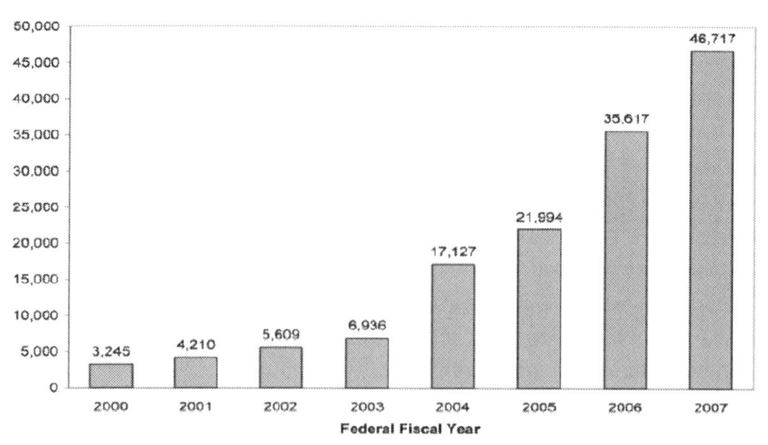

Source: Federal Bureau of Investigation.

Exhibit 14. Number of Suspicious Activity Reports Filed.

In terms of the nature of fraud, the FBI distinguishes between two types of fraud: (1) "for profit," mostly perpetrated by brokers and others to generate profits, and (2) "for housing," perpetrated by homebuyers with the goal of purchasing or retaining a home. The FBI estimates that roughly 80 percent of fraud is "for profit" and conducted by brokers and other professional parties to the transaction (FBI, 2007).[39] Consistent with this conclusion, BasePoint Analytics has concluded that most fraud is driven by mortgage brokers in their efforts to earn profits by originating loans (BasePoint Analytics, 2007). In support of the association between brokers' profit-seeking motives and fraud, their analysis finds a high correlation between the incidence of fraud and above-average interest rates and fees on loans. Furthermore, they find that about 10 percent of brokers account for all the cases of fraud they uncovered in a database of 3 million loans originated between 1996 and 2006.

Based on information on fraud gathered by BasePoint Analytics (2006), the Mortgage Asset Research Institute (2008), and Fitch Ratings Agency (Pendley, Costello, and Kelsch, 2007), the vast majority of fraud involves the misrepresentation of information on loan applications related to income, employment, or occupancy of the home by the borrower. The growth in no- and low-documentation loans appears to be highly related to the growth in fraud. Based on data from both BasePoint Analytics and Fannie Mae, the FBI reports that the fraud rate among Alt-A loans (which include a very high share of no- and low-documentation loans) was three to four times higher than among subprime and prime loans. These same sources also find that another significant share of cases of fraud involve appraisal misrepresentations, where property conditions are materially different than presented in the appraisal or information is used to derive the property value that is typically outside of accepted parameters.

Ultimately, the growing incidence of fraud can be traced back to the lack of adequate underwriting controls by lenders to oversee brokers' activities. A Fitch Rating Agency review of the poor performance of loans originated in 2006 highlighted the importance of poor underwriting performance and fraud in producing high rates of early payment defaults (Pendley, Costello, and Kelsch, 2007). The Fitch report concludes that "poor underwriting processes did not identify and prevent and, therefore, in effect, allowed willful misrepresentation by parties to the transactions." The complicity of lenders practices in the incidence of fraud is also demonstrated by the recent agreement between the New York State Attorney General and Fannie Mae and Freddie Mac to adopt practices to ensure that property appraisals are independent and reliable.[40]

The CRA

Stories and opinion articles in the popular press have identified the CRA as a culprit in the foreclosure crisis. The CRA was passed by Congress in 1977 with the goal of encouraging banks to meet the credit needs of the communities in which they have branches, with a specific emphasis on low- and moderate-income neighborhoods. Banks are subject to reviews to see if they are meeting their CRA goals. Since a bank's CRA rating is considered when banks seek to engage in mergers or acquisitions, CRA's regulations are taken seriously by banks. There is fairly significant evidence that CRA has, in fact, resulted in an increase in credit flows to low- and moderate-income areas where CRA-covered institutions have branches (Apgar and Duda, 2006).

Critics of the CRA claim that the wave of risky lending was generated in no small part by banks having been pushed into making these loans to meet their CRA requirements.[41] While not supported by any in depth empirical analysis, this argument has gained enough prominence that a variety of newspapers have written editorials to counter these arguments.[42] There is a variety of empirical evidence that supports the view that CRA's requirements played little or no role in producing the foreclosure crisis.

One key argument against CRA having played a significant role in the foreclosure crisis is that only a very small share of the high-priced loans that have been a key driver of the crisis were originated by CRA-covered institutions in geographic areas where they are subject to CRA assessment. A recent speech by Governor Randall S. Kroszner (2008) of the Federal Reserve System uses HMDA data to document the fact that only 6 percent of higher priced loans were originated by CRA-covered institutions in their CRA assessment areas. With CRA-motivated loans accounting for such a tiny fraction of higher priced loans, it is hard to argue that CRA played a fundamental role in producing the crisis.

Another weakness in the argument that CRA was an important factor in the crisis is that while CRA lending requirements have been in force for over three decades, the foreclosure crisis is a recent phenomenon. In fact, the rise of the foreclosure crisis came after a period of sustained decline in the share of mortgage lending activity covered under the CRA. As Park (2008) documents, while between 38 and 46 percent of home purchase and refinance mortgages originated in 1994 fell under CRA review, by 2005 these shares had fallen to less than 25 percent. It is hard to argue that CRA produced the foreclosure crisis even as its influence was waning.

Finally, there is also some evidence that loans made to low- and moderate-income homebuyers as part of banks' efforts to meet their CRA obligations have actually performed better than subprime loans. In an analysis of CRA-motivated loans sold to a community development financial institution (Self-Help), Ding, Quercia and Ratcliffe (2008) found that the default risk of these loans was much lower than subprime loans made to borrowers with similar income and credit risk profiles. Similarly, Laderman and Reid (2008) compare the foreclosure risk of home purchase loans made in California in 2004 and 2006 by CRA-covered institutions in their assessment area with loans made by independent mortgage companies while controlling for a range of borrower and loan characteristics. They also find that CRA loans were half as likely to go into foreclosure as loans made by independent mortgage companies. They conclude that this provides evidence that the CRA helped to ensure "responsible lending even during a period of overall declines in underwriting standards."

In short, there is little evidence to support the view that CRA made any contribution worthy of note to the current foreclosure crisis both because the volume of high-priced loans made to meet CRA requirements was very small and because CRA loans had much lower risk of foreclosure than subprime loans generally.

The GSEs

Many of the same voices in the popular press raising questions about CRA' s role in producing the foreclosure crisis have also argued that federal regulations requiring the GSEs (Fannie Mae and Freddie Mac) to devote a sizeable share of their lending to low- and moderate-income homeowners also played a significant role in fostering the growth of risky lending. The serious financial troubles of the GSEs that led to their being placed into conservatorship by the federal government provides strong testament to the fact that the GSEs were, indeed, overexposed to unduly risky mortgage investments. However, there is evidence to suggest that the GSEs' entry into subprime lending was probably more motivated by efforts to chase market share and profits than by the need to satisfy federal regulators.

Much of the GSEs' troubles can be traced to their purchases of Alt-A mortgages offered to prime borrowers who provided little or no documentation of income or assets.[43] Recent congressional hearings into the causes of the GSEs' financial troubles revealed a variety of information from internal documents, suggesting that the agency's own risk managers expressed concerns about the riskiness of these mortgages but that corporate management overlooked these warnings in pursuit of profits and market share. For example, a 2005 internal memorandum from Daniel Mudd, Fannie Mae's CEO, stated that, "the real revenue opportunity was in buying subprime and other alternative mortgages. To pursue this course the company would have to accept higher risk and higher volatility of earnings."[44] While many of these risky loans would help meet the GSEs' housing goals, Freddie Mac's chief enterprise risk officer wrote in an internal memo arguing against purchasing these loans: "what better way to highlight our sense of mission than to walk away from profitable business because it hurts the borrowers we are trying to serve."[45]

That is not to say that the GSEs' expansion of lending to lower income or credit-impaired borrowers was not associated with higher risks. In recent congressional testimony, James B. Lockhart III, Director of the Federal Housing Finance Agency, noted that loans owned or guaranteed by the GSEs to borrowers with credit scores below 660 had 60-day delinquency rates of 10 percent, which was roughly five times larger than the rate among their prime loans (Lockhart, 2009). The delinquency rate among the GSEs' loan portfolios was 2.3 percent for Fannie Mae and 3.2 percent for Freddie Mac, compared to an industry average of 4.7 percent for prime loans and 7.2 percent for all single family mortgages. Overall, the GSEs were taking on less than average risk in recent years.

One way in which the housing goals may have pushed the GSEs into the subprime market was by allowing them to claim credit toward the housing goals by purchasing MBS. Since subprime loans include a high share of low-income borrowers, purchasing the highest rated tranches of subprime MBS offered an easy way for the GSEs to obtain goal credits while seeming to minimize their risks. A *Washington Post* article from June 2008 presents the argument that the GSEs' purchases of subprime MBS, motivated by a desire to meet their federally established housing goals, was a significant source of capital for the subprime market.[46] The article goes on to argue that by spurring the GSEs to purchase subprime MBS, HUD's housing goals may have been an indirect cause of the growth of subprime lending.[47]

The GSEs did play a significant role as purchasers of these securities, although their role greatly diminished even as the market was expanding. *The Washington Post* article reports that the GSEs purchased 44 percent of all subprime securities in 2004, followed by 33 percent in 2005 and 20 percent in 2006. The fact that the GSEs' role as a purchaser of subprime securities was declining during the period when the subprime market grew most rapidly is not consistent with the argument that they fueled the growth of the market. Calomiris (2008) also acknowledges that nonmortgage-backed securities also experienced shrinking risk premiums during the period after 2004, which is evidence that demand by investors other than the GSEs was an important part of market trends. Zandi (2008) argues that demand for MBS by international investors, rather than the GSEs, was an important factor in the growth of this market. While the GSEs certainly contributed to the growth of the subprime market, there was clearly substantial demand for these securities from a wide variety of investors. However, the GSEs' purchase of these subprime securities does appear to have played a significant role in producing their current financial troubles. Lockhart (2009) also reported that in 2008 Freddie Mac recorded realized and unrealized losses of $53 billion in its investments in private-label securities, which was three times bigger than its $16 billion in credit losses across its entire single family book of business.

In evaluating the role of the GSEs' housing goals—which were intended to support increases in homeownership rates among low-income and minority households—in spurring the foreclosure crisis, it is also important to note that most of the rise in homeownership since the early 1990s among low-income and minority households—whom the housing goals were intended to help—occurred prior to 2001 and so before the substantial growth in subprime lending occurred (Joint Center for Housing Studies, 2008). Thus, to the extent that efforts by the federal government to encourage the GSEs to extend credit to low-income and minority homeowners did have an impact on low-income and minority homeownership rates, these benefits were largely realized *before* the problems of the subprime market emerged.

3. Policy Responses to the Foreclosure Crisis

This section describes the existing policy responses to the foreclosure crisis as well as proposals for additional measures that could be undertaken. The first part of this policy discussion will review efforts to address rising foreclosures. The second part will present options that would reduce the future origination of mortgages with unacceptably high risk of foreclosure. The final part will present options for more comprehensive reform of the regulatory structure overseeing mortgage market operations.

3.1. Efforts to Address Rising Foreclosures

Rising mortgage delinquency and foreclosure rates exact a tremendous toll on individual borrowers and their communities. Foreclosures can depress property values, lower local property tax revenue, and impose additional costs on cash-strapped public agencies in the form of additional police, fire, and other municipal services needed to respond to the blighting influence that vacant and foreclosed properties can have on local communities. Aggressive loan modifications and expanded refinancing options can help mitigate these negative impacts. Similar efforts are under way to limit the eviction of tenants from rental properties at risk of foreclosure.

This part briefly discusses these issues, starting with a review of current efforts to promote loan modifications. This is followed by a discussion of several newly proposed, and admittedly highly controversial, initiatives to expand the range of workout options, including more aggressive use of interest rate and even principal writedowns to help households avoid foreclosure.

3.1.1. Efforts to Enhance the Ability of Households to Remain in Their Homes

Over the past 2 years, there have been a growing number of efforts to engage in expanded loan modifications to help consumers remain in their homes. With the assistance of the U.S. Department of Treasury and the active participation of a consortium of banks, mortgage servicing organizations, and other entities led by the Neighborhood Reinvestment Corporation (also know as NeighborWorks America [NWA]), the HOPE NOW Alliance was formed in 2007 to help keep borrowers in their homes by increasing their access to counseling and information and creating a unified private industry plan to facilitate loan workouts. Building on this initiative, in December, 2007, Congress appropriated $180 million to NWA, which it distributed in turn to state agencies and not-for-profit entities to expand the availability of foreclosure prevention counseling services in their areas. This was followed by an additional congressional appropriation of $180 million to NWA in July 2008 for similar purposes.

The federal Government has also availed the use of the Federal Housing Administration's (FHA) mortgage insurance capacity to help provide relief to financially distressed homeowners. Late in 2007, the FHASecure program was launched as an initial response using FHA mortgage insurance to replace risky subprime and high-cost loans with fixed-rate, long-term financing and included some borrowers who were delinquent on their loans due to a payment reset. However, there was limited takeup of this program in part due to eligibility criteria that prevented participation in this program for many borrowers. In July 2008 Congress authorized FHA under the Housing and Economic Recovery Act (HERA) to insure up to $300 billion in loans via a new program: HOPE for Homeowners. This program required existing lenders to accept as payment in full of the original first lien mortgage an amount equal to no more than 90 percent of the current appraised value of the property (87 percent after payment of the upfront premium to FHA)—a substantial principal write-down in many cases. Although some lenders have expressed interest in the program, as of late 2008 the program had insured only one loan. In May 2009, President Obama signed into law the Helping Families Save Their Homes Act. This act modifies HOPE for Homeowners with the goal of helping additional families.

With participation from most of the nation's largest servicers, HOPE NOW members completed nearly 4.4 million loan workouts from July 2007 through May 2009 (HOPE NOW, 2009). Initially, the majority of these workouts consisted of repayment plans, accounting for more than two-thirds of all workouts in the first year of operations. While workouts can help some households meet their mortgage payment obligations, for many subprime borrowers repayment plans offer limited relief. In particular, these plans, by definition, place additional debt repayment obligations on households already struggling to make mortgage payments. The problem is even more severe for those borrowers with an "underwater" mortgage, namely a situation where the value of the property securing the mortgage is less than the amount of their outstanding mortgage debt and deferred payment obligations. Indeed, with home prices falling rapidly in many market areas, one widely cited estimate is that as many as one in six households with a mortgage are "underwater and it appears that a growing number of delinquent owners are simply 'sending the keys back to the lender,' " and accepting the consequences of entering into foreclosure.[48]

Loan modifications that include interest rate and/or principal reductions represent the most powerful tool for keeping borrowers in their homes, yet they pose difficult issues for investors in these loans. Avoiding foreclosure related costs can save investors in the range of $50,000 per property, yet many lenders are reluctant to gain a reputation for reducing interest or principal on loans for fear that all of their customers will seek interest or principal reductions independent of whether they are capable of meeting their mortgage payment obligations. The best available information, however, suggests that only a relatively small fraction of households with loans that are currently underwater in fact "ruthlessly" choose to default on a loan that they could afford to pay. Support for interest and principal write-downs is also limited by concerns about the moral hazard of forgiving debt on homebuyers who overstretched, which may encourage more excessive borrowing in the future.

Based on data reported by HOPE NOW, servicers initially seemed reluctant to pursue loan modifications. Among other things, many servicers lack the capacity to handle the workload associated with elevated requests for loan modifications and write-downs. In any event, servicers have contractual obligations to investors to comply with a series of preset decisionmaking protocols that can limit their flexibility to engage in aggressive loan modification efforts (Eggert, 2007). In the face of these competing interests, there has been rising public pressure on investors and servicers to engage in more aggressive loan modifications to keep more borrowers in their homes. Since mid-2008, HOPE NOW has reported an increasing number of loan modifications by its participating servicers. From July through December 2008 nearly one-half of the loan workouts reported were loan modifications rather than repayment plans.

Yet to date it appears that most of the loan modifications that have been offered have not reduced monthly payments. For example, based on an examination of data from a large cross-section of subprime loan servicers, Allen White (2008) found that voluntary loan modifications of subprime borrowers completed through August 2008 typically increased a borrower's principal debt and virtually none involved a reduction in principal owed.

While servicers did seem willing to lower mortgage interest rates, a recent assessment of the HOPE NOW Alliance program by the Center for Responsible Lending (CRL) estimated that only one in five of all subprime workout plans actually lowered monthly mortgage payments for financially distressed borrowers (Center for Responsible Lending, 2008).

In December 2008, Federal Deposit Insurance Corporation (FDIC) Chairman Sheila Bair called for more aggressive loan modifications that combine both interest rate reduction and principal reduction to enable delinquent borrowers to obtain a 30-year, fixed-rate mortgage while paying no more than an affordable 31 percent of income.[49] She argues that such aggressive restructuring is required to fundamentally change the unsustainable terms of the mortgage and make the loan affordable to the borrowers over the long term.

At the same time, Mason (2007) cautions that there are risks associated with more aggressive use of loan modifications as a foreclosure reduction strategy. Loan modifications can prove effective for those households with good incomes and limited amounts of other debts, but inappropriate loan modifications can also prove harmful, especially as a remedy for those subprime borrowers with heavy mortgage and other debt payments. Mason's main theme is that inappropriate loan modifications can simply draw unsuspecting borrowers deeper into debt and lead to an even bigger default later. In these cases, many borrowers unable to afford homeownership may be better suited by relocating to more affordable rental housing rather than chase what Mason labels as the "unobtainable chimera of homeownership."

The evidence from initial efforts to modify troubled loans suggests many workouts offered in the past were not sustainable. According to the joint Office of the Comptroller of the Currency (OCC) and Office of Thrift Supervision (OTS) *First Quarter 2009 Mortgage Metrics Report*, some 46 percent of recently modified loans were 60 days late just 6 months after the loan was restructured, an increase of 9 percent from the previous quarter. However, this increase in serious delinquencies among modified mortgages was offset by a decline in early stage delinquencies—that is, loans that were 30 to 59 days past due—although the report states that this early state delinquency improvement could be due in part to seasonal effects usually seen in first quarter data.

Making Home Affordable is a comprehensive plan to stabilize the U.S. housing market which was first announced by the federal government on February 18, 2009.[50] The three-part program includes aggressive measures to support low mortgage rates by strengthening confidence in Fannie Mae and Freddie Mac, a Home Affordable Refinance Program to provide new access to refinancing for millions of homeowners, and a Home Affordable Modification Program to offer reduced monthly mortgage payments for up to 3 to 4 million at-risk homeowners.

The Treasury Department released the details of the Making Home Affordable plan on March 4, 2009. The Home Affordable Refinance Program provides access to low-cost refinancing for loans owned or securitized by Fannie Mae and Freddie Mac and for homeowners in areas with declining property value. The refinance option is available for owner-occupied property where the borrower has sufficient income to support the new mortgage debt and the first mortgage is no more than 125 percent of the current market value of the property.[51]

The Home Affordable Modification Program is intended to help those borrowers in imminent danger of default, including those with loans that are not owned or guaranteed by Fannie Mae or Freddie Mac. When evaluating borrowers for a Home Affordable Modification, loan servicers will be required to first determine the homeowner's eligibility for a HOPE for Homeowners refinancing. Where HOPE for Homeowners proves to be viable, the servicer must offer this option to the borrower. If not, then the Home Affordable Modification Program provides aggressive restructuring of troubled loans, reducing mortgage payments to 31 percent of household income primarily through interest rate reductions. The $75 billion program also provides servicers and investors with the option of reducing outstanding principal balance as a means of achieving the 31-percent payment-to-income target. These measures provide borrowers with more sustainable terms that make the loan more affordable over the long term. In addition, the plan involves assistance from the FHA, the FDIC, and other agencies to undertake a multifaceted strategy to help at-risk homeowners stay in their homes.

As noted previously, however, few modifications made prior to the Home Affordable Modification Program reduced monthly payments. As a result, the first quarter 2009 OCC/OTS report does not yet capture the loan performance of the payment-reducing modifications of the Home Affordable Modification program. As of July 1, 2009, more than 200,000 borrowers have received offers for trial loan modifications under the Home Affordable Modification Program. These payment-reducing modifications are expected to experience fewer delinquencies each month following modification than the earlier modifications that left payments unchanged or increased.[52]

3.1.2. Efforts to Enable More Aggressive Loan Modifications

While the greater use of interest and/or principal write-downs may be needed to help stem foreclosures, the ability of loan servicers to offer such write-downs can be stymied by the complex way foreclosure-prone subprime loans were initially securitized, "sliced into pieces," and sold to diverse investors around the world. More than three-quarters of all subprime loans are now held in mortgage-backed securities. Loan servicers, acting as fiduciary agents for investors and bond insurers, collect payments from borrowers and funnel these payments through to investors. These contracts—called pooling and servicing agreements (PSAs)—define the rules concerning how servicers address delinquencies and the use of loan modification tools.

Adding to the complexity is the fact that owners of different risk tranches of a single mortgage pool may be differentially impacted by a proposed mortgage modification or other change in the terms of individual mortgages in the pool. Thus, many servicers have been reluctant to offer interest rate reductions or principal write-downs. In part this reflects concerns that existing PSAs may limit the ability of servicers to engage in loan modification activities that involve mortgage write-downs. Yet, at the same time, many of these agreements contain inconsistent and arguably not enforceable, language as to what actions are permissible under the contracts. The Homeowner Affordability and Stability Plan (HASP) offers subsidies for interest rate reductions, provides bonus payments for successful modifications to lenders and borrowers, and creates clear industrywide standards on how best to interpret these PSAs. Thus, the expectation is that HASP will encourage wider use of loan modification tools.

There remains concern that the Making Home Affordable approach, on its own, is not sufficient to address all situations. For some borrowers, the interest rate subsidies provided through the Home Affordable Modification Program will not be sufficient to allow them to stay in their homes and additional efforts are needed. Some of these borrowers may be helped through the improved HOPE for Homeowners program. But many have argued that bankruptcy reform is needed to allow bankruptcy judges to modify mortgages for families who have run out of other options. Some worry, too, that there may be remaining ambiguities in PSA language that will limit the willingness of servicers to participate in the Home Affordable Modification Program. More aggressive "safe harbor" rules would protect servicers from the threat of litigation as the industry works out the extent to which modifications are consistent with the contractual language in existing PSAs. Other proposals call for changes to the real estate mortgage investment conduit (REMIC) rules. Yet each of these proposals also has its critics, including those who suggest that it is inappropriate to retroactively intervene to override the language of existing contracts.

Proposed Legislative Changes to REMIC Rules

Recognizing both the complexity and variability of pooling and servicing agreements now in force, the extent to which existing agreements limit servicer discretion concerning the use of loan modification tools remains somewhat unclear. Yet there is growing consensus that the rules governing securitization can and do limit the flexibility of servicers to pursue modifications, even in situations where an aggressive modification would benefit both the borrower and investors. To address this issue, Michael Barr and James Feldman (2008) have proposed legislation that would provide servicers with both the legal authority and the appropriate incentives to take distressed loans out of securitized pools and loan portfolios and sell them to the U.S. Department of Treasury or another public purpose organization so that the loan can be restructured or refinanced.

Moreover, because selling mortgage loans to congressionally authorized programs would advance important public interests, Barr (2008) further propose that the Financial Accounting Standards Board (FASB) should modify its Statement 140, which provides accounting rules governing qualified special-purpose entities such as certain mortgage-backed securitization trusts. Barr argues that modifying FASB Statement 140 could provide servicers with further legal comfort in broadly modifying and selling mortgage loans under appropriate mortgage restructuring programs while not conflicting with the underlying purposes of this rule.

Proposed Bankruptcy Reform

Recognizing that restructuring the terms of a mortgage and mortgage security involves the interests of the borrower and potentially scores of distinct investors, not to mention the interests of the public at large, some argue that these matters are best left to a judicial process. Yet, under current law, bankruptcy courts are not authorized to modify the terms of primary mortgages of consumers who file for bankruptcy protection, even though such approaches are common in efforts to resolve delinquency situations involving commercial real estate.

Proponents of bankruptcy reform legislation argue that by altering the payment schedule, reducing the contract interest rate, or reducing the amount of principal owed, these loan modifications would enable borrowers to remain in their home by lowering (and in the case of adjustable-rate loans, stabilizing) their monthly payment to an affordable amount. This not only avoids the costly foreclosure process and benefits delinquent homeowners, it also benefits mortgage servicers and investors if the net present value of the future cash flows from the modified loan exceed the net present value that could be realized via foreclosure. Under current law, similar modifications can be applied to loans secured by cars, boats, second homes, and vacation homes but not by the debtor's principal residence. As a result, the legislation would not set a new precedent but simply would extend to homeowners the same protections in bankruptcy that are now afforded to family farmers, corporations, or others who own investment properties.

Legislation was introduced in the House of Representatives in 2007 to grant bankruptcy judges the authority to reduce outstanding principal balances. This proposal led to the release of a number of studies designed to estimate the impacts of bankruptcy reform on homeowners, loan servicers and investors, and the mortgage market. Although estimating the market implications of such a complex change in rules governing bankruptcy is admittedly difficult, White and Zhu (2008) developed a model and estimated that allowing for mortgage write-downs in bankruptcy could enable an additional 100,000 families to save their homes from foreclosure. In addition, the CRL predicted that allowing bankruptcy judges to mandate principal write-downs would encourage loan servicers and investors to more aggressively pursue loan modifications and mortgage write-downs prior to the commencement of bankruptcy proceeding (Twomey, 2008).

Opponents from the mortgage industry, among others, argued that allowing bankruptcy judges to change the terms of the mortgages would abrograte contractrual requirements, would encourage homeowners to file for bankruptcy to escape mortgage debts, would clog the courts with hundreds of thousands of bankruptcy cases, and would cause lenders to tighten lending standards, thus raising the cost of mortgage credit for all homebuyers and homeowners (Labaton, 2008).

This last objection—namely that allowing judicial modification of loans as part of bankruptcy proceedings will raise mortgage costs for future borrowers—has emerged as perhaps the most hotly contested issue of the debate. While such a change could raise mortgage rates in the future, there is considerable disagreement as to the magnitude. The Mortgage Bankers Association asserts that judicial modification of primary home loans as specified in HR 3609 would raise mortgage rates by 150 basis points (Mortgage Bankers Association, 2008). In contrast, using mortgage market data from the period following previous legislation that first eliminated home mortgages secured by primary residences from being eligible for mortgage modifications, Levitan and Goodman (2008) argue that the market effects of the proposed reversal of these rules would be modest. Levitan and Goodman also note that there is no difference today between the mortgage rates charged for owner-occupied two-family homes, where judicial modifications are allowed in bankruptcy proceedings, and for owner- occupied single-family homes, where judicial modifications are not allowed.

3.1.3. Efforts to Reduce the Negative Impact on Communities

Not only is stemming the tide of foreclosures important to the well-being of millions of at-risk households, reducing the flood of foreclosed properties onto today's housing market is critical to efforts to help stabilize home prices and to halt the resulting loss of housing wealth. Although aggressive mortgage write-downs can help many borrowers remain in their homes, in many instances foreclosure is unavoidable, and the best option is to encourage the owner to sell the home or otherwise convert the property to rental occupancy. In weak market areas where the cost of pursuing a foreclosure exceeds the likely amount recouped from the sale of the foreclosed property, often both the owner and the lender "walk away" from the property in that they do not even bother to complete foreclosure actions or to record the outcome of any foreclosure sale. In these instances, the outcome often is an abandoned property with a title in legal limbo.

It is obviously difficult to disentangle the effects of foreclosures from the effects of the collapse of the housing bubble since 2006. It seems clear, however, that the two reinforce one another—the collapse in house prices has increased the number of foreclosures and the increase in foreclosures has further exacerbated the decline in house prices. By the end of 2008, this vicious cycle was being further reinforced by the onset of a severe recession and associated widespread job losses. Consistent with the forecasts of a deepening recession, forecasts of the likely number of foreclosures grew equally more pessimistic. Indeed, one widely cited estimate suggests that home foreclosures could top 8 million before the current economic downturn has run its course in 2012 (Credit Suisse, 2008).

In addition to direct costs, the rise in foreclosures can impose a wide range of "collateral damage" on communities. In a recent review of the literature on community impact of foreclosure, Alan Mallach (2008) identified several types of damage:

- Diminution of the value of surrounding properties; the more foreclosures in the immediate vicinity, the greater the loss of value.
- Destabilized economic and social conditions in the neighborhood.
- Imposition of additional cost burdens on state and local governments while reducing the revenues available to those entities.

Although local efforts have been under way for several years, the major federal initiative to address these adverse impacts of foreclosure on states and localities was the Neighborhood Stabilization Act, introduced as H.R.58 18 in April 2008 and enacted into law as part of the HERA legislation. Congress appropriated $3.92 billion for the act, dubbed the Neighborhood Stabilization Program, and authorized heavily impacted states and localities to work to mitigate the adverse impacts of foreclosures by acquiring, rehabbing, or converting to rental or other use foreclosed or vacant residential properties. Recognizing that many areas had more foreclosed and vacant properties than could be productively reused, the legislation also authorized the demolition and possible land banking or longer term redevelopment of sites created through the demolition of blighted properties. The recently passed American Recovery and Reinvestment Act of 2009 includes an additional $2 billion to support neighborhood stabilization activities through this program.

3.1.4. Efforts to Protect Renters Affected by Foreclosures

The damage from today's mortgage foreclosure crisis reaches deep into the rental market. Numerous studies document that many of the properties facing foreclosure—including single-family homes and small multifamily properties—are occupied by renters. For example, Harvard's Joint Center for Housing Studies estimates that by the end 2007, one out of every five foreclosure actions nationwide involved absentee owners of one- to four-family rental properties (Joint Center for Housing Studies, 2008). According to another 2008 study by the National Low Income Housing Coalition of 20 metropolitan areas, roughly 40 percent of the recent foreclosures nationwide are on properties likely to be occupied by renters, namely nonowner-occupied single-family and multifamily rental homes (Pelletiere and Wardrip, 2008). Pelletiere (2009) also demonstrates that, given the geographic concentration of multifamily foreclosures in urban communities, these foreclosures are disproportionately affecting low-income and minority renters.

Under current law, foreclosure generally leaves renters at risk of eviction—regardless of whether they paid their rent on a timely and regular basis. Given the limited supplies of affordable rental housing, many housing advocates argue that foreclosure-related evictions will add greatly to the rental cost burden and in extreme instances leave the evicted tenant homeless. On the other hand, the effects of a weak economy on rent levels as well as the increase of rental stock from transferring single-family homes from owner-occupied to rental units (due to the poor sales of single-family homes) may mitigate these effects. Unfortunately, data that trace the postforeclosure occupancy status of families are extremely limited, although there is clearly a potential for a large number of low-income households to experience stress from displacement or posteviction rent increases. Advocacy organizations have conducted surveys of individuals seeking assistance from homeless shelters or other housing assistance program and gathered information from individuals who call foreclosure avoidance hotlines. While many of these studies are anecdotal in nature, they suggest that the ongoing foreclosure crisis combined with increasingly weak economy will exacerbate the economic stress of low-income families and individuals.[53]

Since the foreclosure crisis emerged several years ago, local and state governments have undertaken a variety of initiatives to protect renters from foreclosure related evictions. Although tenant protections vary from one state to the next, the foreclosure process generally overrides existing rental lease provisions. In general, this results from a state's "first in time, first in right" laws, which maintain that if the mortgage was recorded before the tenant signed the lease, then the lease becomes obsolete if the property enters foreclosure. There are several exceptions to this rule, including recipients of Section 8 vouchers and tenants living in rent-controlled units, who are able to maintain their leases after foreclosure by law. In addition, a growing number of states (including the District of Columbia, Massachusetts, Minnesota, New York, New Jersey, and New Hampshire) require "just cause" as a condition for eviction. These laws protect renters by ensuring that landlords can only evict with proper cause, such as not paying rent on time. In general, foreclosure does not count as a "just cause" to justify eviction in these locations.[54]

Increasing the requirements for providing notice to tenants of a pending foreclosure constitutes another approach to protecting tenants from the adverse consequences of eviction. In many instances, renters may not have any warning that the property they are living in is going through foreclosure until they receive a notice of eviction. The new property owner (typically the mortgage lender) can evict the occupants with as little as 3 days' notice in some states. A number of states (including Minnesota and Rhode Island) have enacted or are considering policies to ensure that tenants receive warning of a pending foreclosure and to extend the period that tenants can remain in the home after a foreclosure.

Finally, various federal proposals for comprehensive foreclosure mitigation efforts include special provisions to protect renters. For example, HR 3915, the Mortgage Reform and Anti-Predatory Lending Act of 2007, would not only address homeowner protections but would provide that foreclosures would generally not override tenant leases and that month-to-month tenants would be entitled to 90-day termination notice. In light of the growing federal concern, some loan investors and servicers, including Fannie Mae, have recently announced that they are suspending tenant evictions pending the outcome of new federal regulations governing this matter.

3.2. Efforts to Reduce the Risk of Unacceptably High Rates of Mortgage Foreclosures in the Future

While many factors have undoubtedly contributed to the recent rise in foreclosures, as discussed earlier, no small part of the increase stems from recent increases in abusive forms of subprime lending. In particular, the fact that relatively high shares of loans end in foreclosure less than 2 years after origination is a clear indication that many, although not all, such loans were made with little regard to borrowers' actual ability to repay.

3.2.1. Expanding the Ability of Consumers to Make Wise Choices

In the face of aggressive push marketing by subprime lenders over the past decade, there were numerous efforts to expand homeowner counseling and promote consumer awareness of truly abusive lending practices. Consumer awareness campaigns, including the Don't Borrow Trouble Campaign initiated by Freddie Mac, were designed to prevent unsuspecting buyers and borrowers from falling prey to abusive lenders. Implicitly, these efforts are built on a presumption that once provided with information about alternative loan products, consumers will act "rationally." Yet frequently, the underlying assumptions behind the presumption of rationality can lead to a distorted view about how consumers behave and a faulty basis for generating effective policy approaches that can help consumers avoid falling victim to abuse in the mortgage market.

Essene and Apgar' s (2007) research on consumer behavior provides evidence that many consumers, including many who had access to traditional mortgage counseling and the information distributed through consumer education campaigns, took out mortgages that they did not understand or that were not suitable for their needs. In particular, they find evidence that efforts to educate consumers are all too often overwhelmed by aggressive mortgage sales and marketing efforts that exploit various consumer decisionmaking weaknesses. Notably, some mortgage market participants use their knowledge of consumer decisionmaking tendencies to aggressively market specific mortgage products that may not be in the best interest of the borrower. Instead of supporting informed choices, aggressive and misleading marketing can play on consumer fears and lack of knowledge.

Unfortunately, even the best-designed education and outreach efforts can be easily swamped in a marketplace characterized by aggressive outreach in which some sophisticated and abusive subprime lenders promise to approve a mortgage application in a matter of hours, if not minutes, even for borrowers with "bad credit." In the face of this marketing onslaught, many community groups and counseling organizations are taking a more aggressive approach and expanding their capacity to work with buyers individually to search for the best mortgages. Of course, for such a service to be helpful, community groups must keep abreast of mortgage market trends and developments in mortgage products and must be recognized by potential borrowers as a trusted source of information. Indeed, some community groups already operate a mortgage brokerage business with the explicit goal of using their good standing in the neighborhood to become a "buyer's broker" while at the same time earning a small fee for offering this service like any other mortgage broker.

Borrowing from the automobile blue books, other local counseling agencies make mortgage "rate sheets" available to recent graduates of homebuying courses, participants at fairs, or any homebuyers interested in purchasing a home in their area. Armed with knowledge of their credit score, income, and other characteristics, borrowers use these rate sheets to help shop for the best product and to better evaluate unsolicited offers. Working to enable borrowers or their trusted advisors to be better shoppers and resist such marketing practices would go a long way toward not only reducing the incidence of predatory lending but also to stemming the growth of foreclosures that inevitably follow in the wake of these same predatory lending practices.

Barr, Mullainathan, and Shafir (2008) suggest applying the "opt-in/opt-out" principle identified in the consumer behavior literature to structure more effective mortgage marketing of "good loans"; that is, loans that are fairly priced and that consumers can understand and afford to repay over the life of the loan. For example, many programs first offer a prospective consumer a "safe" level payment fixed-rate mortgage priced in an affordable manner. By starting with the default option of offering a simple and safe product, this approach builds on the observation that consumers often latch onto the first option for which they qualify. Those borrowers who meet a certain set of criteria, (for example, lower income-to-housing-expense ratio) could be allowed to "opt out" of this requirement, a feature that would still allow for mitigating circumstances of some borrowers, but research shows that such an approach is more likely to help consumers make choices that are more likely to be in their (and society's) long-term interest.

3.2.2. Legal and Regulatory Efforts to Ban Deceptive Lending Practices

While expanding the range of consumer counseling and consumer assistance efforts is likely to be helpful, it may also be important to more forcefully counteract aggressive marketing practices and consider banning inherently deceptive loan features. Moreover, since the mortgage market will continue to create new products, efforts to ban specific loan terms or mortgage products may not keep pace with these innovations. Therefore, focusing on efforts to reform the mortgage lending process itself is an equally important strategy.

Disclosure is the major form of regulation for most home mortgages in the United States. The Truth in Lending Act (TILA) requires lenders and brokers to disclose the total finance charge and annual percentage rate of loans. The Real Estate Settlement Procedures Act (RESPA) mandates the disclosure of closing costs for home mortgages. In addition, all mortgage lenders must comply with the Home Ownership and Equity Protection Act (HOEPA) of 1994, which regulates a number of practices, including balloon clauses, loans without regard to the borrower's ability to pay, negative amortization, prepayment penalties, and abusive refinancing. In addition, lenders who make HOEPA loans must provide special truth in lending disclosures to loan applicants in advance of closing. Finally, consumers are also covered by a patchwork of state and federal antipredatory lending laws.

In July 2008, some minor elements of antipredatory lending reform were included in the HERA legislation, along with the act's major reforms of the programs and the oversight of the FHA, the GSEs, and the Federal Home Loan Bank System. HERA also included the Secure and Fair Enforcement (S.A.F.E.) Mortgage Licensing Act of 2008, which provides for a nationwide mortgage licensing system and registry for all state-licensed mortgage originators. This act is intended to enhance consumer protections and reduce fraud by establishing more consistent licensing requirements and oversight of all mortgage lenders. In the same month, after considerable prodding by Congress to more aggressively utilize existing legislative authority, the Federal Reserve Board of Governors issued new rules that would more broadly ban unfair and deceptive mortgage practices and improve TILA disclosures, while in November the U.S. Department of Housing and Urban Development (HUD) issued new RESPA rules designed to increase transparency and enable all borrowers to get firm price quotes on loans and settlement services in order to comparison shop.

But even while applauding these initial efforts, many consumer advocates argue that additional reform is needed. Among areas of greatest concern are efforts to limit or ban yield spread premiums, which provide brokers and loan officers with incentives to sell borrowers higher priced loans, and prepayment penalties, which lock borrowers into high-priced loans and expose them to high fees if they need to refinance or sell their homes. There are also proposals to develop new standards for truth in lending so that mortgage brokers and lenders do not have incentives to get around disclosure rules. Under this approach, federal regulators would evaluate whether a creditor's disclosure was objectively unreasonable, in that the disclosure would fail to communicate effectively the key terms and risks of the mortgage to the typical borrower.

In June 2009, the Treasury Department issued a report outlining detailed recommendations for comprehensive reform of the regulatory structure overseeing the financial sector (U.S. Department of the Treasury, 2009). The report identifies five broad areas where reform is needed, one of which is to provide greater protections for consumers against abusive practices. A central part of the Treasury Department's proposals with regard to consumer protections is the establishment of a new Consumer Financial Protection Agency, which would have broad jurisdiction to protect consumers across the financial sector from unfair, deceptive, or abusive practices. In addition, the Treasury Department recommends that this new agency develop stronger regulations governing consumer disclosures to ensure that they are transparent, simple, and fair.

3.3. Comprehensive Mortgage Market Reform

Arguably, the failure of federal regulation to adapt to the rapid changes in both the primary and secondary market was a key element in the explosion of high-risk lending and resulting surge in mortgage delinquency and default. Over the past several decades, federal legislation and regulation focused much of its energy on regulations that related to deposit-taking institutions, including major commercial banks and thrifts as well as thousands of smaller deposit-taking institutions. For these federally supervised institutions, teams of examiners review loan level records, including Home Mortgage Disclosure Act reports. Examiners also check for lending discrimination and the degree to which the lender evaluates the borrower's ability to repay the mortgage.

This detailed loan-level review did not extend to the growing number of nonbanks chartered by states and not subject to federal supervision, nor even to the many mortgage banking affiliates and subsidiaries of federally regulated banks and thrifts. Similarly, while much attention was given to oversight of the GSEs, increasingly capital was flooding into the mortgage markets through lightly regulated (or even entirely unregulated) Wall Street conduits. The uneven regulation and supervision left what one former Governor of the Federal Reserve Board described as a "gigantic hole in the supervisory safety net" (Gramlich, 2007).

3.3.1. Efforts to Promote Uniform Regulations in the Primary Market

Since the boom and bust of the subprime market was led by nonbank institutions and less fully regulated affiliates and subsidiaries of banks, in large measure the nation's regulatory mechanisms may have been focused on the wrong parts of the system. To realign regulation with today's organization of financial services, greater uniformity of regulation is needed across the lending practices of all segments of the mortgage industry and its regulators. Reforms could reduce the incidence of nonbanks or bank affiliates and subsidiaries playing by different rules and could encourage hands-on oversight to improve fair lending enforcement and compliance monitoring.

An example of harmonizing the rules for all loan originators could be reform of the Community Reinvestment Act (CRA). Such reform would involve expanding the current onsite reviews and detailed file checks now performed on assessment area lending of CRA-regulated entities to all mortgage lending activities. Most importantly, CRA could be expanded to cover independent mortgage banking operations and other newly emerging nonbank lenders.

The Treasury Department's recommendations address these concerns by calling for the Federal Reserve to oversee and set stronger capital requirements for all financial firms, even if they do not own banks (U.S. Department of the Treasury, 2009). In addition, these recommendations also call for the creation of a single National Bank Supervisor to oversee all federally chartered banks as well as the elimination of loopholes that allow some depositories to avoid bank holding company regulation by the Federal Reserve.

3.3.2. Secondary Market Reform Initiatives

As with regulation of the primary market, it is important to take note of the lack of uniformity in the regulation of secondary market participants. The Federal Housing Enterprises Financial Safety and Soundness Act of 1992 established a complex regulatory framework for Fannie Mae and Freddie Mac. Under this system, the Office of Federal Housing Enterprise Oversight was created to oversee safety and soundness regulation of these two GSEs, while HUD was charged with "mission regulation," or the task of overseeing the extent to which the GSEs helped to expand access to affordable housing for the nation's lower income individuals and communities.

At the time the legislation was enacted, the subprime sector barely existed and the secondary market for sub- prime loans was just emerging. Many of the new secondary market institutions and capital market instruments that became the mainstay for funding subprime mortgages did not exist. Similar to potential regulatory changes for the primary market, the changes in mortgage industry structure and the emergence of new mortgage delivery channels imply that federal oversight of the secondary markets must adjust as well.

As a result of this lack of uniformity in regulation, Fannie Mae and Freddie Mac had been subject to extensive federal oversight; however, most of the funding for the subprime market had been flowing through the lightly regulated private-label mortgage-backed securities market. Although the U.S. Securities and Exchange Commission is charged with the responsibility of monitoring the wide range of security transactions linked to the subprime sector, the degree of due diligence in this sector falls short of the more extensive oversight review of the GSEs. Developing a new and comprehensive regulatory structure for the non-GSE segment of the secondary mortgage market will be important.

In considering how best to regulate the GSEs and other secondary market participants, it is important to place these issues in the broader context of how the capital markets channel investment dollars into the subprime mortgage market. Just as is the case in the primary market, the development of detailed secondary market regulations that apply to only one segment of the marketplace can be both counterproductive and unfair. Considering how best to reduce the tendency for capital used to fund higher priced mortgages to flow through less-regulated capital market channels is a worthy addition to the current debate on GSE reform in particular and on capital markets in general.

The recent enactment of GSE regulatory reform under the 2008 HERA legislation and subsequent placement of Fannie Mae and Freddie Mac into conservatorship make examination of the broader issues relating to the regulation of the secondary mortgage market in general a high priority.

With regard to the secondary markets, the Treasury Department's recent recommendations also call for enhanced regulation of securitization markets, including greater oversight of credit rating agencies and a requirement that originators and security issuers retain a financial interest in securitized loans (U.S. Department of the Treasury, 2009). The Federal Reserve would also be granted new authority to supervise all firms that pose a risk to financial stability.

APPENDIX

Table 1. State-Level Trends in Foreclosure Starts and Selected Market Factors (1 of 2)

Category	State	Foreclosure Start Rate			High-Cost Loan Share	Annual Change in FHFA House Price Index		Unemployment Rate	
				Change					
		2005	2008	2005–2008	2006	2005	2008	2005	2008
Group 1: Gain in foreclosure starts > 1.00									
Nevada		0.20	2.34	2.14	34.6%	22.2%	– 23.0%	4.50	6.70
Florida		0.23	2.19	1.96	37.0%	24.6%	– 20.1%	3.80	6.20
Arizona		0.22	1.73	1.51	32.5%	28.8%	– 16.2%	4.60	5.50
California		0.15	1.58	1.43	30.5%	21.2%	– 24.3%	5.40	7.20
Group average		0.20	1.96	1.76	33.6%	24.2%	– 20.9%	4.58	6.40
Group 2: Foreclosure starts >1.00									
Michigan		0.63	1.25	0.61	32.4%	1.9%	– 10.4%	6.80	8.40
Rhode Island		0.27	1.23	0.96	29.8%	10.6%	– 7.5%	5.10	7.80
Indiana		0.92	1.16	0.24	30.4%	3.2%	– 2.4%	5.40	5.90
Ohio		0.84	1.15	0.31	29.1%	2.9%	– 4.5%	5.90	6.50
Illinois		0.47	1.05	0.58	32.1%	7.1%	– 3.9%	5.80	6.50
Georgia		0.57	1.05	0.48	29.4%	5.8%	– 5.5%	5.20	6.20
Group average		0.62	1.15	0.53	30.5%	5.2%	– 5.7%	5.70	6.88
Group 3: Gain in foreclosure starts > 0.40 & <1.00									
Minnesota		0.33	0.93	0.61	26.8%	5.8%	– 6.6%	4.20	5.40
New Jersey		0.29	0.89	0.60	27.6%	14.2%	– 5.3%	4.50	5.50
Maine		0.32	0.89	0.57	26.6%	9.9%	– 1.8%	4.90	5.40
Maryland		0.22	0.83	0.61	33.3%	19.9%	– 9.0%	4.10	4.40
Wisconsin		0.40	0.81	0.41	25.0%	5.6%	– 1.5%	4.80	4.70
District of Columbia		0.21	0.75	0.55	26.2%	19.6%	– 4.3%	6.50	7.00
New Hampshire		0.26	0.74	0.48	23.8%	8.6%	– 6.4%	3.60	3.80
Connecticut		0.29	0.72	0.43	25.9%	10.4%	– 4.4%	4.90	5.70
Virginia		0.16	0.72	0.56	26.0%	15.8%	– 7.1%	3.50	4.00
Hawaii		0.12	0.66	0.54	25.4%	24.2%	– 1.5%	2.70	3.90
Group average		0.26	0.79	0.53	26.7%	13.4%	– 4.8%	4.37	4.98
Group 4: Gain in foreclosure starts > 0.20 & <0.40									
Mississippi		0.55	0.92	0.36	35.6%	6.8%	– 2.2%	7.80	6.90
Colorado		0.53	0.82	0.29	24.2%	5.2%	– 2.4%	5.10	4.90
Kentucky		0.60	0.81	0.22	26.2%	4.2%	0.0%	6.10	6.40

Category	State	Foreclosure Start Rate			High-Cost Loan Share	Annual Change in FHFA House Price Index		Unemployment Rate	
				Change					
		2005	2008	2005–2008	2006	2005	2008	2005	2008
Tennessee		0.55	0.77	0.22	27.8%	6.9%	– 1.8%	5.60	6.40
Missouri		0.46	0.73	0.27	31.2%	5.7%	– 3.2%	5.40	6.10
Idaho		0.32	0.71	0.39	25.0%	14.3%	– 2.9%	3.70	4.90
West Virginia		0.49	0.71	0.22	25.8%	6.8%	1.1%	4.90	4.30
Alabama		0.41	0.69	0.29	29.1%	7.2%	– 1.1%	3.80	5.00
Massachusetts		0.28	0.66	0.39	23.8%	6.7%	– 4.6%	4.80	5.30
Louisiana		0.43	0.64	0.22	31.2%	7.5%	– 0.5%	6.70	4.60
New York		0.33	0.63	0.30	29.5%	9.4%	– 1.2%	5.00	5.40
Delaware		0.34	0.62	0.28	25.5%	13.5%	– 4.5%	4.00	4.80
Oregon		0.25	0.60	0.34	24.1%	16.6%	– 4.2%	6.20	6.40
Washington		0.27	0.55	0.28	24.6%	15.2%	– 3.4%	5.50	5.30
Vermont		0.19	0.51	0.31	20.3%	12.2%	– 1.2%	3.50	4.80
Group average		0.40	0.69	0.29	26.9%	9.2%	– 2.1%	5.21	5.43
Group 5: Gain in foreclosure starts < 0.20									
South Carolina		0.61	0.79	0.18	25.5%	6.9%	– 0.8%	6.70	6.90
Oklahoma		0.63	0.70	0.07	30.4%	5.2%	1.0%	4.50	3.80
Utah		0.56	0.69	0.13	25.7%	11.4%	– 3.0%	4.10	3.40
Texas		0.51	0.64	0.13	30.9%	5.0%	1.5%	5.40	4.90
Pennsylvania		0.48	0.64	0.15	25.2%	11.1%	– 1.6%	5.00	5.40
Kansas		0.53	0.63	0.10	25.3%	4.0%	– 0.4%	5.10	4.40
Arkansas		0.44	0.62	0.19	26.6%	6.7%	– 2.3%	5.10	5.10
Nebraska		0.43	0.62	0.19	25.6%	3.5%	– 2.4%	3.90	3.30
Iowa		0.45	0.62	0.17	25.4%	4.2%	– 0.7%	4.30	4.10
New Mexico		0.44	0.59	0.15	25.7%	12.6%	– 0.6%	5.20	4.20
North Carolina		0.51	0.57	0.07	23.5%	7.0%	– 0.1%	5.30	6.30
Group average		0.51	0.65	0.14	26.4%	7.1%	– 0.9%	4.96	4.71
Group 6: Foreclosure starts < 0.50									
South Dakota		0.27	0.40	0.13	19.5%	6.7%	1.9%	3.60	3.00
Montana		0.25	0.38	0.13	20.7%	11.6%	1.2%	3.70	4.50
Alaska		0.22	0.38	0.16	23.0%	11.1%	– 0.5%	6.90	6.70
Wyoming		0.17	0.30	0.13	25.0%	11.0%	2.0%	3.70	3.10
North Dakota		0.19	0.28	0.09	20.2%	8.4%	3.4%	3.40	3.20
Group average		0.22	0.35	0.13	21.7%	9.8%	1.6%	4.26	4.10
Average, all states		**0.39**	**0.82**	**0.43**	**27.2%**	**10.3%**	**– 3.9%**	**4.91**	**5.30**

FHFA = Federal Housing Finance Agency.

Note: High-cost loans are originated with an annual percentage rate at or above 3 percentage points plus the applicable Treasury yield.

Sources: Federal Housing Finance Agency, House Price Index State-Level; Mortgage Bankers Association; U.S. Census Bureau.

REFERENCES

Ambrose, Brent W., & Charles A. Capone. (1998). "The Conditional Probability of Mortgage Default," *Real Estate Economics, 26* (3), 359–390.

Ambrose, Brent W., Michael LaCour-Little, & Zsuzsa R. Huszar. (2005). "A Note on Hybrid Mortgages," *Real Estate Economics, 33* (4), 765–782.

Anderson, Charles D., Dennis R. Capozza, & Robert Van Order. (2009). *Deconstructing a Mortgage Meltdown: A Methodology for Decomposing Underwriting Quality*. Social Science Research Network. http://ssrn. com/abstract=141 1782.

Apgar, William C., & Mark Duda. (2006). *Collateral Damage: The Municipal Impact of Today's Mortgage Foreclosure Boom*. Minneapolis, MN: Homeownership Preservation Foundation.

Apgar, William C., Jr., Allegra Calder, & Gary Fauth. (2004). *Credit Capital and Communities: The Implications of the Changing Mortgage Banking Industry for Community Based Organizations.* Cambridge, MA: Harvard University, Joint Center for Housing Studies.

Ashcraft, Adam B., & Til Schuermann. (2008). *Understanding the Securitization of Subprime Mortgage Credit.* Staff Report No. 318. New York: Federal Reserve Bank of New York.

Avery, Robert B., Kenneth P. Brevoort, & Glenn B. Canner. (2007). "The (2006) HMDA Data," *Federal Reserve Bulletin*, Vol. *93*, December.

Avery, Robert B., Kenneth P. Brevoort, & Glenn B. Canner. 2008. "The 2007 HMDA Data," *Federal Reserve Bulletin*, Vol. *94*, December.

Barr, Michael S. (2008). Testimony Before the Domestic Policy Subcommittee, U.S. House of Representatives Committee on Oversight & Government Reform, November 14.

Barr, Michael S., & James A. Feldman. (2008). *Issue Brief: Overcoming Legal Barriers to the Bulk Sale of At-Risk Mortgages*. Washington, DC: Center for American Progress. 2008.

Barr, Michael S., Sendhil Mullainathan, & Eldar Shafir. (2008). "Behaviorally Informed Home Mortgage Credit Regulation." In *Borrowing to Live: Consumer and Mortgage Credit Revisited*, edited by Nicolas P. Retsinas and Eric S. Belsky. Washington, DC: The Brookings Institution.

BasePoint Analytics. (2006). *A Study on Mortgage Fraud and the Impacts of a Changing Financial Climate*. Carlsbad, CA: BasePoint Analytics.

BasePoint Analytics. (2007). *Broker-Facilitated Fraud: The Impact on Mortgage Lenders*. Carlsbad, CA: BasePoint Analytics.

Belsky, Eric S., & Ren S. Essene. (2008). "Consumer and Mortgage Credit at a Crossroads: Preserving Expanded Access while Informing Choices and Protecting Consumers." In *Borrowing to Live: Consumer and Mortgage Credit Revisited*, edited by Nicolas P. Retsinas and Eric S. Belsky. Washington, DC: The Brookings Institution.

Bernanke, Ben S. (2008). "Mortgage Delinquencies and Foreclosures." Presentation at Columbia Business School's 32nd Annual Dinner, New York, May 5.

Berry, John M., (2008). "Fed Actions Defuse Subprime ARM Rate Reset Bomb," *Bloomberg*, March 27. Bitner, Richard. 2008. *Confessions of a Subprime Lender*. Hoboken, NJ: John Wiley & Sons.

Bostic, Raphael W., Kathleen C. Engel, Patricia A. McCoy, Anthony Pennington-Cross, & Susan M. Wachter. 2007. State and Local Anti-Predatory Lending Laws: The Effect of Legal Enforcement Mechanisms. Working paper. Social Science Research Network. http://ssrn.com/abstract=1005423.

Bucks, Brian, & Karen Pence. (2006). Do Homeowners Know Their House Values and Mortgage Terms? Working paper no. 2006-03. Washington, DC: Federal Reserve Board of Governors.

Bunce, Harold L., Debbie Gruenstein, Christopher E. Herbert, & Randall M. Scheessele. (2000). "Subprime Foreclosures: The Smoking Gun of Predatory Lending. Presentation at Housing Policies in the New Millennium Conference, Washington, DC, October.

Cagan, Christopher L. (2007). *Mortgage Payment Reset: The Issue and the Impact.* Santa Ana, CA: First American CoreLogic, Inc.

Calhoun, Charles A. (1996). *OFHEO House Price Indexes: HPI Technical Description* Washington, DC: Office of Federal Housing Enterprise Oversight.

Calomiris, Charles W. (2008). "*The Subprime Turmoil: What's Old, What's New, & What's Next.*" Presentation at Federal Reserve Bank of Kansas City Economic Policy Symposium, Jackson Hole, WY, August.

Center for Responsible Lending. (2008). *Solution to Housing Crisis Requires Adjusting Loans to Fair Market Value through Court-Supervised Modifications.*, CRL Issue Brief. Washington, DC: Center for Responsible Lending.

Costello, Glenn, Suzanne Mistretta, & Celcia He. (2007). Drivers of (2006) Subprime Vintage Performance. New York: Fitch Ratings Agency.

Coval, Joshua D., Jakub Jurek, & Erik Stafford. (2009). "The Economics of Structured Finance," *Journal of Economic Perspectives, 23* (1), 3–25.

Credit Suisse. (2008). *Foreclosure Update: Over 8 Million Foreclosures Expected.* New York: Credit Suisse.

Cunningham, Donald F., & Charles A. Capone. (1990). "The Relative Termination Experience of Adjustable to Fixed-Rate Mortgages," *The Journal of Finance, 45* (5), 1687–1703.

Danis, Michelle A., & Anthony Pennington-Cross. (2005)a. The Delinquency of Subprime Mortgages. Working paper (2005)-022A. St. Louis, MO: Federal Reserve Bank of St. Louis, Research Division.

Danis, Michelle A., & Anthony Pennington-Cross. (2005)b. "A Dynamic Look at Subprime Loan Performance," *Journal of Fixed Income, 15* (1), 28–39.

Dell'Ariccia, Giovanni, Deniz Igan, & Luc Laeven., (2008). Credit Booms and Lending Standards: Evidence from the Subprime Market. Working paper W-08-106. Washington, DC: International Monetary Fund.

Demyanyk, Yuliya, & Otto Van Hemert. (2008). Understanding the Subprime Crisis. Working paper. St. Louis, MO: Federal Reserve Bank of St. Louis.

DiMartino, Danielle, John V. Duca, & Harvey Rosenblum. (2007). "From Complacency to Crisis: Financial Risk Taking in the Early 21st Century," Federal Reserve Bank of Dallas, *EconomicLetter, 2* (12).

Ding, Lei, Roberto G. Quercia, & Janneke Ratcliffe. (2008). Risky Borrowers or Risky Mortgages: Disaggregating Effectus Using Propensity Score Models. Working paper. Chapel Hill, NC: University of North Carolina, Center for Community Capital.

Doms, Mark, Fred Furlong, & John Krainer. (2007). Subprime Mortgage Delinquency Rates. Working Paper 2007-33. San Francisco, CA: Federal Reserve Bank of San Francisco.

Eggert, Kurt. (2007). "Comment: What Prevents Loan Modifications?" *Housing Policy Debate*, *18* (2), 79–297.

Elmer, Peter J., & Steven A. Seelig. (1999). "Insolvency, Trigger Events, & Consumer Risk Posture in the Theory of Single-Family Mortgage Default," *Journal of Housing Research*, *10* (1), 1–25.

Engel, Kathleen C., & Patricia A. McCoy. (2004). "Predatory Lending: What Does Wall Street Have to Do with It?" *Housing Policy Debate*, *15* (3), 715–751.

Essene, Ren S., & William C. Apgar. (2007). Understanding Mortgage Market Behavior: Creating Good Mortgage Options for All Americans. Working paper. Cambridge, MA: Harvard University, Joint Center for Housing Studies.

Federal Bureau of Investigation. (2008). *2007 Mortgage Fraud Report*. Washington, DC: Federal Bureau of Investigation.

Fishbein, Allen J., & Patrick Woodall. (2006). *Exotic or Toxic: An Examination of the Non-Traditional Mortgage Market for Consumers and Lenders*. Washington, DC: Consumer Federation of America.

Foote, Christopher L., Kristopher S. Gerardi, Lorenz Goette, & Paul S. Willen. 2009. Reducing Foreclosures. Working paper no. 09-02. Boston: Federal Reserve Bank of Boston.

Foote, Christopher, Kristopher Gerardi, & Paul S. Willen. (2008). "Negative Equity and Foreclosure: Theory and Evidence," *Journal of Urban Economics*, *64* (2), 234–245.

Foote, Christopher, Kristopher Gerardi, Lorenz Goette, & Paul S. Willen. (2008). Subprime Facts: What (We Think) We Know about the Subprime Crisis and What We Don't Know. Public policy discussion paper no. 08-2. Boston: Federal Reserve Bank of Boston.

Foster, Chester, & Robert Van Order. (1984). "An Option-Based Model of Mortgage Default," *Housing Finance Review*, *3* (4), 351–72.

Foster, Chester, & Robert Van Order. (1985). "FHA Terminations: A Prelude to Rational Mortgage Pricing," *AREUEA Journal*, *13* (3), 273–291.

Gerardi, Kristopher S., & Paul S. Willen. (2009). "Subprime Mortgages, Foreclosures, & Urban Neighborhoods," *The B.E. Journal of Economic Analysis & Policy*, *9* (3).

Gerardi, Kristopher, Adam Hale Shapiro, & Paul S. Willen. (2008). Subprime Outcomes: Risky Mortgages, Homeownership Experiences, & Foreclosures., Working Paper no. 07-15. Boston: Federal Reserve Bank of Boston.

Gorton, Gary. (2008). "The Panic of 2007." Presentation at the Federal Reserve Bank of Kansas City Economic Policy Symposium, Jackson Hole, WY, August.

Gramlich, Edward M. (2007). *Subprime Mortgages: America's Latest Boom and Bust*. Washington DC: Urban Institute Press.

Gross, Daniel. (2008). "Subprime Suspects." *Newsweek*, October 7.

Haughwout, Andrew, Richard Peach, & Joseph Tracy. (2008). *Juvenile Delinquent Mortgages: Bad Credit or Bad Economy?* Staff report no. 341. New York: Federal Reserve Bank of New York.

HOPE NOW. (2009). HOPE NOW National Data July (2007) to May (2009). http://www.hopenow.com/industrydata.php.

Husock, Howard. (2008). "Housing Goals We Can't Afford." *The New York Times*, December 11.

Jackson, Howell E., & Jeremy Berry. (2002). *Kickbacks or Compensation: The Case of Yield Spread Premiums. Working paper.* Cambridge, MA: Harvard University, Harvard Law School. http://www.law.harvard.edu/ faculty/hjackson/pdfs/january_draft.pdf.

Jaffee, Dwight M. (2008). The U.S. Subprime Mortgage Crisis: Issues Raised and Lessons Learned. Working Paper no. 28 of The Commission on Growth and Development. Washington, DC: The World Bank,International Bank for Reconstruction and Development.

Joint Center for Housing Studies. (2006). *The State of the Nation's Housing 2006.* Cambridge, MA: Harvard University, Joint Center for Housing Studies.

Joint Center for Housing Studies. (2008). *The State of the Nation's Housing 2008.* Cambridge, MA: Harvard University, Joint Center for Housing Studies.

Keys, Benjamin, Tanmoy Mukherjee, Amit Seru, & Vikrant Vig. (2008). Did Securitization Lead to Lax Screening? Evidence from Subprime Loans. EFA (2008) Athens meetings paper. Social Science Research Network. http://ssrn. com/abstract=1093137.

Kim-Sung, Kellie, & Sharon Hermanson. (2003). "Experiences of Older Refinance Mortgage Loan Borrowers: Broker- and Lender-Originated Loans," AARP Public Policy Institute, *Data Digest 83*.

Kroszner, Randall S. (2008). "*The Community Reinvestment Act and the Recent Mortgage Crisis*." Presentation at the Confronting Concentrated Poverty Policy Forum, Board of Governors of the Federal Reserve System, Washington, DC, December 3.

Labaton, Stephen. (2008). "Loan Industry Fighting Rules on Mortgages," *The New York Times*, April 28, A1.

Laderman, Elizabeth, & Carolina Reid. (2008). *Lending in Low- and Moderate-Income Neighborhoods in California: The Performance of CRA Lending During the Subprime Meltdown*. Working paper presented at Federal Reserve System Conference on Housing and Mortgage Markets, Washington, DC, December 4.

Lax, Howard, Michael Manti, Paul Raca, & Peter Zorn. (2000). Subprime Lending: An Investigation of Economic Efficiency Working paper. Washington, DC: Freddie Mac.

Levitan, Adam J., & Joshua Goodman. (2008). *Mortgage Market Sensitivity to Bankruptcy Modification, Working paper series research paper no. 1087816*. Washington, DC: Georgetown University Law Center, Business, Economics, & Regulatory Law.

Lewis, Michael. (2008). "The End of Wall Street's Boom." *Portfolio. com.*

Lockhart, James B., III. (2009). Statement before the House Financial Services Committee, Subcommittee on Capital Markets, Insurance and Government Sponsored Enterprises, Hearing on The Present Condition and Future Status of Fannie Mae and Freddie Mac, June 3.

Majority Staff of the Joint Economic Committee of the U.S. Senate. (2007). *The Subprime Lending Crisis: The Economic Impact on Wealth, Property Values, & Tax Revenues and How We Got Here*. Washington, DC: U.S. Congress Joint Economic Committee.

Mallach, Alan. (2008). "Saving America's Struggling Communities: Defining the Federal Role in Addressing the Secondary Impacts of the Foreclosure Crisis." Presentation at a Brookings Institution Forum on Policy Responses to the Foreclosure Crisis, Washington, DC, December 5.

Mason, Joseph R. (2007). *Mortgage Loan Modification: Promises and Pitfalls.* Working paper. Social Science Research Network. http://ssrn.com/abstract=1027270.

Mayer, Christopher, Karen Pence, & Shane M. Sherlund. (2009). "The Rise in Mortgage Defaults," *Journal of Economic Perspectives, 23* (1), 27–50.

McCoy, Patricia A., & Elizabeth Renuart. (2008). "The Legal Infrastructure of Subprime and Nontraditional Home Mortgages." In *Borrowing to Live: Consumer and Mortgage Credit Revisited,* edited by Nicolas P. Retsinas and Eric S. Belsky. Washington, DC: The Brookings Institution.

Mian, Atif, & Amir Sufi. (2008). The Consequences of Mortgage Credit Expansion: Evidence from the 2007 Mortgage Default Crisis. Working paper. Chicago: University of Chicago, Booth School of Business.

Miller, Thomas J. (2003). Testimony before the Subcommittee on Financial Institutions and Consumer Credit and the Subcommittee on Housing and Community Opportunity, U.S. House of Representatives, November 3.

Mortgage Asset Research Institute. (2008). *Tenth Periodic Mortgage Fraud Case Report to the Mortgage Bankers Association.* Washington, DC: Mortgage Bankers Association.

Mortgage Bankers Association. (2008). *Bankruptcy is a Last-Ditch Resort, Not a First-rate Remedy.* Washington, DC: Mortgage Bankers Association.

National Low Income Housing Coalition. (2008). "*State-by-State Tenant Foreclosure and Eviction Practice.*" Briefing document. Washington, DC: National Low Income Housing Coalition.

National Training and Information Center (NTIC). (1998). *Preying on Neighborhoods: Subprime Lending and Chicagoland Foreclosures.* Chicago: National Training and Information Center.

Park, Kevin. (2008). *Subprime Lending and the Community Reinvestment Act.* Research note N08-02. Cambridge, MA: Harvard University, Joint Center for Housing Studies.

Pavlov, Andrey, & Susan Wachter. (2008). *Subprime Lending and House Price Volatility.* Research paper no. 08-33. Philadelphia: University of Pennsylvania Law School, Institute for Law and Economics.

Pelletiere, Danilo, & Keith Wardrip. (2008). "Renters and the Housing Crisis," *Poverty and Race, 17* (40), July/ August.

Pelletiere, Danilo. (2009). *Renters in Foreclosure: Defining the Problem, Identifying Solutions.* Washington, DC: National Low Income Housing Coalition.

Pendley, M. Diane, Glenn Costello, & Mary Kelsch. (2007). *The Impact of Poor Underwriting Practices and Fraud in Subprime RMBS Performance.* New York: Fitch Ratings Agency.

Pennington-Cross, Anthony, & Giang Ho. (2006). The Termination of Subprime Hybrid and Fixed-Rate Mortgages. Working paper (2006)-042A. St. Louis: Federal Reserve Bank of St. Louis, Research Division.

Pennington-Cross, Anthony. (2003). "Credit History and the Performance of Prime and Nonprime Mortgages," *Journal of Real Estate Finance and Economics, 27* (3), 279–302.

President's Working Group on Financial Markets. (2008). *Policy Statement on Financial Market Developments.* Washington, DC: U.S. Department of the Treasury.

Quercia, Roberto G., & Michael A. Stegman. 1992. "Residential Mortgage Default: A Review of the Literature," *Journal of Housing Research, 3* (2), 341–379.

Quercia, Roberto, Michael Stegman, & Walter R. Davis. (2005). *The Impact of Predatory Loan Terms on Subprime Foreclosures: The Special Case of Prepayment Penalties and Balloon Payments*. Chapel Hill, NC: University of North Carolina, Kenan-Flagler Business School.

Rajan, Uday, Amit Seru, & Vikrant Vig. (2008). *The Failure of Models that Predict Failure: Distance, Incentives, & Defaults*. Research paper no. 08-19. Chicago: University of Chicago, Booth School of Business.

Reeder, William J., & John P. Comeau. (2008). "Using HMDA and Income Leverage to Examine Current Mortgage Market Turmoil," *U.S. Housing Market Conditions*, August.

Renuart, Elizabeth, Carolyn L. Carter, Alys I. Cohen, & Chi Chi Wu. (2005). *Cost of Credit: Regulation, Preemption, & Industry Abuses*. Boston: National Consumer Law Center.

Renuart, Elizabeth. (2004). "An Overview of the Predatory Mortgage Lending Process," *Housing Policy Debate*, *15* (3), 467–501.

Schloemer, Ellen, Wei Li, Keith Ernst, & Kathleen Keest. (2006). *Losing Ground: Foreclosures in the Sub- prime Market and Their Cost to Homeowners*. Washington, DC: Center for Responsible Lending.

Sherlund, Shane M. (2008). *The Past, Present, & Future of Subprime Mortgages*. Washington, DC: Federal Reserve Board, Finance and Economics Discussion Series, Divisions of Research & Statistics and Monetary Affairs.

Shiller, Robert J. (2007). "Understanding Recent Trends in House Prices and Home Ownership." Presentation at Federal Reserve Bank of Kansas City Economic Policy Symposium, Jackson Hole, WY, August.

State Foreclosure Prevention Working Group. (2008). "Analysis of Subprime Servicing Performance." http:// www.mass

Stein, Eric. (2008). "*Turmoil in the U.S. Credit Markets: The Genesis of the Current Economic Crisis*." Testimony before the 110th Congress, U.S. Senate Committee on Banking, Housing, & Urban Affairs, October 16.

Stiglitz, Joseph. (2007). "House of Cards," *The Guardian*, October 9.

Twomey, Tara. (2008). "*The Implementation of the Hope for Homeowners Program and a Review of Foreclosure Mitigation Efforts*." Testimony before the U.S. House of Representatives, Committee on Financial Services, September 17.

U.S. Department of Housing and Urban Development (HUD). 1999. "Table 18. Mortgage Originations, 1-4 Family Units by Lender Type: 1970-1997," *U.S. Housing Market Conditions*, May.

U.S. Department of Housing and Urban Development. (HUD) (2008). *Regulatory Impact Analysis and Final Regulatory Flexibility Analysis. FR-5180-F-02. Final Rule to Improve the Process of Obtaining Mortgages and Reduce Consumer Costs*. Washington, DC: U.S. Department of Housing and Urban Development. http://www. hud.gov/offices/hsg/ramh/res/impactanalysis.pdf.

U.S. Department of the Treasury. (2009). *Financial Regulatory Reform: A New Foundation*. Washington, DC: U.S. Department of the Treasury. http://www.financialstability.gov /docs/regs/FinalReport_web.pdf.

U.S. Government Accountability Office (GAO). (2004). *Federal and State Agencies Face Challenges in Confronting Predatory Lending.* GAO-04-280. Washington, DC: Government Accountability Office.

U.S. Government Accountability Office (GAO). (2006). *Alternative Mortgage Products: Impact on Defaults Remains Unclear, But Disclosure Risks to Borrowers Could Be Improved.* Washington, DC: U.S. General Accountability Office.

U.S. Government Accountability Office (GAO). (2007). *Information on Recent Default and Foreclosure Trends for Home Mortgages and Associated Economic and Market Developments.* GAO-08-78R. Washington, DC: Government Accountability Office.

Vandell, Kerry D. (1995). "How High is Mortgage Default: A Review and Synthesis of the Evidence," *Journal of Housing Research, 6* (2), 245–264.

Wardrip, Keith. (2008). "*Foreclosure's Invisible Victims: Recent Research on the Foreclosure Crisis.*" Power- Point presentation.

Wheaton, William C., & Gleb Nechayev. (2008). "The 1998-(2005) Housing "'Bubble" and the Current "Correction": What's Different This Time?" *Journal of Real Estate Research, 30* (1), 1–26.

White, Alan M. (2008). "Rewriting Contracts, Wholesale: Data on Voluntary Mortgage Modifications from (2007) and (2008) Remittance Reports," *Fordham Urban Law Journal, 35.* http://ssrn.com/ abstract=1259538.

White, Michelle J., & Ning Zhu. (2008). Saving Your Home in Chapter 13 Bankruptcy. Working paper 14179. Cambridge MA: National Bureau of Economic Research.

Wilmarth, Arthur E., Jr. (2004). Testimony before the Committee on Banking, Housing, & Urban Affairs, U.S. Senate, April 7.

Woodward, Susan E. (2003). *Consumer Confusion in the Mortgage Market. Sand Hill Econometrics.* http:// sandhillecon.com/consumer_ confusion.pdf.

Zandi, Mark. (2008). *Financial Shock.* Upper Saddle River, NJ: Pearson Education.

Additional Reading

Ambrose, Brent W., & Charles A. Capone. (2000). "The Hazard Rates of First and Second Defaults," *Journal of Real Estate Finance and Economics, 20* (3), 275–293.

Apgar, William C. (2008). *The Mortgage Market Meltdown and Older Americans.* Cambridge, MA: Harvard University, Joint Center for Housing Studies.

Apgar, William C., Amal Bendimerad, & Ren S. Essene. (2007). *Mortgage Market Channels and Fair Lending: An Analysis of HMDA Data.* Working paper. Cambridge, MA: Harvard University, Joint Center for Housing Studies.

Apgar, William C., Jr., & Allen J. Fishbein. (2005). "Changing Industrial Organization of Housing Finance and Changing Role of Community-Based Organizations." In *Building Assets, Building Credit: Creating Wealth in Low-Income Communities*, edited by Nicolas P. Retsinas and Eric S. Belsky. Washington, DC: The Brookings Institution.

BasePoint Analytics. (2007). *Early Payment Default: Links to Fraud and Impact on Mortgage Lenders and Investment Banks.* Carlsbad, CA: BasePoint Analytics.

Belsky, Eric S., Karl E. Case, & Susan J. Smith. (2008). "Identifying, Managing, & Mitigating Risks to Borrowers in Changing Mortgage and Consumer Credit Markets." In

Borrowing to Live: Consumer and Mortgage Credit Revisited, edited by Nicolas P. Retsinas and Eric S. Belsky. Washington, DC: The Brookings Institution.

Bernanke, Ben S. (2007). "*The Subprime Mortgage Market*." Presentation at the Federal Reserve System's 43rd Annual Conference on Bank Structure and Competition, Chicago, IL, May 17.

Brinkmann, Jay. (2008). *An Examination of Mortgage Foreclosures, Modifications, Repayment Plans and Other Loss Mitigation Activities in the Third Quarter of (2007)*. Washington, DC: Mortgage Bankers Association.

Calhoun, Charles A., & Yoheng Deng. (2002). "A Dynamic Analysis of Fixed- and Adjustable-Rate Mortgage Terminations," *Journal of Real Estate Finance and Economics*, *24* (1/2), 9–33.

Calhoun, Michael D. (2008). "*Helping Families Save their Homes: The Role of Bankruptcy Law*," Testimony on the behalf of the Center For Responsible Lending Before the U.S. Senate Judiciary Committee, November 19.

Cohen, Alys. (2008). Testimony Before the Domestic Policy Subcommittee, U.S. House of Representatives Committee on Oversight & Government Reform, November 14.

Cordell, Larry, Karen Dynan, Andreas Lehnert, Nellie Liang, & Eileen Mauskopf. (2008). *The Incentives of Mortgage Servicers: Myths and Realities.* Working paper 2008-46. Washington, DC: Federal Reserve Board, Finance and Economics Discussion Series.

Courchane, Marsha J., Brian J. Surette, & Peter M. Zorn. (2004). "Subprime Borrowers: Mortgage Transitions and Outcomes," *Journal of Real Estate Finance and Economics*, *29*(4), 365–392.

Cutts, Amy C. (2003). *Loss Mitigation Technology and Homeownership Sustainability.* Paper prepared for the LISC (2003) Homeownership Summit. Washington, DC: Freddie Mac.

Cutts, Amy C., & Richard K. Green. (2005). "Innovative Servicing Technology: Smart Enough to Keep People In their Houses?" In *Building Assets, Building Credit: Creating Wealth in Low-Income Communities*, edited by Nicolas P. Retsinas and Eric S. Belsky. Washington, DC: The Brookings Institution.

Cutts, Amy C., & Robert Van Order. (2003). *On the Economics of Subprime Lending.* McLean, VA: Freddie Mac. http://www.freddie mac.com/ corporate/reports/.

Cutts, Amy C., & William A. Merrill. (2008). "Interventions in Mortgage Default: Policies and Practices to Prevent Home Losses and Lower Costs." *In Borrowing to Live: Consumer and Mortgage Credit Revisited*, edited by Nicolas P. Retsinas and Eric S. Belsky. Washington, DC: The Brookings Institution.

DiMartino, Danielle, & John V. Duca. (2007). "The Rise and Fall of Subprime Mortgages," Federal Reserve Bank of Dallas, *EconomicLetter*, *2* (11).

Eggum, John, Katherine Porter, & Tara Twomey. (2008). "Saving Homes in Bankruptcy: Housing Affordability and Loan Modification," *Utah Law Review*, 2008 (3).

Faris, John, & Christopher A. Richardson. (2004). "The Geography of Subprime Mortgage Payment Penalty Patterns," *Housing Policy Debate*, *15* (3), 687–714.

Federal Bureau of Investigation. (2007). *Financial Crimes Report to the Public, Fiscal Year 2007.* Washington, DC: Federal Bureau of Investigation.

Furman Center for Real Estate and Urban Policy. (2008). *Transforming Foreclosed Properties into Community Assets.* Furman Center white paper. New York: New York University.

Goldberg, Michael, & Ann B. Schnare. (2008). *An Alternative Look at the Financial Strength of the FHA Single Family Insurance Program.* Encino, CA: Genworth Financial Asset Management, Inc.

Greenspan, Alan, (2005). "*Consumer Finance.*" Remarks at the Federal Reserve System's Fourth Annual Community Affairs Research Conference, Washington, DC, April 8.

Harding, John P., Eric Rosenblatt, & Vincent W. Yao. (2008). The Contagion Effect of Foreclosed Properties. Unpublished paper. Social Science Research Network. http://papers.ssrn.com/sol3/papers.cfm? abstract_id=1 160354.

Harney, Kenneth R. (2005). "Agency Sounds Warning on Stated-Income and Interest-Only Mortgages," *Realty- Times*, January 10.

Immergluck, Dan. (2008c). "From the Subprime to the Exotic: Excessive Mortgage Market Risk and Foreclosures," *Journal of the American Planning Association*, *74* (1), 59–76.

Immergluck, Dan. 2(008b). *Community Response to the Foreclosure Crisis: Thoughts on Local Interventions.* Community Affairs discussion paper. no. 01-08. Atlanta: Federal Reserve Bank of Atlanta.

Immergluck, Dan. 2008a. *The Accumulation of Foreclosed Properties: Trajectories of Metropolitan REO Inventories during the 2007-2008 Mortgage Crisis.* Community Affairs discussion paper. no. 02-08. Atlanta: Federal Reserve Bank of Atlanta.

Lin, Zhenguo, Eric Rosenblatt, & Vincent W. Yao. (2009). "Spillover Effects of Foreclosures on Neighborhood Property Values," *Journal of Real Estate Finance and Economics*, *38* (4), 387–407.

Liu, David, & Shumin Li. (2006). *Alt-A Credit: The Other Shoe Drops?* Santa Ana, CA: First American LoanPerformance, *The MarketPulse.*

McCoy, Patricia A. (2007). "Rethinking Disclosure in a World of Risk-Based Pricing," *Harvard Journal on Legislation*, *44*, 123–154.

Mortgage Asset Research Institute. (2006). *Eighth Periodic Mortgage Fraud Case Report to the Mortgage Bankers Association.* Washington, DC: Mortgage Bankers Association.

Office of the Comptroller of the Currency and Office of Thrift Supervision. (2008). *OCC and OTS Mortgage Metrics Report, Third Quarter 2008.* Washington, DC: Office of the Comptroller of the Currency; Office of Thrift Supervision.

Office of the Comptroller of the Currency. (2008). "*Comptroller Dugan Highlights Re-Default Rates on Modified Loans.*" Press release. Washington, DC: Office of the Comptroller of the Currency.

Pagano, Michael, & Christopher Hoene. (2008). *City Fiscal Conditions in 2008.* Washington, DC: National League of Cities.

Renuart, Elizabeth, & Dianne E. Thompson. (2008). "The Truth, The Whole Truth, & Nothing but the Truth: Fulfilling the Promise of Truth in Lending," *Yale Journal of Regulation*, *25* (2), 181–245.

Schwartz, Steven L. (1994). "The Alchemy of Structured Finance," *Stanford Journal of Law, Business & Finance*, *1*, 133–154.

Tatom, John. (2008). The U.S. Foreclosure Crisis: A Two-Pronged Assault on the U.S. Economy. Working paper 2008-WP-10. Terre Haute, IN: Indiana State University, Networks Financial Institute.

Terhune, Chad, & Robert Berner. (2008). "FHA-Backed Loans: The New Subprime," *Business Week*, November 19.

Tripoli, Steve, & Elizabeth Renuart. (2005). *Dreams Foreclosed: The Rampant Theft of Americans' Home Through Foreclosure "Rescue" Scams*. Boston: National Consumer Law Center.

U.S. Department of the Treasury and U.S. Department of Housing and Urban Development. 2000. *Curbing Predatory Home Lending: A Joint Report.* Washington, DC: U.S. Department of the Treasury; U.S. Department of Housing and Urban Development.

U.S. Securities and Exchange Commission (SEC). (2008). *Summary Report of Issues Identified in the Commission Staff's Examination of Select Credit Rating Agencies.* Washington, DC: U.S. Securities and Exchange Commission.

End Notes

[1] The term "Alt-A" refers to loans made to borrowers that require little or no documentation of borrowers' income or assets and entail other features that may expose borrowers to large increases in loan payments over time.

[2] Generally, mortgage "default" occurs when a borrower has missed three payments and a fourth is due. The default leads lenders to initiate the foreclosure process, but historically a majority of defaults are resolved without a foreclosure occurring.

[3] Quercia and Stegman (1992) and Vandell (1995) provide detailed reviews of the literature researching the option-based theory of mortgage defaults.

[4] Reeder and Comeau (2008) and Demyanyk and Van Hemert (2008) provide evidence of weakening credit quality of loan originations. Other research finds denial rates declined in recent years at the metropolitan-area level (Dell'Ariccia, Igan, and Laeven, 2008) and at the ZIP-Code level (Mian and Sufi, 2008).

[5] For example, Gramlich (2007), Essene and Apgar (2007), McCoy and Renaurt (2008), and Barr (2008).

[6] GAO (2004) also describes the inadequacy of the mortgage lending disclosure system.

[7] Rating agencies only began registering with the Securities and Exchange Commission in September 2007 as mandated under the Credit Agency Reform Act of 2006.

[8] Zandi (2008) discusses how the U.S. trade deficit left international investors with a flood of dollars to invest.

[9] See Bitner (2008); BasePoint Analytics (2006); Mortgage Asset Research Institute (2008); and Pendley, Costello, and Kelsch (2007).

[10] One source of this claim is in *The New York Times* by Husock (2008). Counter editorials include *The New York Times* (October 15, 2008) and *The Los Angeles Times* (October 25, 2008).

[11] The February 18, 2009, announcement was originally entitled the Homeowner Affordability and Stability Plan and has since become known as Making Home Affordable.

[12] A detailed discussion of opt-in/opt-out loans is provided in Barr, Mullainathan, and Shafir (2008).

[13] Uneven regulation and supervision left what one former governor of the Federal Reserve Board described as a "gigantic hole in the supervisory safety net" (Gramlich, 2007).

[14] "Mortgage Sector Withstands Subprime's Fallout," Danielle Reed and Anusha Shrivastava, *The Wall Street Journal*, December 9, 2006.

[15] "Tremors at the Door," Vikas Bajaj and Christine Haughney, *The New York Times*, January 26, 2007.

[16] "Late Mortgage Payments and Foreclosures Rise," *The New York Times*, December 14, 2006.

[17] "US Mortgage Crisis Goes into Meltdown," *The Daily Telegraph*, February 24, 2007.

[18] "Mortgage Crisis Spirals, and Casualties Mount," Julie Creswell and Vikas Bajaj, *The New York Times*, March 5, 2007.

[19] "Record Foreclosures Hit Mortgage Lenders," *USA Today*, March 13, 2007.

[20] "Mortgage Troubles Rise to Record Levels," Renae Merle, *The Washington Post*, December 6, 2008.

[21] In part, the sharp rise in the subprime market share reported in the Mortgage Bankers Association data may reflect changes in reporting practices among lenders participating in the *National Delinquency Survey* to include more subprime loans that were previously excluded from the survey. Nonetheless, the sharp rise in market share from 2003 to 2005 is consistent with data from *Inside Mortgage Finance* showing the subprime market's share of mortgage originations more than doubling to 20 percent over this period. When this high share of new originations is coupled with a huge wave of refinancing in 2003 due to historically low mortgage rates, it is not improbable that the subprime share of all outstanding mortgages could have doubled over this period.

[22] "Option" adjustable-rate mortgages give the borrower several options for each monthly pay-ment during the early years of the loan: a fully amortizing payment, an interest-only payment, or a payment that is less than the interest owed that month, leading to an increase in the outstanding loan balance.

[23] "Delinquencies Increase, Foreclosure Starts Flat in Latest MBA National DelinquencySurvey," Mortgage Bankers Association, December 5, 2008.

[24] See, for example, "Alt-A Credit: The Other Shoe Drops," David Liu, Shumin Li, *The MarketPulse*, December 2006, LoanPerformance; "Mortgage Crisis Spreads Past Subprime Loans," *The New York Times*, February 12, 2008; and "Fannie Having Debt Woes," *National Mortgage News*, November 17, 2008.

[25] High-cost loans are originated with an annual percentage rate at or above 3 percentage points plus the yield of a Treasury security of comparable maturity. Not all high-cost loans are necessarily subprime; however, high incidence of high-cost lending is generally indicative of high incidence of subprime lending.

[26] Technically, mortgage "default" occurs when a borrower has missed three payments and a fourth is due. The default leads lenders to initiate the foreclosure process, but historically a majority of defaults are resolved without a foreclosure occurring.

[27] Option-theory also focuses on borrowers' ability to exercise a "call" option by prepaying the mortgage when interest rates fall. Thus, pure option-theoretic models focus heavily on trends in house prices and interest rates to explain both defaults and prepayments.

[28] Foote, Girardi, and Willen (2008) present theoretical examples comparing the financial returns from maintaining ownership in the face of declining home prices with the alternative of renting a home of the same quality to show that it can be logical for homeowners to choose to default on their mortgage.

[29] Hybrid adjustable-rate mortgages are loans where interest rates are fixed for an initial 2- or 3-year period, following which interest rates adjust every 6 months to a year based on trends in an index rate (commonly the London Interbank Offer Rate) plus a margin specified for each loan.

[30] In an analysis of the performance of fixed-rate subprime loans from a similar time period, Danis and Pennington-Cross (2005) find that delinquent loans had a very high probability of prepayment as long as the borrower had some positive equity in the home. This result is consistent with the finding that subprime adjustable-rate mortgages from this period did not experience high defaults at the time of reset as rapidly rising house prices in most areas of the country would have provided most owners with a positive equity cushion.

[31] There are several interesting features of this study. First, the data analyzed cover a period of nearly two decades from 1987 to 2007 that span two periods of substantial decline in nominal home prices. Second, the data come from public real estate records that track spans of property ownership rather than just the lifespan of an individual loan.

[32] One limitation of this study is that it only includes data on Massachusetts and so may not be representative of other areas of the country. For example, Massachusetts has experienced fairly volatile house prices over this period compared to other areas of the country (such as the Midwest) and did not have the same degree of subprime or Alt-A lending as other areas (such as California or the south-central regions). Another limitation is that the study did not have any information on loan terms other than whether the loan was originated by a lender on a list of subprime lenders compiled by the U.S. Department of Housing and Urban Development.

[33] A plausible explanation is that growth in the values of individual properties is distributed around the measured market area index, which represents the mean growth for the market area. Even with a positive mean growth in a market, there will be some properties in that market that experience negative growth. When the mean for the market grows less rapidly, there are likely to be a higher number of individual properties with negative growth. According to Calhoun (1996), "it is now standard practice in the housing research literature to characterize individual house prices as arising from a stochastic process in which the average rate of change or drift in housing values is represented by a market index and the dispersion and volatility of values around the market average are modeled as a log normal diffusion process. In this approach, one assumes that the price, Pit, of an individual house i at time t, can be expressed in terms of a market price index βt, a Gaussian random walk Hit, and white noise Nit, such that $\ln(Pit) = \beta t + Hit + Nit$."

[34] Pp. 32-33.

[35] P. 23.

[36] The federal banking regulators do issue and enforce regulations relating to fair lending and equal credit opportunity intended to protect borrowers from many abusive practices, but these protections were not oriented toward helping borrowers avoid inappropriate housing and mortgage product choices in the years leading up to the crisis. For example, the Office of Thrift Supervision has rules to prohibit discrimination and false advertising. See 12 C.F.R. part 528 and 12 C.F.R. § 563.27. Furthermore, stronger consumer protections have been put in place by federal banking regulators in response to the crisis. See 74 Fed. Reg. 5489, 5506 (January 29, 2009).

[37] As previously noted, the agencies do issue and enforce regulations that provide consumer protections (for example, see Office of Thrift Supervision rules to prohibit discrimination and false advertising at 12 C.F.R. part 528 and 12 C.F.R. § 563.27) but bank safety and soundness are their primary concern. Recent additions to their regulations have strengthened the depository regulators' consumer protection role.

[38] The three main rating agencies registered with the U.S. Securities and Exchange Commission are Fitch Ratings, Moody's Investor Services, and Standard & Poor's Rating Services (SEC 2008). These firms are referred to collectively as the "rating agencies."

[39] Of course, in some cases homeowners may be complicit in broker fraud, for example by allowing their income to be misrepresented so the borrower is able to either take more cash out of their homes or to purchase a more expensive home than they might otherwise have been able to. However, to the extent that the broker is helping to perpetrate the misrepresentation, the act of fraud is deemed to have been committed by the broker.

[40] For details, see the press release from the Office of the New York State Attorney General, March 3, 2008.

[41] Gross (2008) identifies a number of sources of this criticism. One notable example is a recent editorial in *The New York Times* by Husock (2008).

[42] See, for example, The New York Times (October 15, 2008) and *The Los Angeles Times* (October 25, 2008).

[43] Turmoil in the U.S. Credit Markets: The Genesis of the Current Economic Crisis, Senate Committee on Banking, Housing, and Urban Affairs (Stein, 2008).

[44] "Former GSE Chiefs Scolded for Careless Lending," *The Washington Post*, December 9, 2008.

[45] "Internal Warnings Sounded on Loans at Fannie, Freddie," *The Washington Post*, December 9, 2008.

[46] "How HUD Mortgage Policy Fed the Crisis," The Washington Post, June 10, 2008.

[47] Calomiris (2008) also argues that the government-sponsored enterprise purchase of subprime securities made a significant contribution to the growth of the subprime market.

[48] See Moody's Economy.com as published in *The Wall Street Journal*, October 8, 2008 ("Housing Pain Gauge: Nearly 1 in 6 Owners 'Under Water.'").

[49] Remarks by Federal Deposit Insurance Corporation Chairman Sheila Bair to The New America Foundation conference: "Did Low-income Homeownership Go Too Far?": Washington, DC, December 17, 2008.

[50] The February 18 announcement was originally entitled the Homeowner Affordability and Stability Plan, which has since become known as Making Home Affordable.

[51] The original Home Affordable Refinance Program was limited to 105 percent of the current market value, but this limit was raised to 125 percent on July 1, 2009.

[52] "OCC and OTS Mortgage Metrics Report, First Quarter 2009," Office of the Comptroller of the Currency and Office of Thrift Supervision, Washington, DC, June 2009.

[53] For an overview on what is known about what happens to displaced tenants, see Wardrip (2008).

[54] For a comprehensive review of state and local tenant protections, see National Low Income Housing Coalition (2008).

In: America's Foreclosure Crisis
Editors: Russell Burns and Roy A. Foster
ISBN: 978-161942- 271-1

Chapter 2

MORTGAGE FORECLOSURES: DOCUMENTATION PROBLEMS REVEAL NEED FOR ONGOING REGULATORY OVERSIGHT*

United States Government Accountability Office

WHY GAO DID THIS STUDY

Mortgage servicers—entities that manage home mortgage loans—halted foreclosures throughout the country in September 2010, finding that documents required to be provided to courts in some states may have been improperly signed or notarized. In addition, academics and court cases are raising questions over whether foreclosures are being brought properly because of concerns over how loans were transferred into mortgage-backed securities (MBS). GAO was asked to examine (1) the extent to which federal laws address mortgage servicers' foreclosure procedures and federal agencies' past oversight, (2) federal agencies' current oversight and future oversight plans, and (3) the potential impact of these issues on involved parties. GAO reviewed federal laws, regulations, exam guidance, agency documents, and studies, and conducted interviews with federal agencies, mortgage industry associations, investor groups, consumer advocacy groups, and legal academics.

WHAT GAO RECOMMENDS

GAO recommends that banking regulators and the Bureau of Consumer Financial Protection (CFPB) develop plans for overseeing mortgage servicers and include foreclosure practices in any servicing standards that are developed. GAO also recommends that regulators

---

* This is an edited, reformatted and augmented version of the United States Government Accountability Office Publication, GAO-11-433, dated May 2011.

assess the risks that documentation problems pose for their institutions. The agencies generally agreed with the recommendations.

What GAO Found

Federal laws do not specifically address the foreclosure process, and federal agencies' past oversight of servicers' foreclosure activities has been limited and fragmented. State laws primarily govern the foreclosure process and specify what, if any, documentation is required to foreclose on a property. Several federal laws include mortgage servicing provisions, but they largely are focused on consumer protection at mortgage origination, not specific foreclosure requirements. Although various federal agencies have authority to oversee most mortgage servicers, past oversight of their foreclosure activities has been limited, in part because banking regulators did not consider these practices as posing a high risk to banks' safety and soundness, and some servicers have not been under direct federal oversight. Federal housing and other agencies typically do not monitor servicers' foreclosure activities.

In response to the disclosed documentation problems, federal agencies have recently increased attention to servicing activities. Banking regulators conducted a coordinated review of 14 mortgage servicers and identified pervasive problems with their document preparation and oversight of foreclosure processes, although they did not find widespread instances of foreclosures that should not have proceeded. The regulators issued enforcement actions requiring servicers to improve these practices and plan to assess their compliance, but have not fully developed plans for the extent of future oversight. Further, regulators are considering the need for uniform servicing standards, but whether such standards will address foreclosure activities is yet unclear. Federal housing and other agencies are also reviewing servicer foreclosure practices and considering corrective actions. In July 2011, the newly created CFPB also will have responsibility for mortgage servicing, including over certain nondepository firms currently without federal oversight. How regulators and CFPB will interact and share responsibility for ongoing oversight of servicers is yet unclear, leaving the potential for continued gaps and inconsistency in oversight until final plans are developed.

Foreclosure documentation problems have slowed the pace of foreclosures across the United States, but most entities GAO interviewed indicated that such errors were correctable and that affected foreclosures would proceed. Delays in the pace of foreclosures as servicers correct and refile cases and implement more rigorous processes may benefit borrowers by providing more time to modify loans, but communities may be negatively affected as any vacant properties in foreclosure remain unoccupied for longer periods. Some foreclosures are also being delayed because of allegations that practices commonly used for transferring loans when creating MBS were not completed properly, which some commentators argue may affect whether servicers can prove legal authority to foreclose. Regulators did not always verify these transfer practices during their reviews or assess the potential risks of transfer problems to institutions. The potential financial costs resulting from these issues for investors, institutions that create MBS, and the overall financial system likely will remain uncertain until sufficient numbers of courts render decisions on the appropriateness of these practices.

ABBREVIATIONS

CFPB	Bureau of Consumer Financial Protection
FDIC	Federal Deposit Insurance Corporation
FHA	Federal Housing Administration
FHFA	Federal Housing Finance Agency
FIRREA	Financial Institutions Reform, Recovery, and Enforcement Act
GSE	government-sponsored enterprise
HAMP	Home Affordable Modification Program
HUD	Department of Housing and Urban Development
LPS	Lender Processing Services
MBS	mortgage-backed securities
MERS	Mortgage Electronic Registration System
MHA	Making Home Affordable
OCC	Office of the Comptroller of the Currency
OTS	Office of Thrift Supervision
RESPA	Real Estate Settlement Procedures Act of 1974
SAFE Act	Secure and Fair Enforcement for Mortgage Licensing Act of 2008
SCRA	Servicemembers Civil Relief Act
SEC	Securities and Exchange Commission
TILA	Truth in Lending Act
UCC	Uniform Commercial Code

May 2, 2011

Congressional Requesters

With record numbers of borrowers in default and delinquent on their loans, mortgage servicers—entities responsible for managing home mortgage loans—are initiating a large number of foreclosures throughout the country. As of December 2010, an estimated 4.63 percent of the about 50 million first-lien mortgages outstanding nationwide were in some stage of foreclosure—an increase of over 370 percent since the first quarter of 2006, when just 1 percent of mortgages were in foreclosure.[1] Requirements for proceeding with foreclosure are largely contained in state laws, and some states require the party seeking foreclosure to prepare documents that are notarized or signed by someone with knowledge of the case and submit them to a court. Beginning in September 2010, several servicers announced that they were halting or reviewing their foreclosure proceedings throughout the country after allegations that the documents accompanying judicial foreclosures may have been inappropriately signed or notarized. The servicers subsequently began resuming some foreclosure actions after reviewing their processes and procedures, but following these allegations, some homeowners have challenged the validity of foreclosure proceedings brought against them. In other states, foreclosures may be processed without the involvement of courts, but challenges to the documentation associated with foreclosures can occur and are occurring in these states as well. In addition, questions over whether documents for loans that were sold and packaged into mortgage-backed securities were properly handled have prompted additional challenges regarding whether the parties filing for foreclosure have the necessary authority to do so.[2] In response, numerous federal agencies have initiated reviews of foreclosure practices at major servicers. Additionally, state attorneys general are engaged in a review of servicers' foreclosure practices.

In light of these developments, you asked us to examine various aspects of federal oversight of the residential mortgage foreclosure process. In response to your request, this report addresses (1) the extent to which federal laws address mortgage servicers' foreclosure procedures and federal agencies' authority to oversee activities and the extent of past oversight; (2) federal agencies' current oversight activities and future oversight plans; and (3) the potential impact of foreclosure documentation issues on homeowners, servicers, regulators, and mortgage-backed securities investors.

To address these objectives, we reviewed relevant federal laws, regulations, examination guidance, and other agency documents. We also reviewed relevant literature, examples of reported court cases involving these issues, congressional testimonies, and other relevant publicly available documentation. In addition, we examined agency documentation on current oversight activities, such as an examination worksheet, checklists, and supervisory letters summarizing examination findings. We conducted interviews with representatives of federal agencies, including the Bureau of Consumer Financial Protection (CFPB), Department of Housing and Urban Development (HUD), Department of Justice (Justice), Department of the Treasury (Treasury), Federal Deposit Insurance Corporation (FDIC), Federal Housing Finance Agency (FHFA), Board of Governors of the Federal Reserve System (Federal Reserve), Office of the Comptroller of the Currency (OCC), Office of Thrift Supervision (OTS), and Securities and Exchange Commission (SEC). We also interviewed legal experts and representatives of the mortgage industry—including the Federal National Mortgage Association (Fannie Mae) and the Federal Home Loan Mortgage Corporation (Freddie Mac), investor groups, and consumer advocacy groups.

We conducted this performance audit from October 2010 through April 2011 in accordance with generally accepted government auditing standards. Those standards require that we plan and perform the audit to obtain sufficient, appropriate evidence to provide a reasonable basis for our findings and conclusions based on our audit objectives. We believe that the evidence obtained provides a reasonable basis for our findings and conclusions based on our audit objectives.

BACKGROUND

Mortgages and Mortgage Market Participants

When individuals purchase residential real property with borrowed funds, they usually enter into a contractual agreement, typically called a promissory note, in which they agree, among other things, to make principal and interest payments to the originating lender for a period of time. To secure their debt, lenders obtain a lien on the underlying property as collateral against borrower default, which grants the holder of the lien the right to seize, and usually sell, the property should the borrower fail to pay.[3] In other words, what may be commonly referred to as a mortgage consists of both a promissory note evidencing the debt to be paid by the borrower and the lien or security interest in the underlying property, which generally is provided for in a deed of trust or a mortgage document. In the past, the institution providing the loan was typically a bank or thrift and would normally hold the loan as an interest-earning asset in its portfolio. All activities associated with servicing the loan—including accepting payments, initiating collection actions for delinquent payments, and conducting foreclosure if necessary—would have been performed by this originating institution.

Over the last few decades, the number of participants in and the complexity of the market for home mortgage loans in the United States have increased. Now, institutions that originate home mortgages generally do not hold such loans as assets on their balance sheets but instead sell them to others, who then acquire the right to receive borrowers' monthly payments. In recent years, originating lenders generally have sold or assigned their interest in both the note and the deed of trust to other financial institutions for the purpose of securitizing the mortgage. Through securitization, the purchasers of these mortgages then package them into pools and issue securities known as mortgage-backed securities (MBS) for which the mortgages serve as collateral. These securities pay interest and principal to their investors, which include other financial institutions, pension funds, or other institutional investors.

Multiple entities—including the mortgage servicer, a trustee for the securitized pool (trust), and the investors in the MBS that were issued based on the pooled loans—have specific roles regarding loans. After a mortgage originator sells its loans to another investor or to an institution that will securitize them, another financial institution or other entity is usually appointed as the servicer to manage payment collections and other activities associated with these loans. Mortgage servicers, which can be large mortgage finance companies or commercial banks, earn a fee for acting as the servicer on behalf of the owner of a loan.[4] In some cases, the servicer is the same institution that originated the loan and in other cases it may be a different institution. The duties of servicers for loans securitized into MBS are specified in a contract called a pooling and servicing agreement, which can vary widely, but may mirror the servicing guidelines issued by the government-sponsored enterprises (GSE) Fannie Mae and Freddie Mac.[5] Servicing duties can involve sending borrowers monthly account statements, answering customer service inquiries, collecting monthly mortgage payments, maintaining escrow accounts for property taxes and hazard insurance, and forwarding proper payments to the mortgage owners. In the event that a borrower becomes delinquent on loan payments, servicers also initiate and conduct foreclosures in order to obtain the proceeds from the sale of the property on behalf of the owners of the loans.

When loans are sold, they are generally packaged together in pools and held in trusts pursuant to the terms and conditions set out in the underlying pooling and servicing agreement. These pools of loans are the assets backing the securities that are issued and sold to investors in the secondary market. Another entity will act as trustee for the securitization trust. Trustees act as asset custodians on behalf of the trust, keeping records of the purchase and receipt of the MBS and holding mortgage liens that secure the investment. Trustees are also the account custodians for the trust—pass-through entities that receive mortgage payments from servicers and disperse them among investors according to the terms of the pooling and servicing agreement. Although trustees may be the legal owners of record of the mortgage loans on behalf of the trust, they do not have a beneficial interest in the underlying loans of the securitization.[6] However, any legal action a servicer takes on behalf of the trust, such as foreclosure, generally may be brought in the name of the trustee. The beneficial interests in these loans accrue to or "are held by" purchasers of the MBS, typically large institutions such as pension funds, mutual funds, and insurance companies.

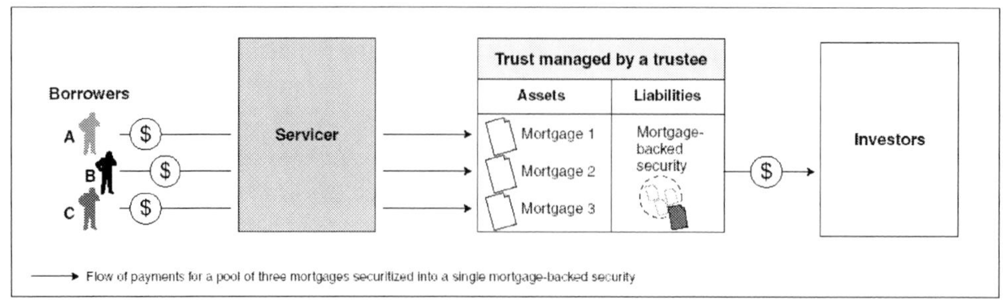

Source: GAO (analysis); Art Explosion (images).

Figure 1. Flow of Payments in a Basic Securitized Transaction .

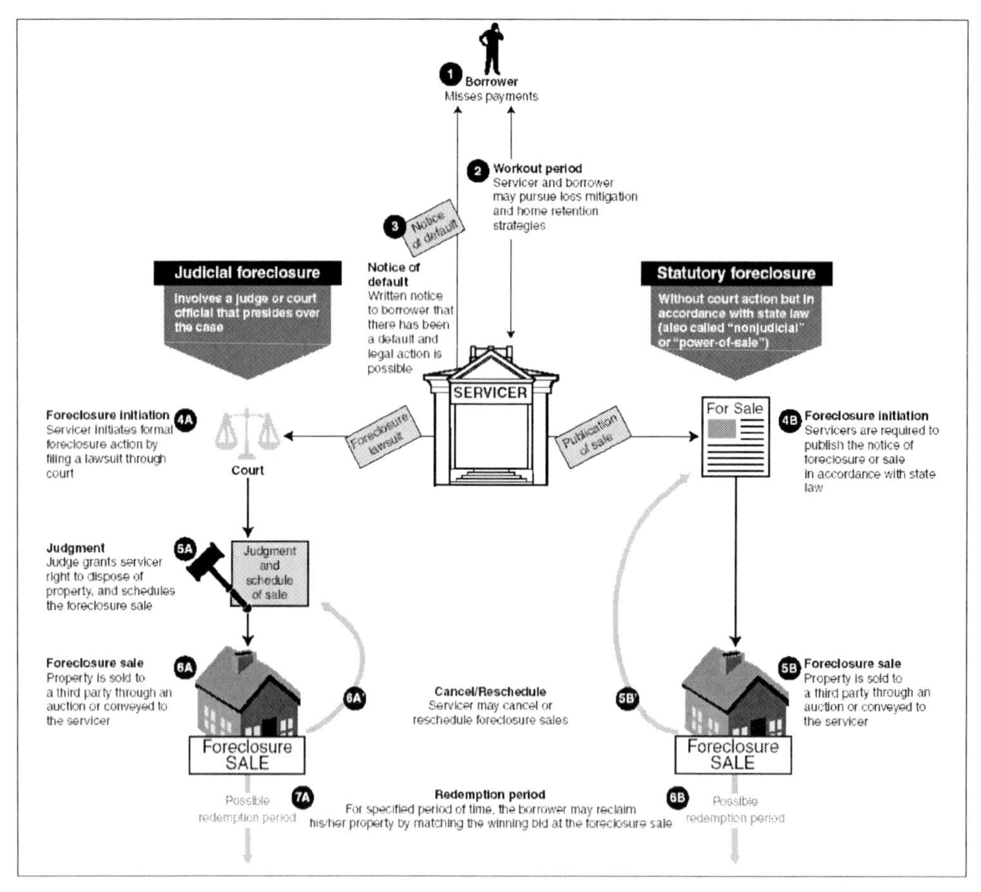

Source: GAO (analysis); Art Explosion (images).

Figure 2. Typical Judicial and Nonjudicial Foreclosure Processes.

The Foreclosure Process: Overview and Recent Concerns

If a borrower defaults on a mortgage loan secured by the home, the mortgage note holder is entitled to pursue foreclosure for the property to be sold at auction and obtain title to the property and sell it on behalf of the mortgage owner to repay the loan. Once the borrower is in default, the servicer must decide whether to pursue a home retention workout or other foreclosure alternative or to initiate foreclosure.[7] The mortgage owner or servicer generally initiates foreclosure once the loan becomes 90 days or more delinquent. As shown in figure 2, states generally follow one of two foreclosure methods. In a judicial foreclosure, a judge presides over the process in a court proceeding. Servicers initiate a formal foreclosure action by filing a lawsuit with a court and in some states may submit supporting documents, such as notarized sworn statements, or affidavits, as part of the lawsuit.[8] A nonjudicial foreclosure process takes place outside the courtroom, typically by the trustee named in the deed of trust.[9] Trustees, and sometimes servicers, generally send a notice of default to the borrower and publish a notice of sale in area newspapers or legal publications.

Beginning in September 2010, several major servicers announced potential problems with their internal procedures for executing documents required to be submitted in a judicial foreclosure. These procedural problems referred to servicers' practice of having a small number of employees sign a large number of affidavits and other legal documents that mortgage companies subsequently submitted to courts and other public authorities to execute foreclosures, so-called robosigning. This practice has raised concerns as to whether individuals who claimed in affidavits to have personal knowledge of the facts necessary to legally foreclose on a property actually had that knowledge and whether legal documents were properly notarized in accordance with state law. As a result, questions were raised about whether mortgage companies had met the necessary prerequisites to foreclose on certain properties, particularly in the judicial foreclosure states that have such documentation requirements.

In addition, questions have been raised about servicers being able to prove that they have authority to act on behalf of the mortgage owner, or are able to prove who the owner is in order to foreclose. State laws may vary on who has authority to bring a foreclosure action, but in all cases the legal holder of the mortgage note (and its legal representatives, acting in the name of the mortgage holder) generally has the right to foreclose on the property. Challenges over this authority, or standing, in foreclosure actions have been raised.[10] Some of these challenges may center on whether the servicer has acquired the rights of a mortgage holder when paperwork documenting a sale or assignment of interest in a mortgage is missing or deficient in some way—for example, if it is not properly endorsed by the parties or if the assignment occurred after the foreclosure complaint was filed.

Federal Agencies Involved in Overseeing Institutions That Originate and Service Loans

Several federal agencies share responsibility for regulating the banking industry in relation to the origination and servicing of mortgage loans.[11] Chartering agencies oversee federally and state-chartered banks and their mortgage lending subsidiaries. At the federal level, OCC has authority to oversee nationally chartered banks. OTS oversees state- and federally chartered savings associations, or thrifts, (including mortgage operating subsidiaries) as well as savings and loan holding companies and lenders owned by a savings and loan holding company.[12] The Federal Reserve oversees insured state-chartered member banks, while FDIC oversees insured state-chartered banks that are not members of the Federal Reserve System. Both the Federal Reserve and FDIC share oversight with the state regulatory authority that chartered the bank. In addition, OTS shares oversight for state-chartered savings associations with the state regulatory authority that chartered the savings association. The Federal Reserve also has general authority over entities that may be owned by federally regulated holding companies but are not federally insured depository institutions. The Federal Trade Commission has authority to enforce certain federal consumer protection laws for nonbank financial services providers. Upon assumption of its full authorities on July 21, 2011, CFPB will have the authority to regulate mortgage servicers with respect to federal consumer financial law.[13] On that date, consumer financial protection functions from seven existing federal agencies will transfer to the new agency.[14] For mortgage servicers that are depository institutions with more than $10 billion in assets or their affiliates, CFPB will have exclusive supervisory authority and primary enforcement authority to ensure compliance with federal consumer financial law.[15] Additionally, if a servicer is a nondepository institution, CFPB will have both supervisory and enforcement authority to ensure compliance with federal consumer financial law.[16] Finally, CFPB will have rulemaking authority with respect to mortgage servicers, including authority that transfers from other federal agencies such as the Federal Reserve and the Federal Trade Commission.[17]

Other agencies are also involved in overseeing certain aspects of U.S. mortgage markets but do not have supervisory authority over mortgage servicers. For example, FHFA has direct supervisory authority over Fannie Mae's and Freddie Mac's activities, but does not have supervisory authority over servicers in general.[18] The Federal Housing Administration (FHA) oversees institutions approved to service loans that FHA insures for the servicers' compliance with servicing regulations on, for example, the timing of foreclosure initiation. Similarly, Treasury has a contractual relationship with servicers that voluntarily participate in the Home Affordable Modification Program (HAMP) and can review these servicers' compliance with Treasury's loan modification guidelines.[19] In addition, staff from SEC also review some of the registered offerings that private issuers of MBS file. Justice has authority to investigate and prosecute civil or criminal enforcement cases. In particular, the Financial Fraud Enforcement Task Force, led by Justice, is charged with coordinating an interagency effort to combat mortgage, loan, and lending fraud committed against the U.S. Treasury, among other financial crimes. Additionally, the Federal Trade Commission is responsible for enforcing certain federal consumer protection laws for brokers, lenders, and servicers that are not depository institutions, including state-chartered independent mortgage lenders.

FEDERAL LAWS DO NOT SPECIFICALLY ADDRESS THE FORECLOSURE PROCESS, AND PAST FEDERAL OVERSIGHT OF FORECLOSURE ACTIVITIES HAS BEEN LIMITED AND FRAGMENTED

Requirements for Foreclosure Processes and Needed Evidence Are Governed Mostly by State rather than Federal Laws

State rather than federal laws largely govern foreclosure processes in the United States. Foreclosure proceedings, including specifying who can bring foreclosure actions and what procedures must be followed as part of such actions, are generally governed by state laws. State foreclosure laws establish certain procedures that mortgage servicers must follow in conducting foreclosures and minimum time periods for various aspects of the foreclosure process. State laws on who has authority, or standing, to bring a foreclosure action generally provide that the legal holder of the mortgage note (and its legal representative, such as a servicer or trustee acting in the name of the mortgage holder) has the right to foreclose on the property.[20] In addition, although state laws vary greatly, in order to foreclose on a property, servicers generally may need evidence that (1) they are the original owner of (or are a holder in due course of) the mortgage on the property or have authority to act on behalf of the owner (or holder) and (2) the borrower is in default on the mortgage.

State laws also vary on the evidence required to support a foreclosure. In states with judicial foreclosure processes, the state laws generally require that a foreclosing party file an action—which may have to include certain documentation—with a court. For example, mortgage holders often are required to prove the amount of the borrower's outstanding obligation and that the borrower is in default through notarized affidavits. In addition, to prove the authority, or standing, to foreclose, a foreclosing entity may be required to submit to the court the original promissory note and mortgage.

State laws may allow foreclosing entities to submit other evidence to establish standing. For instance, the relevant state law may allow for the submission of affidavits attesting to the fact that the entity had the note but that the original note is lost, destroyed, or otherwise cannot be produced for the court. In other instances, mortgage holders may produce copies of the original note and mortgage, or deed of trust, accompanied by an affidavit attesting to the fact that the holder has physical possession of the originals. Affidavits may require a testament that the signers have personal knowledge of the facts to which they are swearing or that they have personally examined the attested facts. Affidavits usually must be signed in the presence of a notary or other witnesses.

In states that allow parties to bring foreclosure actions without court approval—nonjudicial foreclosure states—foreclosing parties are generally required to adhere to all of the procedural and notice requirements established by state law. Mortgage holders are expected to be able to meet the same two criteria that are required in a judicial foreclosure process—that they have authority, or standing, to foreclose and that the borrower is in default. However, evidence documenting these facts is not usually required to be filed with a court or any other entity. If the borrower being foreclosed upon believes that the action is unjustified, he or she must file a lawsuit with a court to contest the foreclosure. In nonjudicial foreclosure states, therefore, servicers might not need to produce documentation supporting their right to foreclose or proving the borrower's default unless a foreclosure is contested.

Federal Laws That Apply to Mortgage Lending Focus on Loan Origination and Do Not Specifically Address the Foreclosure Process

Because state laws primarily govern the foreclosure process, federal laws related to mortgage lending are focused on protecting consumers at mortgage origination and during the life of a loan, but not necessarily during foreclosure. Among the federal laws that apply to residential mortgage lending and subsequent servicing of such loans are the Fair Housing and Equal Credit Opportunity Acts, which address granting credit and ensuring nondiscrimination in lending; the Truth in Lending Act (TILA), much of which addresses disclosure requirements for consumer credit transactions; the Real Estate Settlement Procedures Act of 1974 (RESPA), which focuses primarily on the regulation and disclosure of mortgage closing documents; the Fair Credit Reporting Act, which addresses consumer report information, including use of such information in connection with mortgage lending; and the Secure and Fair Enforcement for Mortgage Licensing Act of 2008 (SAFE Act), which requires licensing and/or registration of mortgage loan originators.[21]

These various federal consumer protection laws address some aspects of mortgage servicers' interactions with borrowers, but do not include specific requirements for servicers to follow when executing a foreclosure. For example, TILA, as amended by the Dodd-Frank Wall Street Reform and Consumer Protection Act (Dodd-Frank Act), requires servicers to notify borrowers of impending interest rate changes on hybrid adjustable rate mortgages and will require certain disclosures in monthly statements to borrowers.[22] Amendments to the regulations implementing TILA that took effect in October 2009 also prohibit, for certain loans, imposing a late fee on a late fee.[23] In addition, RESPA requires a servicer of a federally related mortgage loan to provide initial and annual escrow account statements, notices of transfer of servicing, and timelines for responding to certain written requests from borrowers, such as requests for the identity, address, and other relevant contact information of the lien holder.[24] RESPA also outlines rules regarding referring borrowers to affiliated businesses for services and requirements for maintaining escrow accounts that the servicer establishes or controls on behalf of a borrower to pay taxes, insurance premiums, or other charges.[25] With respect to foreclosure processing specifically, according to Federal Reserve officials, among the only federal laws that address the foreclosure process they had identified were the Protecting Tenants at Foreclosure Act of 2009, which protects certain tenants from immediate eviction by new owners who acquire residential property through foreclosure; the Servicemembers Civil Relief Act (SCRA), which restricts foreclosure of properties owned by active duty members of the military; and federal bankruptcy laws.[26]

Past Oversight of Foreclosure Activities by Bank Regulators Has Been Limited and Fragmented

Bank regulators are responsible for overseeing most entities that conduct mortgage servicing, but their oversight of foreclosure activities generally has been limited. As part of their mission to ensure the safety and soundness of financial institutions, banking regulators have the authority to conduct reviews of any aspect of banks' activities, including mortgage servicing activities. The majority of the mortgage servicing in the United States is performed by financial institutions and other subsidiaries of holding companies that are under the oversight of OCC, OTS, Federal Reserve, or FDIC. Federal banking regulators have responsibility for helping ensure the safety and soundness of the institutions they oversee, promoting stability in the financial markets, and enforcing compliance with applicable consumer protection laws. To achieve these goals, regulators establish capital requirements for banks and conduct on-site examinations and off-site monitoring to assess their financial condition, including assessing their compliance with applicable banking laws, regulations, and agency guidance.[27] Additionally, federal bank regulators can take a variety of enforcement actions to rectify any identified deficiencies, including deficiencies in financial institutions' mortgage origination, transfer, securitization, and foreclosure processes.[28] These enforcement actions include the ability to issue cease-and-desist orders, to impose civil money penalties, and to suspend or prevent entities or individuals from conducting business on behalf of a financial institution, under certain circumstances. Although federal laws do not specifically address the foreclosure process, officials at the federal banking regulatory agencies stated that their agencies have the necessary authority to oversee the compliance of institutions under their jurisdiction with any applicable state laws, including those pertaining to foreclosing on a home mortgage.

As part of overseeing the safety and soundness of banks, the banking regulators have developed a variety of guidance that outlines expectations for banks to follow in conducting their operations, but the extent to which this guidance addresses how foreclosures should be conducted has been limited. Each of the banking regulators has guidance that addresses various aspects of lending, including for home mortgages, and that establishes expectations regarding extending credit, conducting appraisals of properties, and other activities. For example, the federal banking regulators have developed uniform real estate lending standards that require depository institutions to establish and maintain comprehensive, written real estate lending policies that are consistent with safe and sound banking practices.[29] These policies must address certain lending considerations, loan administration procedures, and portfolio diversification standards, among other requirements. Regarding foreclosure, these lending guidelines noted only that institutions should have procedures that address foreclosure timing and compliance with servicing agreements. Further, the Interagency Guidelines Establishing Standards for Safety and Soundness state that institutions should have loan documentation practices that ensure that any claim against a borrower is legally enforceable.[30]

The examination handbooks that FDIC, Federal Reserve, OCC, and OTS examiners follow when conducting examinations of banks' servicing activities do not address the specifics of how foreclosures are to be conducted, but the guidance does address a number of foreclosure-related activities. For example, these regulators' examination guidance addresses such topics as how to assess the costs of foreclosure or the value of the homes for which ownership is acquired through foreclosure. In addition, the guidance addresses how to value servicing rights, which provide the stream of income that servicers receive from conducting servicing on behalf of other loan owners, such as MBS trusts. The value of this income is shown as an asset on the balance sheet of the servicer. Each of the regulators' guidance also notes that institutions should have foreclosure procedures and that examiners should assess whether the institutions' procedures address the timing of foreclosure. For example, the Federal Reserve guidance suggests selecting a sample of loans to determine whether foreclosure was instituted in a timely manner. The regulators' examination guidance also expects institutions to consider the risks that arise when contracting with third parties to conduct any business activities on their behalf and the controls and monitoring that should be established throughout the arrangement. The guidance for OCC, OTS, and the Federal Reserve also instructs their examiners to assess the methods—such as policies and procedures or management reports—that institutions use to ensure that their foreclosure procedures comply with applicable laws, regulations, and investor guidelines. Finally, OCC and OTS guidance notes that examiners should review internal bank reports on foreclosure trends.

The extent to which bank regulators have conducted reviews of the foreclosure activities of banks or banking subsidiaries that perform mortgage servicing has been limited because these practices generally were not considered as posing a high risk to the safety and soundness of the institutions. Because mortgage servicers generally manage loans that are actually owned or held by other entities, they are not exposed to significant losses if the loans become delinquent.[31] In addition, we have previously reported that the percentage of loans in foreclosure had historically been very low (less than 1 percent) from 1979 to 2006.[32] According to OCC and Federal Reserve staff, these agencies conduct risk-based examinations that focus on areas of greatest risk to their institutions' financial positions, as well as some other areas of potential concern, such as consumer complaints. Because they determined that the risks from mortgage servicing generally had not indicated the need to conduct more detailed reviews of these operations, federal banking regulators have not regularly examined servicers' foreclosure practices on a loan-level basis. Instead, previous federal regulatory examinations of mortgage servicers have focused on loan modifications or on the income banks earn from servicing loans.

Oversight also has been fragmented, and not all servicers have been overseen by federal banking regulators. Multiple agencies have regulatory responsibility for most of the institutions that conduct mortgage servicing, but until recently, some nonbank institutions have not had a primary federal or state regulator. As shown in figure 3, of the top 25 servicers in 2010 that represent 75 percent of the market, the majority—over 90 percent—were depository institutions that are subject to oversight by one of the federal banking regulators. For example,

- OCC is the primary regulator for banks that service 78.3 percent of loans serviced by the top 25 servicers.
- The Federal Reserve oversees bank holding companies or their depository institution subsidiaries and state-chartered member banks that may conduct servicing that together account for 4.1 percent of the loans serviced by the top 25 servicers.
- OTS, whose functions are scheduled to be transferred to OCC, FDIC, and the Federal Reserve on July 21, 2011, oversees servicers that are savings associations, which account for 4.7 percent of the volume of the top 25 servicers.[33]
- FDIC acts as the primary regulator for servicers that represent 1.1 percent of the loans serviced by the top 25 servicers.

In addition, many federally regulated bank holding companies that have insured depository subsidiaries, such as national or state-chartered banks, may have nonbank subsidiaries, such as mortgage finance companies. Under the Bank Holding Company Act of 1956, as amended, the Federal Reserve has jurisdiction over such bank holding companies and their nonbank subsidiaries that are not regulated by another functional regulator.[34] These nonbank subsidiaries accounted for about 5.9 percent of the top 25 servicers' volume in 2010. In some cases nonbank entities that service mortgage loans are not affiliated with financial institutions at all, and therefore were not subject to oversight by one of the federal banking regulators. These entities accounted for about 6 percent of the top 25 servicers' volume in 2010.

In addition to fragmented oversight among multiple regulators, past oversight of servicers has been uneven, particularly with respect to nonbank entities. Although the Federal Reserve has authority over nonbank subsidiaries that are affiliates of bank holding companies, until recently the Federal Reserve had generally not included these entities in its examination activity because their activities were not considered material risks to the bank holding company. In a previous report on predatory lending, we raised questions about the activities of some of these less regulated nonbank entities and recommended that federal regulators actively monitor their activities.[35] However, regulators continued to view the firms as not posing material risks. In 2007, after widespread defaults on mortgage loans began occurring, the Federal Reserve conducted a targeted review of consumer compliance supervision at selected nonbank subsidiaries that originate loans. Additionally, in October 2009, the Federal Reserve began a loan modification initiative, including on-site reviews, to assess whether certain servicers, including nonbank subsidiaries of bank holding companies, were executing loan modification programs in compliance with relevant federal consumer protection laws and regulations. A Federal Reserve official recently testified that the current foreclosure documentation problems underscore the importance of using the agency's authority to send examiners into nonbank affiliates of bank holding companies.[36] Further, the Federal Reserve received certain authority in the Dodd-Frank Act to supervise certain nonbank financial institutions that have been determined to pose a potential threat to the financial stability of the United States.[37]

There also have been gaps in past oversight. For example, nonbank servicers have historically been subject to little or no direct oversight by state or federal regulators. We have previously reported that some states require mortgage servicers (including state-chartered banks) to register with the state banking department.[38] State banking regulators generally oversee independent lenders and mortgage servicers by requiring business licenses that mandate meeting net worth, funding, and liquidity thresholds. According to officials representing state banking supervisors, bank examinations focus on loan origination and, until recently, did not include an evaluation of servicing or foreclosure practices. In our 2009 report on how the U.S. financial regulatory system has not kept pace with the major developments in recent decades, we noted that the varying levels, and in some cases complete lack, of oversight of nonbank institutions that originated mortgages created problems for consumers or posed risks to regulated institutions.[39]

Other Federal Agencies' Involvement in Reviewing Servicing Activities Also Has Been Limited

In addition to federal banking regulators, federal housing agencies and others have oversight responsibilities for various aspects of mortgage servicing, but these agencies' past efforts also focused primarily on servicers' loan modification and preforeclosure activities rather than the processes associated with foreclosure.

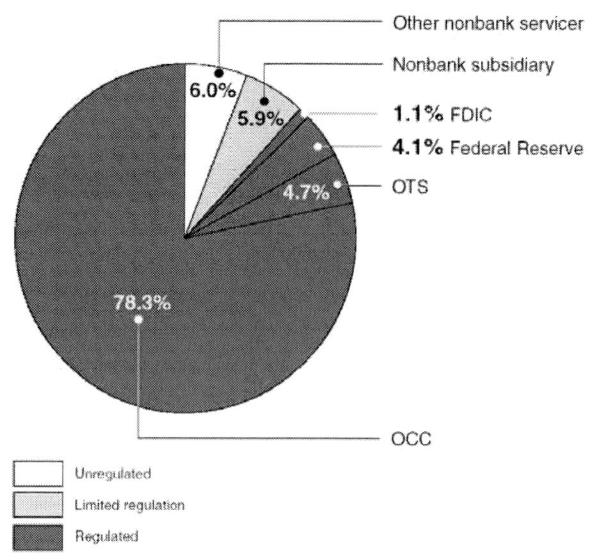

Source: GAO analysis of Inside Mortgage Finance data.

Note: We identified institutions' share of the mortgage servicing market as reported in an industry publication, *Inside Mortgage Finance*. According to our analysis of these data, the home mortgage loans serviced by the top 25 institutions accounted for about 75 percent of all loans outstanding.

Figure 3. Regulatory Oversight of Top 25 Servicers, by Percentage of Mortgage Loans Serviced, December 2010.

- FHA, which oversees mortgage servicers that manage the home mortgage loans insured by that agency, uses a risk-based approach to monitor those institutions. Furthermore, according to FHA staff, the agency's mortgage insurance contract provisions do not authorize direct oversight of the mortgage foreclosure process. FHA does have regulations that provide expectations for servicers related to foreclosure activities.[40] These regulations address the timely initiation of foreclosure, completion of foreclosure within specified time frames, and conveyance to HUD of properties with clear and marketable title following foreclosure sale.[41] According to FHA staff, past servicer reviews have focused on monitoring compliance with requirements for assisting delinquent borrowers to remain in their homes by considering loan modifications, payment plans, or other options to avoid foreclosure, called loss mitigation. For example, FHA examiners would review whether servicers considered all loss mitigation alternatives before foreclosure was initiated. The staff noted, however, that examiners have not previously conducted in-depth reviews of servicers' foreclosure practices.
- FHFA also conducts housing oversight activities, but its past oversight of foreclosure activities has also been limited. FHFA has no direct authority over servicers, but does have authority to ensure that the housing GSEs are being run in a safe and sound fashion, as well as the power to impose operational, managerial, and internal control standards on the companies.[42] According to FHFA staff, their agency has monitored foreclosure trends and policies at Fannie Mae and Freddie Mac, but the agency did not in the past routinely examine these enterprises' oversight of their servicers'

foreclosure procedures. Like the banking regulators and FHA, FHFA has focused its past efforts on the institutions' loan modification and preforeclosure efforts. For example, according to FHFA staff, recent oversight activities have included an operational risk assessment of the GSE's HAMP program as well as reviews of GSE oversight of servicer performance in adhering to foreclosure timeline standards and oversight of retained foreclosure attorney networks and examinations of foreclosure claim filing performance. Similarly, the GSEs also were not actively taking steps to ensure that the servicers they contracted with to manage the loans they purchased or pooled into MBS were following appropriate foreclosure practices. Representatives from the GSEs reported that they conduct targeted reviews of servicers that focus on evaluating processes and procedures. While the GSEs conducted reviews of delinquent loans and tested whether certain key elements of the servicers' management of loans in default were being properly followed, the reviews did not specifically check that servicers were in compliance with foreclosure practices based on state-specific laws and guidance. They said that they require servicers to follow proper legal procedures with respect to all aspects of their business operations, including their foreclosure documentation practices, as part of their contractual obligations with the GSEs and expect servicers to report problems with their activities.

- Treasury ordinarily does not have any direct role in oversight over entities that conduct mortgage servicing. However, under HAMP, which was initiated in 2009, mortgage servicers contract with Treasury to help troubled homeowners obtain modifications of their mortgage loans. As part of this program, Treasury has conducted compliance reviews and is assessing servicer compliance with HAMP requirements. These requirements, and thus Treasury's oversight, do not cover foreclosure activities.
- SEC is involved in ensuring that appropriate public disclosures are made as part of the issuance of MBS, but it does not have a direct role with respect to foreclosure activities related to the loans in these pools. SEC staff told us they receive a first annual report on publicly traded residential MBS that includes information such as the overall performance and status of loans in the pool.[43] When MBS are underwritten and issued, a company (usually an investment bank) must disclose certain information about the securities to inform potential investors of the risks involved. SEC has the authority to enforce civil securities fraud statutes related to any inaccurate disclosures, such as about the performance or ownership of the loans in the pool.[44] However, we previously reported that officials from SEC told us that they did not examine servicers' policies or activities for these securitized assets. SEC staff told us that they also reviewed information included in the publicly filed financial statements of publicly traded companies engaged in mortgage servicing. This information generally included aggregate trends in foreclosure activity but did not address actions taken related to individual loans.
- The Federal Trade Commission is responsible for enforcing certain federal consumer protection laws for entities that are not depository institutions, including state-chartered independent mortgage lenders. As a result, it can take enforcement actions against nonbank mortgage servicers if it receives a complaint and then determines that such an entity had violated one of the various federal consumer protection laws.

In recent years, the Federal Trade Commission has completed a number of enforcement actions against mortgage servicers.[45] However, the Federal Trade Commission is not a supervisory agency and thus does not conduct ongoing monitoring of compliance, including of nonbank mortgage servicers.

- Justice has general authority to investigate and prosecute instances of fraud, through both civil and criminal enforcement, and thus can be involved in mortgage-related activities if fraud against the government, lenders, borrowers, or investors occurs. However, according to Justice staff, their agency does not have bank regulatory authorities; therefore, it does not engage in routine review of servicers' activities as bank regulators do.[46] Justice staff could not comment on any ongoing investigations, but said that cases completed in the past involving mortgage servicers involved issues other than foreclosure.[47] In 2009, the Obama administration established the Financial Fraud Enforcement Task Force in response to the financial crisis. The task force's Mortgage Fraud Working Group is focused on a wide array of mortgage fraud, including mortgage lending fraud and foreclosure rescue schemes. To date, this group's activities have focused on investigating issues related to mortgage origination, short sales, and appraisals and tracking the market for indications of mortgage fraud.

FEDERAL REGULATORS HAVE CONDUCTED REVIEWS IN RESPONSE TO FORECLOSURE DOCUMENTATION PROBLEMS, BUT EXTENT OF AND ROLES IN FUTURE OVERSIGHT ARE UNCLEAR

Federal Regulators Have Recently Increased Attention on Servicing Activities and Identified Problems through a Coordinated Review

In response to the foreclosure process deficiencies that various mortgage servicers publicly announced beginning in September 2010, federal banking regulators have conducted specific reviews of certain servicers' foreclosure activities. When reports of foreclosure documentation problems surfaced, banking regulators initially ordered servicers to conduct self-assessments of their foreclosure management processes and correct any deficiencies. Consequently, some servicers temporarily halted foreclosure proceedings in order to review their foreclosure processes and to verify the soundness of documentation preparation procedures. Further, OCC, the Federal Reserve, OTS, and FDIC began a coordinated on-site review of 14 mortgage servicers to evaluate the adequacy of controls over servicers' foreclosure processes and to assess servicers' policies and procedures for compliance with applicable federal and state laws.[48]

Regulatory staff told us that as part of these reviews, their examiners evaluated internal controls and procedures for processing foreclosures and reviewed samples of individual loan files to better ensure the integrity of the document preparation process and to confirm that files contained appropriate documentation. Examiners reviewed more than 2,800 loan files—which they noted was a relatively small number of foreclosure files given the volume of recent foreclosures processed by these servicers—comprising approximately 200 foreclosure loan files with a variety of characteristics from each servicer. According to one of the banking agencies, 9 of the servicers included in the file review had completed about 608,000 foreclosures in 2010.[49] The foreclosure files selected for review included ongoing and completed foreclosures, foreclosures conducted in both judicial and nonjudicial states, and a judgmental sample of files based on the findings of initial file reviews and consumer complaints. The on-site reviews were conducted largely in November 2010.

The reviews uncovered similar weaknesses in many of the mortgage servicers' foreclosure practices, although one regulator noted that each weakness was not evident at every servicer, nor was every deficiency uncovered in each loan file. Generally, the examinations revealed severe deficiencies in three primary areas:

- First, examiners identified shortcomings in the preparation of foreclosure documents. For example, according to agency officials, affidavits used in foreclosures frequently were signed by persons who did not satisfy personal knowledge requirements and were not properly notarized, which represented practices not conducted in accordance with state laws.
- Second, regulators found that most servicers did not have adequate policies, staffing, or oversight of their internal foreclosure processes. Regulators' reviews revealed that most servicers lacked sufficient policies to guide personnel engaged in foreclosure activities, including policies that outlined how affidavit documents should be legally prepared and notarized. Additionally, examiners found that most servicers did not have effective quality controls or internal review processes in place to detect deficiencies in foreclosure procedures. Regulatory staff reported that servicers did not generally review document execution processes or verify compliance with regulations and state and local laws during internal audits of foreclosure processes. Further, the regulators' reviews also revealed that most servicers did not maintain sufficient staffing levels to process the increasing volume of foreclosures, nor were staff adequately trained to perform this work in compliance with relevant laws and regulations. For example, regulators found that one servicer that had previously understaffed this function and had not provided adequate training increased its document-signing staff from 5 to 80 and revised its training to include guidance for judicial foreclosures to address deficiencies in foreclosure processing.
- Third, regulators found that all the servicers had not sufficiently overseen the activities of third-party service providers, particularly in oversight of foreclosure attorneys, who were performing foreclosure activities on behalf of these servicers. Regulatory staff said that their reviews indicated that servicers had relied on attorneys to execute foreclosures in compliance with applicable laws, but had failed to conduct due diligence assessments of these attorneys' foreclosure practices. Many servicers had also failed to adequately supervise other firms that also conducted foreclosure activities on behalf of servicers, such as firms that track loan ownership or process foreclosure-related documents.

As a part of the reviews of foreclosure documentation problems, banking regulators also conducted on-site reviews of two bank service providers that were involved with processing or maintaining foreclosure-related documents and found similar weaknesses. In conjunction with staff from other regulatory agencies, OCC staff led an examination of MERSCORP and its wholly owned subsidiary, Mortgage Electronic Registration System (MERS), an electronic registry established by the mortgage finance industry that tracks mortgage ownership and transfers of servicing rights, and Federal Reserve staff led a similar on-site review of foreclosure-related activities at Lender Processing Services (LPS), which provides various data and document processing services to mortgage lenders and servicers.[50] The regulators identified some weaknesses in governance and oversight at both firms and found that internal controls were insufficient to identify deficiencies. To address these issues, the agencies are taking formal enforcement actions against MERS and LPS.[51]

Bank Examiners Found That Borrowers in Files Reviewed Were Delinquent and Servicers Generally Had Necessary Documents to Foreclose

While the bank regulators' examinations of the 14 servicers revealed material weaknesses in these entities' overall foreclosure management processes, examiners generally did not find in the files they reviewed cases in which the borrowers were not seriously delinquent on the payments on their loans or that the servicers lacked the documents necessary to demonstrate their authority to foreclose. The reviews did not include an analysis of the payment history of each loan prior to foreclosure or potential mortgage-servicing issues outside of the foreclosure process.[52] For example, examiners focused their reviews on foreclosure procedures and documentation preparation and did not examine whether servicers had followed other requirements, such as FHA requirements for assessing the borrower for a loan modification or other loss mitigation alternatives, before initiating foreclosure. Nonetheless, regulatory staff told us that examiners or internal servicer reviews of foreclosure loan files had identified a limited number of cases in which foreclosures should not have proceeded—even though the borrower was seriously delinquent—and servicers' internal controls over, for example, procedures for staff knowledge of the case, could have made a difference.[53] For example, one supervisory letter noted that one servicer's internal review had identified instances of foreclosures that proceeded despite the borrower having received a loan modification, which should have halted the foreclosure process. A Federal Reserve official told us that while its examiners uncovered only one case in its file review where foreclosure was initiated against a borrower in a loan modification status, the examinations raised concerns about the level of communication between servicers' foreclosure and loan modification staff. In addition, regulatory staff told us that some servicers reported instances where foreclosures proceeded against military service members on active duty in violation of SCRA.[54] According to regulatory staff, violations of SCRA were not reported by all servicers. According to our discussions with regulatory staff, 2 servicers of the 14 included in the regulators' review preliminarily identified almost 50 instances of foreclosures proceeding against military service members on active duty in violation of SCRA. They noted that some of these cases may have been prevented had servicers had better internal controls, such as procedures to ensure that staff reviewing files took steps to obtain information to verify active duty status and borrower eligibility for SCRA protection prior to taking foreclosure action.

From the sample loan reviews of the 14 servicers, the bank regulatory officials said that examiners generally did not identify any concerns related to transfers of loan documents that would impede the servicer's ability to initiate foreclosure. On the basis of their reviews of more than 2,800 files, examiners determined that servicers generally were able to effectively demonstrate ownership of promissory notes and were generally able to locate original notes and mortgage documents that are required to be in the possession of the foreclosing party under most state laws. However, bank regulatory officials told us that examiners did not always verify, as part of the loan file review process, whether documentation included a record of all previous mortgage transfers from loan origination to foreclosure initiation, as may be required by some state laws or contracts.[55] In addition, with some exceptions, examiners found that notes appeared properly endorsed and mortgages appeared properly assigned. In a few instances, examiners uncovered notes that were not properly endorsed, which could subject the servicer to challenges on its authority or standing to foreclose. Additionally, while each of the regulators stated that servicers could generally produce requested documentation, servicers at times had required some time to find necessary documents. In part, these difficulties in locating necessary documents quickly was likely exacerbated by the examiners' finding that many servicers did not maintain formal foreclosure files, but relied on third parties such as foreclosure attorneys to maintain documents, including judicial affidavits and promissory notes, on behalf of the servicer.

Future Oversight Plans of Regulators and the Degree to Which Potential National Servicing Standards Would Address Documentation Issues Are Yet Unclear

On the basis of their findings from the coordinated review, regulators are taking formal enforcement actions against each of the 14 servicers, but the extent of their future oversight of servicing activities has yet to be determined.[56] Regulators recently issued formal enforcement orders to these servicers, and these servicers are required to take corrective actions to address identified deficiencies and weaknesses.[57] According to bank regulatory staff and these enforcement orders, each of the 14 servicers is required to enhance its compliance program with respect to oversight of foreclosure processes and to ensure that mortgage servicing and foreclosure practices comply with applicable laws and regulations. In addition, enforcement orders require servicers to align staffing levels with servicing volume and to enhance training to ensure that personnel involved in processing foreclosures are aware of compliance obligations. Regulators' enforcement actions also require servicers to reassess and strengthen their vendor management processes to improve supervision over third-party service providers, including external law firms and MERS. Because examiners reviewed a relatively small number of foreclosure files, enforcement orders require each servicer to retain an independent firm to conduct a comprehensive review of past foreclosure actions from January 1, 2009 to December 31, 2010 to identify borrowers who were financially harmed by servicer deficiencies identified in the independent review, and to remediate those borrowers, as appropriate.[58] Further, the servicers are required to retain an independent firm to assess the compliance, legal, and reputational risks in their servicing operations, in particular the risks of deficiencies in foreclosure activities and loss mitigation. According to the regulators, some servicers have already begun to implement new foreclosure policies and procedures, including strengthening internal controls, increasing the number of staff, and enhancing training. For example, OTS found that one servicer had revised its affidavit processing and notarization procedure to come into compliance with state law by requiring signing officers to review supporting documentation, including documents used by attorneys in preparing affidavits, before signing affidavits and to require an authorized notary to witness the affiant's signature.

Although regulators have taken enforcement actions against servicers, they have not identified specifically how they will change the extent and frequency of future oversight of servicers going forward. According to the regulators' report on their coordinated review, regulators will take steps to help ensure that corrective actions taken by servicers and as required by the enforcement orders are fully implemented.[59] Staff at one of these agencies told us that they will substantially revise their supervisory strategy to include plans to assess servicer compliance with any enforcement orders and to evaluate servicers' implementation of corrective action plans. However, although regulatory staff recognized that additional oversight would likely be necessary for servicers' foreclosure activities in the future, as of April 2011 they had not determined what changes would be made to guidance or to the extent and frequency of examinations. For example, staff from the Federal Reserve acknowledged that the recent Dodd-Frank Act directs them to conduct additional oversight of bank holding companies and their nonbank subsidiaries, including those that perform mortgage servicing.[60] These staff said that they were developing a standardized work plan for examinations of all mortgage servicers supervised by the Federal Reserve, but they said that they had not finalized plans for the extent and timing for conducting such ongoing oversight.

Moreover, regulators with whom we spoke expressed uncertainty about how their organizations will interact with and share responsibility with the new CFPB regarding oversight of mortgage servicing activities. This agency was established in the Dodd-Frank Act and, once it assumes its full authority, will have direct authority to conduct examinations of and enforce consumer protection regulations for the largest depository institutions and their affiliates as well as nonbank institutions, with regard to servicing activities. This includes authority to enforce various consumer protection statutes currently overseen by other regulators—including authority to enforce TILA and RESPA. Although bank regulatory staff told us that they will continue to look at banks' mortgage servicing activities to assess the potential impact on such institutions' safety and soundness, they have not yet determined how this oversight will be shared with CFPB, which is to focus on ensuring that consumers are adequately protected. According to regulatory staff and the staff standing up CFPB, the agencies intend to coordinate oversight of mortgage servicing activities as CFPB assumes its authorities in the coming months. In addition, the staff standing up CFPB said that supervision of mortgage servicing will be a priority for the new agency, but as of April 2011 oversight plans had not been finalized. As previously discussed, fragmentation among the various entities responsible for overseeing mortgage servicers heightens the importance of coordination on plans for future oversight. In recent testimony, the Acting Comptroller of the Currency expressed concern about the lack of clarity regarding CFPB's regulatory role and stated the need for CFPB to clearly define its role and responsibilities so that regulatory agencies can practice appropriate oversight.[61] Some of the elements we identified as important for ensuring effective regulation in our 2009 report on reforming the U.S. financial regulatory system highlight the importance of regulatory coordination as part of the oversight of foreclosure practices. In that report, we noted that effective oversight requires regulators to develop appropriately comprehensive regulations and clearly defined goals so that they can effectively conduct activities to implement their missions. This report also noted that when regulators have different goals, such as the banking regulators with their focus on institutions' safety and soundness and CFPB's focus on consumer protection, having mechanisms for regulators to coordinate oversight is important to prevent gaps and inconsistencies in oversight.[62] CFPB staff told us they are aware of these concerns and said that they would continue to communicate with other regulators on servicing issues and general coordination of examinations.

As part of addressing the problems associated with mortgage servicing, including those relating to customer service, loan modifications, and other issues, various market participants have begun calling for the creation of national servicing standards, but the extent to which any final standards would address foreclosure documentation and processing is unclear. For example, a December 2010 letter from a group of academics, industry association representatives, and others to the financial regulators noted that such standards are needed to improve the certainty associated with mortgage securitizations and ensure appropriate servicing for all loans, including those in MBS issuances and those held either in portfolios of the originating institution or by other owners. This letter outlined various areas that such standards could address, including requirements that servicers submit written attestations that foreclosure processes comply with applicable laws and that loan modifications be pursued whenever economically feasible.

Similarly, some regulators have made statements in support of such standards. For example, OCC has developed draft standards, and in his February 2011 testimony, the Acting Comptroller of the Currency expressed support for such standards, noting that they should provide the same safeguards for all consumers and should apply uniformly to all servicers. He also stated that standards should require that servicers have strong foreclosure governance processes that ensure compliance with all legal standards and documentation requirements and establish effective oversight of third-party vendors. In addition, a member of the Board of Governors of the Federal Reserve System testified that consideration of national standards for mortgage servicers was warranted.[63] Further, in a recent speech on the urgent need for mortgage reform, FDIC's Chairman urged servicers and federal and state regulators to act now to create national servicing standards.[64] Most of the regulators with whom we spoke indicated that such national servicing standards could be beneficial. For example, staff from one of the regulators told us that national standards would create clear expectations for all servicers, including nonbank entities that are not overseen by the banking regulators, and would help establish consistency across the servicing industry. The regulators' report on the coordinated review also states that such standards would help promote accountability and appropriateness in dealing with consumers and strengthen the housing finance market. In response to our draft report, multiple agencies commented that an interagency effort to develop national servicing standards is currently under way. While the banking agencies, HUD, Treasury, and FHFA are collaborating to create standards that would address problems in mortgage servicing, including deficiencies in foreclosure processing, as of April 2011 it was still uncertain what any final standards would address and how they would be implemented. According to CFPB staff, whatever the outcome of the interagency negotiations, CFPB will have substantial rulemaking authority over servicing and under the Dodd-Frank Act is required to issue certain rules on servicing by January 2013. In the past, we have reported that opportunities for problems involving financial institutions and consumers increase when activities are not subject to consistent oversight and regulatory expectations.[65] As a result, including specific expectations regarding foreclosure practices in any standards that are developed could help ensure more uniform practices and oversight in this area.

In response to recently disclosed foreclosure documentation problems, federal housing agencies and entities also conducted reviews of servicer practices. For example, FHA recently returned to the six largest servicers of FHA-insured mortgage loans, following earlier examinations on servicers' loss mitigation practices, to review servicer foreclosure processes.[66] According to agency officials, FHA issued questionnaires to targeted servicers—all of which were also being reviewed as part of the bank regulators' reviews—to obtain information on their foreclosure practices, and the agency performed on-site examinations that included review of individual loan files. Agency officials also reported that examiners reviewed servicing transfer documentation to ensure that assignments were properly recorded and exhibited no break in chain of title. FHA officials stated that they are in the process of consolidating and reviewing exam findings and plan to issue an executive summary report. While FHA plans to issue letters to servicers requesting corrective action plans, agency officials noted that many of the servicers had already implemented corrective measures to remedy deficiencies in foreclosure processes. Internally, FHA is also considering changes in servicing guidance to better ensure the soundness and timeliness of the foreclosure process.

FHFA is also responding to revelations of foreclosure documentation problems. In October 2010, FHFA issued a statement of support for the GSEs' efforts in addressing documentation concerns after both Fannie Mae and Freddie Mac issued letters to their respective servicers reminding them of their legal and contractual obligations and requiring that they assess their foreclosure processes and correct any deficiencies. Subsequently, FHFA issued a four-point policy framework to the GSEs and servicers for assessing and remedying foreclosure process deficiencies that asked them to

- verify that their foreclosure processes were working properly,
- remediate any deficiencies identified in their foreclosure processing,
- refer suspicions of fraudulent activity to appropriate regulatory officials, and
- avoid delaying the processing of foreclosures in the absence of identified problems.

According to GSE officials, in response, some servicers reported problems with their foreclosure procedures and are taking steps to remediate deficiencies.

In addition, FHFA and the GSEs are evaluating future measures to improve mortgage servicing. As announced by FHFA in a recent press release, FHFA directed Fannie Mae and Freddie Mac to work on a joint initiative, in coordination with FHFA and HUD, to consider alternatives for future mortgage servicing structures and servicing compensation for single family loans; however, any changes are not expected to be implemented before 2012.[67] Separately, FHFA also directed the GSEs to work together to align their guidelines to servicers to establish, among other things, consistent timelines and requirements for communications with borrowers.[68] Moreover, both Fannie Mae and Freddie Mac have already begun to enhance oversight of their attorney networks. According to an official from one of the GSEs, changes in oversight include increased staffing levels in the GSEs' legal and business units and on-site staff at servicer locations in one state.

Other federal agencies are also taking steps to address foreclosure documentation issues.

- In October 2010, Treasury issued a reminder letter to Making Home Affordable (MHA) servicers reiterating servicer obligations to comply with applicable federal and state laws.[69] As a consequence of reported irregularities in the foreclosure process, Treasury instructed its compliance agent, MHA-Compliance, to review internal policies and procedures governing preforeclosure activities at the 10 largest servicers.[70] While Treasury's efforts are primarily focused on loss mitigation efforts and compliance with HAMP requirements, Treasury is also working to improve servicer processes and to help borrowers.

- SEC also responded in October 2010 by reaching out to certain companies about the adequacy of the disclosures that publicly traded companies that perform mortgage servicing, which includes many of the largest servicers, have made to their shareholders about the potential financial risks to their companies that are associated with mortgage foreclosure documentation issues. SEC issued a letter to public companies engaged in mortgage servicing activities reminding them of their disclosure obligations and identifying items to consider in disclosure statements, including potential material impacts on operations because of liabilities resulting from documentation problems. SEC officials noted that reporting companies did include disclosures regarding foreclosure documentation issues in recent filings. For example, 2 of the largest servicers disclosed that they had instituted a moratorium on foreclosures because of alleged irregularities in foreclosure documentation processing.
- Justice is also taking actions to address foreclosure documentation issues. Justice staff could not comment on investigations, but told us that they are working with investigatory and regulatory partners to look into the servicers' foreclosure practices. While they said that federal civil and criminal statutes could apply in complaints or charges in areas of mortgage fraud, including mail and wire fraud, false statements, Financial Institutions Reform, Recovery, and Enforcement Act (FIRREA) civil actions, and fraud against the government, if the mortgage loans involved were federally insured or guaranteed, Justice staff told us that the state attorneys general and other regulators also have enforcement authority to address these issues.

As multiple investigations into mortgage servicer activities are under way, numerous federal agencies and state officials recently formed a group to help coordinate these efforts. Participants include the federal banking regulators as well as agencies such as Justice, Treasury, FHFA, HUD, SEC, and FTC, with input from CFPB. Additionally, some of these agencies are coordinating with state officials, including representatives from the 50-state Attorney General group formed to investigate robosigning allegations and other deficient servicer practices. Agencies participate in weekly check-ins, and meetings are conducted as needed. The goal of this group is to provide a comprehensive and coordinated process for conducting reviews of mortgage servicing activities, developing solutions, and enforcing accountability. The group enables agencies to share information across agencies and to minimize duplication in investigative efforts and to coordinate remedial actions.

Multiple federal agencies with the state attorneys general are considering resolution options with the largest servicers. According to media reports, a concept paper aimed to facilitate discussion and input from the servicers was provided to these servicers. Among the discussion topics in the paper were potential steps to improve foreclosure processes and comply with affidavit preparation standards and note transfer requirements as enumerated in the concept paper. However, some lawmakers have expressed concerns about some of the topics in this paper. As of March 2011, no resolution has been reached.

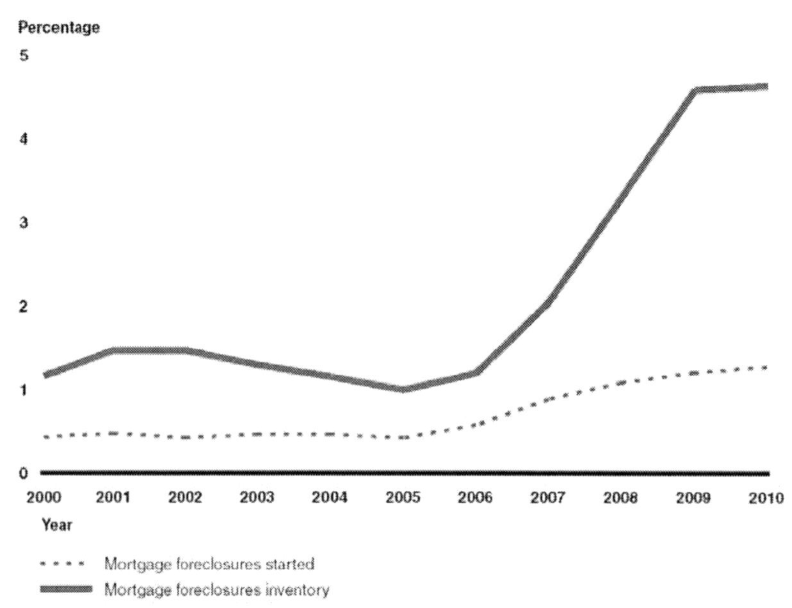

Source: GAO analysis of Mortgage Bankers Association National Delinquency Survey data.

Note: The Mortgage Bankers Association's quarterly National Delinquency Survey covers about 80 percent of the mortgage market and presents default and foreclosure rates (i.e., the number of loans in default or foreclosure divided by the number of loans being serviced).

Figure 4. Year-End Foreclosure Starts and Foreclosure Inventory, 2000 to 2010.

DOCUMENTATION PROBLEMS WILL LIKELY RESULT IN DELAYS IN THE FORECLOSURE PROCESS, BUT THE IMPACT ON FINANCIAL INSTITUTIONS AND OTHERS IS LESS CLEAR

Improper Documentation Practices Will Likely Add Delays in the Foreclosure Process, but as Problems Are Corrected, Foreclosures Will Proceed

To date, a key impact of the problems relating to affidavits and notarization of mortgage foreclosure documents appears to be delays in the rate at which foreclosures are proceeding, but many foreclosures are expected to be completed eventually. One reason that the rate at which foreclosures are being completed has slowed is that servicers have been performing internal reviews of their procedures and, in some cases, have implemented moratoriums on foreclosures in both judicial and nonjudicial states. In addition, several states have called for moratoriums on foreclosures or otherwise taken actions that could stall the foreclosure process in these states. As shown in figure 4, the percentage of loans in some stage of foreclosure (foreclosure inventory) increased to a year-end historical high of 4.63 percent in December 2010. According to legal academics, financial industry representatives, and government regulators, servicers' missteps in foreclosure documentation are, in large part, responsible for the delays in foreclosure completions. In addition, a recent report issued by

OCC and OTS notes that the number of foreclosures completed during the fourth quarter of 2010 decreased 49.1 percent from the previous quarter largely as a result of the foreclosure moratoriums implemented by the largest servicers.[71] Further, we have reported that data on new foreclosure filings and delinquencies suggest that servicers are not initiating foreclosures on many loans normally subject to such actions.[72] New foreclosure starts declined from 1.42 percent in September 2009 to 1.27 percent in December 2010.

Despite these initial delays, some regulatory officials as well as legal academics and industry officials we interviewed indicated that foreclosure documentation issues are correctable. Once servicers have revised their processes and corrected documentation errors, most delayed foreclosures in judicial states will likely proceed. For example, in cases where affidavits were signed by a person without the required personal knowledge of the case or were not signed in the presence of a notary, legal representatives and industry observers said that courts generally may allow the foreclosures to proceed once the affidavits are refiled with the appropriate signatures and notarization. In addition, some legal representatives told us that because almost all foreclosures involved borrowers who were seriously delinquent on their loans, most would likely proceed once the paperwork is corrected. Revising and refiling the required documentation will take time, however, as servicers may potentially have thousands of cases to review. For example, Fannie Mae representatives said that one of its servicers plans to file over 100,000 revised affidavits and another plans to file 50,000 revised affidavits, even though not all of the documents were necessarily defective.

Increased scrutiny of documents by servicers and courts may reduce inaccuracies, but the increased demand on judicial resources could contribute to further delays. Some legal academics and attorneys we spoke with told us that state courts previously assumed the accuracy of documents provided by servicers as part of foreclosure cases, but some courts are increasingly skeptical of foreclosure documentation and are now looking more closely at documents submitted in foreclosure cases. In certain circumstances, judges are insisting that servicers more rigorously adhere to foreclosure strictures, such as requirements that the original note be produced. Additionally, some courts have been imposing their own new requirements to help ensure the accuracy of filings; for example, in New York state and Cuyahoga County, Ohio, attorneys are required to sign statements affirming that the facts in affidavits are accurate. Although these requirements may be intended to help ensure the accuracy of information submitted to the court, some market observers have argued that these additional procedures are contributing to the delay in processing foreclosures. However, some banking industry representatives, attorneys, and government officials that we interviewed noted that cases with documentation problems should diminish with improved attention to accuracy on the part of servicers and courts.

In nonjudicial states where production of foreclosure documentation in court generally may not be required, information on the prevalence and impact of foreclosure documentation problems is unavailable because documents, such as affidavits, that have been called into question in judicial states may not typically be required to complete foreclosures. Without judicial review of documentation supporting foreclosures or certification that foreclosures are justified, some academics and others indicated that errors may go unchecked unless borrowers contest foreclosures, an action that would prompt a judicial review. Further, those we spoke with noted that, unlike in judicial states, where a judge must approve foreclosures, in nonjudicial states, the borrowers must contest foreclosures, which can be expensive and difficult.

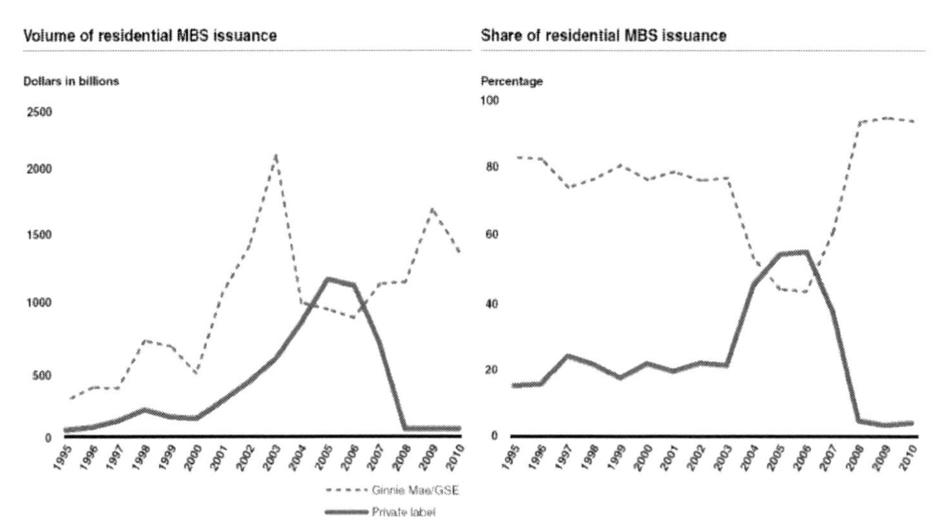

Source: GAO analysis of data from Inside Mortgage Finance, *2010 and 2011 Mortgage Market St atistical Annual, Volume II.*

Figure 5. Volume and Share of Enterprises and Private Label MBS Issuances, 1995 to 2010.

Delays in the Foreclosure Process May Have Both Positive and Negative Effects on Homeowners, Communities, and the Mortgage Market

Legal academics and representatives of the mortgage industry reported mixed views on the implications of delays in the foreclosure process for borrowers. Borrowers whose mortgage loans are in default may benefit from the additional delays in the foreclosure process if the additional time allows them to obtain income that allows them to bring mortgage payments current or cure the default, or to work out other payment solutions, such as loan modifications. According to representatives of housing counseling and legal aid groups we spoke with, mortgage default and foreclosures are often caused by borrowers' inability to make mortgage payments because of unemployment. An extended period before a foreclosure is completed may allow borrowers to obtain employment and to begin making mortgage payments again. Additionally, as foreclosures stall, lenders and borrowers may have additional time and opportunity to work out loan modifications. However, according to legal services attorneys we interviewed, these delays also leave borrowers unsure about how long they may be able to remain in their homes. Even if a court dismisses a foreclosure based on faulty documentation, the borrower may still be subject to a new foreclosure proceeding if the bank assembles the necessary paperwork and resubmits the case. In addition, mortgage industry participants noted that fees such as taxes and insurance may continue to accrue on borrowers' loans during the delay, making it more difficult for them to catch up on payments. Even if a foreclosure action can be completed properly, weaknesses in servicers' foreclosure processes could otherwise adversely impact borrowers. For example, according to the banking regulators' report on their coordinated review, these weaknesses could result in inaccurate fees and charges assessed against a borrower. In addition, borrowers could find their loss mitigation options curtailed because of dual-track processes that result in foreclosure even when a borrower has been approved for a loan modification.

Delayed foreclosures resulting from documentation problems could have negative impacts on communities as more properties may become vacant. When borrowers are unable to make mortgage payments and foreclosure appears imminent, they sometimes vacate properties to secure new housing. Our previous work has demonstrated that properties are more likely to become vacant once foreclosure is initiated.[73] As such, properties may become vacant before foreclosure is completed. We have reported that neighborhood and community problems stemming from vacancy include heightened crime, blight, and declining property values.[74] Additionally, such problems result in increased costs to local governments in policing and securing vacant homes. Delays in the foreclosure process, though temporary, could exacerbate the problems communities are facing from vacancy because of foreclosure.

Various market observers and regulators also indicated that the delays caused by the foreclosure documentation problems could negatively affect the recovery of U.S. housing prices in the long term. According to one rating agency's analysis, the recovery of the housing market could be delayed as servicers work through the backlog of homes in foreclosure. In addition, according to the rating agency's analysis, the foreclosure documentation problems and resulting delays in foreclosures being completed were likely to reduce the number of home sales at the end of 2010, but not necessarily home prices during that period because fewer foreclosed homes—which typically sell for less than other homes—would be on the market. Once the issues are resolved and foreclosures are completed, however, the analysis projected that the backlog of foreclosed homes would delay the recovery of the housing market. The regulators' report on their coordinated review also notes that the deficiencies and weaknesses leading to delays in foreclosure processing have had an adverse impact on the functioning of the mortgage market. Regulators reported that such delays could be an impediment for communities working to stabilize local neighborhoods and housing markets. The regulators' report on their coordinated review states that these delays could lead to extended periods of depressed home prices.

Impacts on Servicers, Trusts, and Investors because of Loan Transfer Documentation Problems Are Unclear

On the basis of servicers' disclosures of problems with foreclosure documentation and recent court decisions, some academics and others have argued that the way that mortgage loans were transferred in connection with some MBS issuances could affect servicers' ability to complete foreclosures and create financial liability for other entities, such as those involved in creating securities. As previously discussed, when a loan is originated, a lender can choose to hold the loan as an income-producing asset in its own portfolio or it can sell the loan to another institution that intends to pool it with other loans and create an MBS that can be sold to investors. In a typical MBS issuance, the documents that represent the loan—the promissory note and the mortgage deed that secures the property as the collateral for the loan—are required to be transferred to an entity known as a document custodian. The document custodian holds these loan documents on behalf of the trustee for the MBS trust, which is the legal owner of the loans in the pool. The trustee acts on behalf of the trust and receives the payments from the pooled loans underlying the MBS issuance and distributes them to the securities investors. Between loan origination and the time when a mortgage is placed in an MBS trust, both the note and mortgage may be sold and transferred several times between various entities that facilitate the creation of loan pools for MBS issuances before being physically delivered to the document custodian designated by the MBS trustee.

Some cases decided in 2007 and 2008 found that servicers were not able to present sufficient evidence that they had the right to foreclose on properties owned by MBS trusts. For example, courts dismissed complaints to foreclose on the mortgages of 46 properties in two federal court cases in Ohio because the servicer (on behalf of the trust) failed to submit to the court a copy of the assignment of the note and mortgage evidencing its status (on behalf of the trust) as holder of the note for these loans.[75] According to real estate attorneys who researched these issues, these cases led real estate lawyers and courts to reexamine the paperwork necessary to foreclose. Simultaneously, at least one legal academic began researching discrepancies in servicers' preparation and management of documentation as these issues arose in and related to bankruptcy proceedings involving foreclosure matters.[76] Further, investors have made claims about servicer irregularities regarding securitized loans.[77] As reports of other discrepancies in the preparation and notarization of foreclosure documentation surfaced in September 2010, questions about the documentation related to mortgage transfers similarly came to national attention.

According to GSE officials, the potential problems related to transfers of loans as part of MBS issuances do not appear to affect the purchases and subsequent securitization of loans by housing GSEs. As shown in figure 5, most of the MBS issuances in 2008 were by the GSEs.[78] According to staff from Fannie Mae and Freddie Mac, the GSEs' policies, procedures, and processes used to obtain the underlying supporting documents for the loans that these two GSEs purchase provide substantial assurance that they will have adequate proof of ownership of the loans and could provide required documents as needed for foreclosing on their loans. Representatives of Fannie Mae and Freddie Mac noted that they have strict note delivery requirements and oversight of document custodians. For example, Fannie Mae and Freddie Mac staff said that they require that notes be endorsed without designating a payee—as provided for in the Uniform Commercial Code (UCC) and known as endorsing in blank—so that when the GSEs purchase loans, take possession of the notes, and become the owner and holder, they can give temporary possession of the notes to their servicers, as necessary, so that the servicers can (1) be holders, (2) commence enforcement actions, and (3) readily provide a court with the note endorsed in blank as evidence of their status as holder if required. In addition, the GSEs stated that the document custodian is required to complete a prepurchase certification that it, among other things, has taken physical possession of the notes. Further, the staff either review the adequacy of the documentation of any previous transfers at the time of the purchase or rely on servicers' statements that they own the loans when they sell them under penalty of having to repurchase the loans if the ownership is not clear. The GSEs also require that either the servicer or MERS be listed as the mortgagee of record in local public land recording offices.[79] Finally, the GSEs require that the notes and certain other documentation be held by approved document custodians, and Fannie Mae and Freddie Mac occasionally examine these custodians. Fannie Mae and Freddie Mac staff indicated that as a result of their documentation requirements, the potential problems related to transfers of loans have not been, nor are likely to be, a concern regarding mortgage-backed securities issued by Fannie Mae and Freddie Mac.

After other documentation problems and questions involving potential loan transfer problems surfaced, some legal academics began arguing that loans that were sold into pools and then securities issued primarily by non-GSE entities—known as private label MBS—may not have always been transferred properly. According to these academics, the contracts—known as pooling and servicing agreements—that govern loan transfers in private label securitization deals often called for the notes and mortgage deeds supporting the pooled loans to be transferred into the MBS trust by having each party in the securitization process endorse the note.[80] They argue that a servicer may not be able to prove its right to foreclose on a property if the trust on whose behalf it is servicing the loan is not specifically named in the transfer documentation. In addition, one academic recently testified before Congress that a specific chain of transfers identifying the loan originator, securitization sponsor, depositor, and finally the MBS trust may be necessary to ensure that the loans placed in the trust will remain in the trust if one of the parties in the chain files for bankruptcy.[81] Further, these legal academics argue that in order to provide such protections in the event of bankruptcy, pooling and servicing agreements also generally require documentation to be physically delivered to the trustee.

According to some legal academics, if the transfer of the mortgages and notes into private label MBS trusts are found to be insufficient to prove that the trusts own the loans, then MBS investors, trusts, the servicers working on their behalf, and the institutions that originated these mortgage loans or created the MBS issuances could be subject to potentially serious consequences. For example, according to some academics, if loans were not properly transferred, then the trusts may not actually own the loans and they (and the servicers acting on their behalf) would not have the right to foreclose on the property of borrowers in default. Furthermore, if the MBS trusts did not properly obtain ownership of the loans underlying the securities in accordance with the terms of the pooling and servicing agreement, these academics argue that the tax-exempt structure of the MBS trust may be voided, and thus the trusts may owe taxes on the income to the trust. In addition, attorneys, a representative of investors, and other studies noted that if the investors in the MBS issuance may not have received what they were promised when they purchased the securities, they may press legal claims against the creators of the trusts or force them to reimburse the investors for some amount of improperly transferred loans. With almost $1.3 trillion of private label securities outstanding at the end of 2010, if these arguments are correct this liability could be significant.

However, other market participants have an opposing view and argue that mortgages were pooled into securities using standard industry practices that were sufficient to create legal ownership on behalf of MBS trusts. According to these market participants, the practices that were typically used to transfer loans into MBS trusts comply with the Uniform Commercial Code, which generally has been adopted in every state. Among other things, provisions in the UCC govern the transfer of negotiable instruments, such as checks and mortgage promissory notes.[82] As a result, according to their argument, if mortgage notes being transferred into MBS pools were endorsed in blank, then this would be sufficient under the UCC, and thus the transfers of loans to the private label securities' trusts would be legally sufficient to establish the trusts' ownership. According to these market participants, these practices were the customary means by which loans were transferred as part of creating private label MBS.

Additional Court Decisions May Determine Ultimate Effect of MBS Loan Transfer Problems, and Regulators Have Not Assessed the Extent of This Risk

Although some courts may have addressed MBS loan transfer practices in certain contexts, the varying circumstances of these cases limit their use in determining whether such problems are widespread or what effects they may have on foreclosures or on market participants. For example, in a bankruptcy case recently decided in New Jersey, the judge concluded that the loan in question had not been properly endorsed and transfered to the trust of the particular private label MBS pool that had purchased the loan as required by both the UCC and the trust's own pooling and servicing agreement and disallowed the servicer's proof of claim against the borrower.[83] Banking industry analysts told us that this ruling should not lead to permanent dismissals of foreclosures. For example, analysts from one rating agency told us that based on their review of several securitizations—including the security that included the loan involved in the New Jersey case—these problems might not be widespread. Specifically, the rating agency determined that out of 9,233 loans in the security, only 180 had some discrepancies in the paperwork such as missing assignments of mortgage, notes, endorsements, deeds of trust, or powers of attorney.[84] In a different case, the Supreme Judicial Court of Massachusetts found that the lower court did not err in concluding that the securitization documents submitted by the plaintiffs failed to demonstrate that they were the holders of the subject mortgages at the time of foreclosure.[85] The court also stated, regarding an argument that assignments in blank evidenced and confirmed the assignments, that it does not "regard an assignment of land in blank as giving legal title in land to the bearer of the assignment" (which was a statement of Massachusetts law and not necessarily the law in other jurisdictions). Some attorneys representing mortgage servicers pointed out that the court's opinion seems to suggest that had the servicers been able to show sufficient supporting documentation listing these particular loans and properties, this would have supported proof of ownership despite the failure to properly endorse the loans when originally transferred to the MBS trusts. According to one rating agency, this Massachusetts case will not significantly prevent foreclosures from going forward because it does not invalidate the fundamental principles of loan transfers during securitization; rather, this decision upholds that MBS trusts can prove mortgage ownership in more than one way. Another attorney we spoke with who works on MBS issuances further noted that it was uncertain whether this ruling would have a broad impact in states outside of Massachusetts.

The impact of these problems likely will remain uncertain until definitive, controlling court decisions are issued, establishing whether typical processes for transferring loans into private label MBS were legally effective or how such problems can be resolved. Adding to this uncertainty may be differing views on court decisions on the appropriateness of foreclosures being initiated in the name of MERS.[86] In the near term, industry observers noted that these cases could lead to increased litigation and servicing costs for servicers and more foreclosure delays. According to SEC filings and risk analyses and reporting by some servicers, some financial institutions have set aside funds or performed estimations of the potential risk and liability from lawsuits. Several large servicers' annual SEC filings that we reviewed noted the possibility of increased litigation and other costs resulting from regulatory reviews of servicing activities, but servicers did not provide estimates of the potential amounts because of the uncertainty in the number and types of cases they may be involved in.

Another reason the impact of these problems remains uncertain is that investors face challenges in bringing claims against servicers. Representatives of investors noted that although investors may have viable claims against servicers for inappropriate documentation practices, it is difficult for investors to obtain the information needed to prove that documentation inaccuracies have occurred. In addition, investors may not want to pursue legal claims against servicers because of the impact large-scale claims could have in the market, as new private label securitization issuances have recently declined.

Although tasked with overseeing the financial safety and soundness of institutions under their jurisdiction, some banking regulators stated that they have not yet fully assessed the extent to which MBS loan transfer problems could financially affect their institutions. Federal Reserve staff said that the agency has conducted an assessment of the extent to which any of its institutions may be required to repurchase loans. The Federal Reserve also required the institutions it supervises that originated large numbers of mortgages or sponsored significant MBS to assess and provide for these risks as part of their overall capital planning process. Regarding the extent to which loan transfer problems can affect their institutions, banking regulatory staff at OCC, the Federal Reserve, and OTS told us that their servicer reviews generally did not uncover problems with servicers' authority to foreclose, although examiners noted instances where documentation in the foreclosure file alone may not have been sufficient to prove authority to foreclose without reference to additional information. However, according to staff at one of the agencies, while examiners reviewed files to determine whether the name of the entity on the foreclosure initiation paperwork matched the name on the mortgage note to confirm that the foreclosing entity was the owner of the note and had standing to foreclose, they did not always verify that loan files included accurate documentation of all previous note and mortgage transfers—leaving open the possibility that such transfer problems exist in the files they reviewed. According to the regulators' report on the coordinated review, servicers may bear legal costs related to disputes over note ownership or authority to foreclose and may be subject to claims by investors as a result of delays or other damages caused by weaknesses in foreclosure processes. The enforcement orders resulting from the coordinated review require servicers to retain an independent firm to assess risks such as these. In addition, the regulators' report states that the agencies will more frequently monitor the servicers involved in the reviews until they have corrected the identified weaknesses. For example, OCC staff said that as part of their assessment of servicers' compliance with the enforcement orders, examiners will review servicer processes to ensure that mortgages are assigned properly before initiating foreclosure. However, regulators have not definitively determined how mortgage transfer problems might financially affect other institutions they regulate, including if any of the institutions involved in the creation of private label MBS could face any financial repercussions. With almost $1.3 trillion in private label securities outstanding as of the end of 2010, the institutions and the overall financial system could face significant risks. Given the banking regulators' role in helping ensure the safety and soundness of regulated institutions in order to protect the deposit insurance fund, having affected institutions complete such assessments, analyzing their results, and requiring institutions to take any necessary steps to mitigate their risks could reduce the magnitude of any resulting problems.

CONCLUSIONS

Until the problems regarding foreclosure documentation came to light, federal regulatory oversight of mortgage servicers had been limited, as such activities were viewed as low risk to safety and soundness. However, regulators' examinations since then have revealed that servicers had generally failed to properly prepare required documentation and lacked effective supervision and controls over their foreclosure processes. The resulting delays in completing foreclosures and increased exposure to litigation highlight how the failure to oversee whether institutions follow sound practices can heighten their risks and create problems for the communities in which these foreclosures are occurring. Banking regulators plan to follow up with servicers to better ensure that they implement agreed-upon corrective actions, and the new CFPB also plans to conduct oversight of mortgage servicing activities. However, the extent to which these regulators will conduct ongoing supervision of mortgage servicers in the future, as well as the goals for this supervision and the roles that each regulator will play, have not been definitively determined. Until such plans are developed, the potential for continued fragmentation and gaps in oversight remains.

Recently, some regulators and market participants have begun working to develop national servicing standards that could provide consistent expectations for how servicers conduct many activities and interact with borrowers. Such standards could cover a wide range of servicer activities, including those at loan origination and throughout the ongoing life of a loan.

However, the extent to which such standards will address the weaknesses and lack of consistency among servicers' foreclosure practices is not yet clear. If such standards are developed, ensuring that they also provide expectations for servicers to follow as part of the foreclosure process could be a way to improve uniformity in the servicers' practices.

Finally, the extent to which foreclosures and the financial standing of some mortgage market participants will be affected by legal challenges to the way that loans were transferred as part of creating private label MBS is uncertain. Some observers argue that the typical practices could render some securitizations invalid, which could prevent justified foreclosures and create significant financial liabilities on the part of various institutions that created MBS issuances. In contrast, other market participants have indicated that loan transfer practices were acceptable. Until additional court decisions provide definitive guidance, the extent of the impact is unclear, as is the potential that regulated financial institutions will face losses arising from increased litigation or the need to repurchase loans from MBS trusts if improper transfers are discovered. Although such losses could be substantial, the affected financial institutions have not completed assessments of the possible impact on their firms, and banking regulators have not fully assessed the possible impact on the safety and soundness of these institutions if such problems are found to be legitimate. Such assessments could focus on institutions that sold significant numbers of loans to creators of private label securities, which appear to be at greater risk of loan transfer problems than those sold to GSEs. Completing the assessments of these potential risks and fully ensuring that regulated institutions are taking steps to proactively address them could reduce the potential threat to the soundness of these institutions, the deposit insurance fund, and the overall financial system.

RECOMMENDATIONS FOR EXECUTIVE ACTION

To help ensure strong and robust oversight of all mortgage servicers, we recommend that the Comptroller of the Currency, the Chairman of the Board of Governors of the Federal Reserve System, the Director of the Office of Thrift Supervision, the Chairman of the Federal Deposit Insurance Corporation, and the Bureau of Consumer Financial Protection take the following actions:

- develop and coordinate plans to provide ongoing oversight and establish clear goals, roles, and timelines for overseeing mortgage servicers under their respective jurisdiction, and
- if national servicing standards are created, include standards for foreclosure practices.

In addition, to reduce the likelihood that problems with mortgage transfer documentation problems could pose a risk to the financial system, we recommend that the Comptroller of the Currency, the Chairman of the Board of Governors of the Federal Reserve System, the Director of the Office of Thrift Supervision, and the Chairman of the Federal Deposit Insurance Corporation assess the risks of potential litigation or repurchases due to improper mortgage loan transfer documentation on institutions under their jurisdiction and require that the institutions take action to mitigate the risks, if warranted.

AGENCY COMMENTS AND OUR EVALUATION

We requested comments on a draft of this report from CFPB, FDIC, FHFA, Federal Reserve, Federal Trade Commission, HUD, Justice, OCC, OTS, SEC, Treasury, Fannie Mae, and Freddie Mac. We received written comments from CFPB, FDIC, the Federal Reserve, OCC, and Treasury that are presented in appendixes II through VI. We also received technical comments from CFPB, FDIC, Federal Trade Commission, FHFA, Freddie Mac, HUD, OCC, Treasury, Federal Reserve, and Justice, which we incorporated where appropriate. Fannie Mae, OTS, and SEC did not have any comments on the draft report.

The agencies generally agreed with our recommendation on developing and coordinating plans to provide ongoing oversight of mortgage servicers. The Associate Director for Research, Markets & Regulations at CFPB said in his letter that CFPB has already been engaged in discussions about mortgage servicing with various federal agencies as part of preparing to take on the authorities that will transfer to it in July 2011 and is committed to coordinating constructively with other federal and state agencies to ensure that oversight responsibilities are exercised in an efficient and effective manner. The Director of the Division of Risk Management Supervision at FDIC said in her letter that FDIC agrees with our recommendation and noted the importance of a thorough regulatory review of servicers' loss mitigation efforts given that the scope of the coordinated review was limited to the foreclosure process. The letter also states that FDIC will continue to monitor servicers under its jurisdiction for these issues and will work with the other regulators to ensure a more coordinated and comprehensive approach to the review of mortgage servicers going forward.

The Director of the Division of Consumer and Community Affairs for the Board of Governors of the Federal Reserve System said in her letter that the Board agrees with the recommendation and noted that the recent enforcement actions require servicers to implement significant revisions to mortgage loan servicing and foreclosure processing practices. In his letter, the Acting Comptroller of the Currency stated that OCC agreed with our recommendations and noted that the agency will continue to oversee the mortgage servicers under its jurisdiction, and will emphasize in the near term ensuring that these entities are taking steps to remedy any deficiencies in their foreclosure processes.

The agencies also generally agreed with our recommendation on including standards for foreclosure practices in any national servicing standards that are created. The Associate Director for Research, Markets & Regulations at CFPB noted in his letter that CFPB has effective authority to adopt national mortgage servicing rules for all mortgage servicers, including those for which CFPB does not have supervisory authority. The Director of the Division of Risk Management Supervision at FDIC agreed with this recommendation and noted that FDIC successfully proposed the inclusion of loan servicing standards in the proposed rules to implement the securitization risk-retention requirements of the Dodd-Frank Act that address several servicing issues. She also said that any servicing standards should ensure that appropriate loss mitigation activities are considered when borrowers are experiencing financial difficulties. The Director of the Division of Consumer and Community Affairs for the Board of Governors of the Federal Reserve System said in her letter that the intent of the interagency effort to develop national standards for mortgage servicing was to address the problems found in the servicing industry, including in foreclosure processing. She also noted that the agencies would coordinate their efforts. The Acting Comptroller of the Currency noted that efforts are under way to develop national servicing standards, and that these are intended to include provisions covering both foreclosure abeyance and foreclosure governance. The Under Secretary for Domestic Finance at Treasury said that the agency has been closely engaged with the interagency group reviewing errors in mortgage servicing and that it supports national servicing standards that align incentives and provide clarity and consistency to borrowers and investors regarding their treatment by servicers. In response to these comments we added a reference to the interagency efforts to develop national servicing standards in the body of the report.

Regarding our recommendation that the regulators assess the risks of potential litigation or repurchases due to improper mortgage loan transfer documentation on institutions under their jurisdiction, the Director of the Division of Risk Management Supervision at FDIC said that the agency strongly supports this recommendation and noted the agency's particular interest in assessing the potential litigation associated with servicing deficiencies to protect the interests of the deposit insurance fund. The Director of the Division of Consumer and Community Affairs for the Board of Governors of the Federal Reserve System said in her letter that the Federal Reserve has conducted a detailed evaluation of the risk of potential litigation or repurchases to the financial institutions it supervises. She also noted that the agency will continue to monitor the affected institutions' capital and reserves and take information from reviews servicers are required to complete as part of the enforcement orders into account when assessing this risk in the future, including reviewing the risks that servicers may suffer losses because of the lack of legally enforceable documentation of ownership. OCC and Treasury did not comment on this recommendation.

As we agreed with your offices, unless you publicly announce the contents of this report earlier, we plan no further distribution of it until 30 days from the date of this report. At that time we will send copies of this report to interested congressional committees, CFPB, FDIC, FHFA, Federal Reserve, Federal Trade Commission, HUD, Justice, OCC, OTS, SEC, and Treasury. The report also is available at no charge on the GAO Web site at http://www.gao.gov.

If you or your staff have any questions about this report, please contact me at (202) 512-5837 or clowersa@gao.gov. Contact points for our Offices of Congressional Relations and Public Affairs may be found on the last page of this report. Key contributors to this report are listed in appendix VII.

A. Nicole Clowers
Acting Director, Financial Markets and Community Investment

List of Requesters
The Honorable Robert Menendez
Chairman
Subcommittee on Housing, Transportation and Community Development
Committee on Banking, Housing, and Urban Affairs
United States Senate

The Honorable John Conyers, Jr.
Ranking Member
Committee on the Judiciary
House of Representatives

The Honorable Luis V. Gutierrez
Ranking Member
Subcommittee on Insurance, Housing and Community Opportunity
Committee on Financial Services
House of Representatives

The Honorable Michael Capuano
Ranking Member
Subcommittee on Oversight and Investigations
Committee on Financial Services
House of Representatives
The Honorable Al Franken
United States Senate

Appendix I. Objectives, Scope, and Methodology

This report focuses on various aspects of federal oversight of the mortgage foreclosure process. Specifically, this report addresses (1) the extent to which federal laws address mortgage servicers' foreclosure procedures and federal agencies' authority to oversee activities and the extent of past oversight; (2) federal agencies' current oversight activities and future oversight plans; and (3) the potential impact of foreclosure documentation issues on homeowners, servicers, regulators, and mortgage-backed securities investors.

To determine the extent to which federal laws address foreclosure procedures, we reviewed relevant federal laws and our prior reports. We also conducted interviews with representatives of federal agencies and asked for their insight on relevant federal laws. The federal agencies we interviewed include the Department of Housing and Urban Development (HUD), Department of Justice (Justice), Department of the Treasury (Treasury), Federal Deposit Insurance Corporation (FDIC), Federal Housing Finance Agency (FHFA), Board of Governors of the Federal Reserve System (Federal Reserve), Office of the Comptroller of the Currency (OCC), Office of Thrift Supervision (OTS), and Securities and Exchange Commission (SEC).

To determine federal agencies' oversight authority and extent of past oversight, we analyzed the relevant sections of agencies' authorizing laws and agency regulations and exam guidance. We also interviewed agency officials for their views on the extent to which their current authority allows the agency to oversee institutions conducting servicing and servicers' compliance with state foreclosure laws. In addition, we asked agency representatives about the extent and substance of their past oversight activities regarding mortgage servicers. We compared and contrasted the agencies' authorities to identify any gaps in their ability to oversee mortgage servicing and foreclosure activities and summarized their previous oversight actions. We also reviewed our past reports and other studies on federal oversight of the mortgage servicing industry.

To determine what actions the federal banking regulators have taken to address deficiencies in foreclosure processes, we interviewed officials from the four federal banking regulatory agencies (Federal Reserve, FDIC, OCC, and OTS). To obtain additional information on the regulators' coordinated review and to further understand the scope of their efforts, we evaluated regulators' examination review worksheet and analyzed the supervisory letters and draft enforcement orders issued to servicers following the reviews. In addition, we interviewed officials from the federal housing agencies and the government-sponsored entities, Treasury, SEC, and Justice to report on other agencies' recent efforts to address foreclosure process deficiencies and to understand the extent of interagency coordination in addressing weaknesses in mortgage servicing practices. We also reviewed and analyzed relevant congressional testimonies and other publicly issued statements from agency officials. Further, we interviewed representatives of state attorneys general and state banking supervisors. To report on future oversight of mortgage servicers, we conducted follow-up interviews with OCC, OTS, and the Federal Reserve to discuss the findings of their coordinated reviews and to determine what changes, if any, regulators planned to make in future oversight based on these findings. Since the new Bureau of Consumer Financial Protection (CFPB) will accept responsibilities for overseeing mortgage servicing activity in the future, we contacted CFPB representatives to clarify the extent of CFPB's regulatory authority and to determine what role this new agency will play in future oversight of mortgage servicers. We also discussed the guidance and extent of oversight conducted by the two large housing government-sponsored enterprises, the Federal National Mortgage Association (Fannie Mae) and the Federal Home Loan Mortgage Corporation (Freddie Mac).

To determine the potential impacts and implications of foreclosure documentation issues, we reviewed various studies from other agencies and organizations conducting similar work. We also searched for reported cases in the "Federal and State Cases combined" database of Lexis and Westlaw and limited the time frame to the last 5 years. Our search attempted to identify examples of relevant cases to estimate the prevalence of challenges to foreclosures or challenges to proof of claims submitted in bankruptcy matters related to foreclosures, which involved mortgage documentation and chain-of-title issues. We did identify some potentially relevant cases, but determined that not enough cases were found or materially on point to definitively indicate the prevalence. We also reviewed congressional testimonies, and other relevant publicly available documentation. In addition, we interviewed legal academics and attorneys representing both borrowers and servicers and representatives of rating agencies, the mortgage industry, investor groups, and consumer advocacy groups about the impacts of these issues on their constituencies. Because of servicers' involvement in ongoing litigation in various state courts, we did not directly interview servicers about these issues. Therefore, we obtained information about actions mortgage servicers are taking and the impacts of these issues on servicers from legal academics and representatives of industry associations, such as the Mortgage Bankers Association and Association of Mortgage Investors. In addition, we obtained the insight of staff from banking regulatory agencies who have directly examined mortgage servicers on these issues and from mortgage servicers' public statements and SEC filings. We categorized the information we gathered from these various sources to identify the most common types of impacts and implications of foreclosure documentation issues these sources attributed to different stakeholder groups.

To provide context and additional support for our findings throughout the report, we gathered and analyzed data on financial market trends from two industry sources, *Inside Mortgage Finance* and Mortgage Bankers Association. We analyzed data on servicing volume and securitization issuances from *Inside Mortgage Finance*. We discussed the reliability of these data with an official from *Inside Mortgage Finance*. In addition, we have relied on data from *Inside Mortgage Finance* for past reports and determined that they are sufficiently reliable for the purpose of presenting and analyzing trends in financial markets.[87] We analyzed data on foreclosure filings and foreclosure inventory from Mortgage Bankers Association National Delinquency Survey. In a previous report, we assessed the reliability of these data by reviewing existing information about the quality of the data, performing electronic testing to detect errors in completeness and reasonableness, and interviewing Mortgage Bankers Association officials knowledgeable about the data.[88] To assess the reliability of the data for this report we reviewed prior assessments of the data and contacted an MBA official about any potential limitations to the use of the data or changes in data collection methods. We determined that the data were sufficiently reliable for purposes of the report.

We conducted this performance audit from October 2010 through April 2011 in accordance with generally accepted government auditing standards. Those standards require that we plan and perform the audit to obtain sufficient, appropriate evidence to provide a reasonable basis for our findings and conclusions based on our audit objectives. We believe that the evidence obtained provides a reasonable basis for our findings and conclusions based on our audit objectives.

APPENDIX II. COMMENTS FROM THE BUREAU OF CONSUMER FINANCIAL PROTECTION

DEPARTMENT OF THE TREASURY
WASHINGTON, D.C. 20220

April 19, 2011

Ms. A. Nicole Clowers
Acting Director, Financial Markets and Community Investment
U.S. Government Accountability Office
441 G Street, N.W.
Washington, D.C. 20548

Dear Ms. Clowers:

Thank you for the opportunity to comment on the GAO's draft report titled *Mortgage Foreclosures: Documentation Problems Reveal Need for Ongoing Regulatory Oversight*. I want to note up front that the Consumer Financial Protection Bureau (CFPB) does not currently have authority with regard to the issues covered within the report. When CFPB receives its full authorities, however, it will have authority to set standards for mortgage servicing.

The report sets forth an important analysis of the documentation problems that emerged last year in residential mortgage foreclosures. The report finds that past federal oversight of mortgage servicers' activities has been "limited and fragmented." In this regard, the report describes lack of comprehensive federal standards for mortgage servicers, the absence of any direct federal oversight of some servicers, and the fact that federal banking regulators did not consider mortgage servicing practices as presenting high risk to bank safety and soundness.

While the report acknowledges that the CFPB will play a role with regard to oversight of mortgage servicing practices, we wish to emphasize the extent to which the Dodd-Frank Wall Street Reform and Consumer Protection Act (Dodd-Frank Act) addressed the problem of limited and fragmented federal oversight of mortgage servicers by vesting new jurisdiction and powers in the CFPB for consumer protection.

In particular, Congress gave the CFPB effective authority to adopt national mortgage servicing rules for all mortgage servicers (including mortgage servicers for which CFPB does not have supervisory authority). This rulemaking power includes authorities under various federal laws to be transferred to the CFPB from other federal agencies – such as the Board of Governors of the Federal Reserve System, the Department of Housing and Urban Development, and the Federal Trade Commission – as well as new rulemaking authorities conferred upon the CFPB in the Dodd-Frank Act. In addition, the CFPB will have exclusive supervisory authority and primary enforcement authority over any mortgage servicer that is a depository institution with total assets of over $10 billion, or an affiliate of such a depository institution, to ensure that it complies with the Federal consumer financial laws (including any rules in this area adopted by the CFPB). For the first time, moreover, the Dodd-Frank Act placed non-depository mortgage servicers under direct federal authority. The Act accomplished this by giving the CFPB supervisory as well as enforcement authority over non-depository servicers with respect to the Federal consumer financial laws.

The Dodd-Frank Act is quite clear with respect to both the extent and the limits of the CFPB's jurisdiction over mortgage servicers. As a practical matter, the CFPB is still in the process of establishing its infrastructure, hiring staff, and making other preparations to take on the authorities that will transfer to it on the designated transfer date of July 21, 2011. We are fully committed to coordinating constructively with the prudential regulators to ensure that we exercise these responsibilities in an efficient and effective manner.

Indeed, we have already been engaged in discussions about mortgage servicing with various federal agencies as part of our preparatory efforts. Given the complexity of the issues raised concerning servicer operations and the historical role that the states have played in regulating foreclosure activities, we also believe federal-state coordination will be critical to addressing the issues raised in the report. The CFPB stands ready to partner with the other agencies and the states to make significant progress in this area.

Sincerely,

Rajeev Date
Associate Director
Research, Markets & Regulations
Consumer Financial Protection Bureau

APPENDIX III. COMMENTS FROM THE FEDERAL DEPOSIT INSURANCE CORPORATION

Federal Deposit Insurance Corporation
550 17th Street NW, Washington, D.C. 20429-9990 Division of Risk Management Supervision

April 28, 2011

Mr. Richard J. Hillman
Managing Director, Financial Markets and Community Investment
United States Government Accountability Office
411 G Street NW
Washington, DC 20548

Dear Mr. Hillman:

Thank you for the opportunity to comment on the GAO's draft report titled "Mortgage Foreclosures: Documentation Problems Reveal Need for Ongoing Regulatory Oversight" (GAO-11-433). We agree with the recommendations provided in the report and are committed to working to improve regulatory oversight of mortgage foreclosure practices.

The report focused on the findings of the interagency review of the 14 largest mortgage servicers. While we are not the primary federal regulator for any of the largest mortgage servicers, the Federal Deposit Insurance Corporation (FDIC) participated in the interagency reviews at the invitation of the primary regulator, as the back-up regulator to protect the interests of the deposit insurance fund. As noted in the report, the findings of the interagency review clearly show that the largest mortgage servicers had significant deficiencies in numerous aspects of their foreclosure processing. Accordingly, on April 13, 2011, the three primary federal regulators of the 14 largest servicers published final Consent Orders against these servicers based on the findings of this review. The FDIC was signatory to one of the Orders as the primary federal regulator of an insured depository whose loans were serviced by an affiliated servicer under the holding company. The effect of this Order is to require the bank to ensure that its affiliated servicer takes corrective measures to fully address deficiencies identified in the interagency review.

We support GAO's recommendation that the federal banking agencies develop and coordinate plans to provide ongoing oversight and establish clear goals, roles, and timelines for overseeing mortgage servicers under their jurisdiction. The Orders incorporate requirements that, if fully implemented, will help prevent a recurrence of the most significant problems with foreclosure processing. It is essential that the implementation of the Orders incorporate specific, measurable actions of these servicers to address the deficiencies identified in the interagency review.

It is also important to note that the interagency review was limited in scope. The horizontal review and resulting Consent Orders did not encompass issues beyond the foreclosure process. As a result, the review did not review allegations of improper servicing or loss mitigation, such as misapplied payments, unreasonable fees, inappropriate force-placing of insurance, failure to adequately consider a borrower for a loan modification, or requiring a borrower to be delinquent in order to qualify for a loan modification. The Orders require the servicers to undertake a comprehensive third party review of risk in servicing operations and to reimburse borrowers injured by servicer errors. Furthermore, investigations by State and Federal law enforcement agencies related to these allegations are on-going.

A thorough regulatory review of loss mitigation efforts is needed to ensure processes are sufficiently robust to prevent wrongful foreclosure actions and to ensure servicers have identified

Appendix III. (Continued)

the extent to which individual homeowners are harmed. The FDIC will continue to use its full range of authorities to work with the primary federal regulators to promote these results.

As noted in the report, the FDIC directly supervises only a limited portion of the mortgage servicing industry, which collectively service less than four percent of residential mortgages. The FDIC has issued guidelines for an institution's real estate lending policies and standards for safety and soundness, including guidance related to foreclosure timing, loss mitigation, enforceability of claims against borrowers, and loan administration procedures. FDIC examiners review selected loans and supporting loan documentation during examinations to ensure an institution is complying with such guidelines. Significant exceptions are commented upon in the reports of examination.

When evidence of foreclosure documentation issues such as "robo-signing" came to light in the fall of 2010, the FDIC commenced a review of FDIC-supervised banks engaged in mortgage servicing. The review has not identified "robo-signing" or any other deficiencies that would warrant formal enforcement actions. The FDIC will continue to monitor these servicers, as well as the performance of institutions servicing loans through FDIC securitizations or resolution programs.

We also support GAO's recommendation that, if national servicing standards are created, the federal banking agencies include standards for foreclosure practices. To that end, in developing the proposed rules to implement the securitization risk-retention requirements of the Dodd-Frank Wall Street Reform and Consumer Protection Act, the FDIC successfully proposed the inclusion of loan servicing standards in the Qualified Residential Mortgage (QRM) requirements. Long-term confidence in the securitization process can only be restored by including loan servicing standards that result in a proper alignment of servicing incentives with the interests of investors, and that are designed to achieve the best value for all investors, and not for any particular class or tranche. The servicing standards included as part of the QRM requirements address many of the most significant servicing issues. In addition to aligning incentives between investors and servicers, the proposed standards also should promote greater fairness to borrowers by ensuring that appropriate loss mitigation activities, including loan modifications, are considered when borrowers are experiencing financial difficulties.

Lastly, we strongly support GAO's final recommendation that the federal banking agencies assess the risks of potential litigation repurchases due to improper mortgage loan transfer documentation on institutions under their jurisdiction and require that the institutions take action to mitigate the risks, if warranted. To protect the interests of the deposit insurance fund, the FDIC has an especially keen interest in assessing the potential litigation associated with servicing deficiencies at the largest servicers.

In summary, although various federal agencies have authority to oversee most mortgage servicers, past oversight of their foreclosure activities has been limited. We fully support a more coordinated and comprehensive approach to the review of mortgage servicers going forward.

Thank you again for the opportunity to review this report and submit comments.

Sincerely,

Sandra L. Thompson
Director

APPENDIX IV. COMMENTS FROM THE BOARD OF GOVERNORS OF THE FEDERAL RESERVE

BOARD OF GOVERNORS
OF THE
FEDERAL RESERVE SYSTEM
WASHINGTON, D. C. 20551

SANDRA F. BRAUNSTEIN
DIRECTOR
DIVISION OF CONSUMER
AND COMMUNITY AFFAIRS

April 20, 2011

A. Nicole Clowers
Acting Director
Financial Markets and Community Investment
U.S. Government Accountability Office
Washington, DC 20548

Dear Ms. Clowers:

Thank you for the opportunity to comment on the draft report entitled "Mortgage Foreclosures: Documentation Problems Reveal Need for Ongoing Regulatory Oversight," GAO-11-433. The draft report finds that foreclosure documentation problems have slowed the pace of foreclosures across the United States; and while the delay may benefit borrowers by providing more time to modify loans as servicers correct and refile cases, it may also negatively impact communities as vacant properties in foreclosure remain unoccupied for longer periods. Additionally, the draft report states that the potential financial impact resulting from investor allegations regarding the improper transfer of securities in mortgage-backed securitizations (MBS) remain uncertain until outstanding litigation is fully adjudicated.

The draft report notes that the banking agencies coordinated reviews of large mortgage servicers and identified pervasive problems with documentation preparation and oversight of the foreclosure process. To begin to address those problems, on April 13, 2011 the Board of Governors of the Federal Reserve System (the Board) announced formal enforcement actions requiring 10 banking organizations to address a pattern of misconduct and negligence related to deficient practices in residential mortgage loan servicing and foreclosure processing.

The Board's actions also require each servicer to take a number of remedial steps, including making significant revisions to certain residential mortgage loan servicing and foreclosure processing practices. Each servicer must, among other things, submit plans acceptable to the Federal Reserve that:

- Strengthen coordination of communications with borrowers by providing borrowers the name of the person at the servicer who is their primary point of contact;
- Ensure that foreclosures are not pursued once a mortgage has been approved for modification, unless repayments under the modified loan are not made;
- Establish robust controls and oversight over the activities of third-party vendors that provide to the servicers various residential mortgage loan servicing, loss mitigation, or foreclosure-related support, including local counsel in foreclosure or bankruptcy proceedings;

Appendix IV. (Continued)

- Provide remediation to borrowers who suffered financial injury as a result of wrongful foreclosures or other deficiencies identified in a review of the foreclosure process; and
- Strengthen programs to ensure compliance with state and federal laws regarding servicing, generally, and foreclosures, in particular.

The draft report recommends three actions that the Chairman of the Federal Reserve Board should take, two of which are to be taken with the Comptroller of the Currency, the Director of the Office of Thrift Supervision, the Chair of the Federal Deposit Insurance Corporation, and the Director of the Bureau of Consumer Financial Protection. These recommendations direct the agencies to:

- Develop and coordinate plans to provide ongoing oversight and establish clear goals, roles, and timelines for overseeing mortgage servicers under their respective jurisdiction; and
- Include standards for foreclosure practices if national servicing standards are created.

The Board agrees with these recommendations. Indeed, in December 2010, Governor Daniel Tarullo, in testimony on behalf of the Board before the Senate Banking Committee, called for the development of national mortgage servicing standards. Since that time, the Federal Reserve has initiated an interagency effort with the other financial regulators, including the Office of the Comptroller of the Currency, the Federal Deposit Insurance Corporation, the Federal Housing Finance Agency, and the Consumer Financial Protection Bureau, to develop a set of national standards for mortgage servicing for all consumer mortgage lenders and servicers. The intent of the proposed standards would be to address the problems that we have found in the servicing industry, including in foreclosure processing, and to coordinate the efforts of the multiple regulatory agencies to ensure that in the future consumers will be treated properly and consistently. Of note, the enforcement actions announced last week require servicers to implement significant revisions to mortgage loan servicing and foreclosure processing practices.

The third recommendation is that the Board, in conjunction with the Comptroller of the Currency, the Director of the Office of Thrift Supervision, and the Chair of the Federal Deposit Insurance Corporation, assess the risks to institutions under their jurisdiction of potential litigation or repurchases due to improper mortgage loan transfer documentation and require that the institutions take action to mitigate the risks, if warranted. The Federal Reserve has conducted a detailed evaluation of this risk, the so-called "put-back" risk, to financial institutions supervised by the Federal Reserve. We have also required institutions we supervise that originated large numbers of mortgages or sponsored significant MBS to assess and provide for these risks as part of their overall capital planning process. This exercise was included in the recently completed Comprehensive Capital Analysis and Review (CCAR), which involved 19 bank holding companies. In addition, as part of the recently announced foreclosure orders, the servicers will be required to conduct a review of foreclosures conducted from January 2009 through December 2010. The Federal Reserve will also take that information into account in assessing put-back risk to the institutions we supervise.

This will include a review of risks that servicers may suffer losses because of the lack of legally enforceable documentation of ownership.

The ultimate financial loss for any originator or securitizer subject to put-back risk is dependent upon a wide range of factors that can be firm or transaction specific, such as the quality of initial underwriting, the incidence of fraud, the performance of sold mortgages, whether the mortgages were sold to Fannie Mae and Freddie Mac or as private label securitizations, the relative strength of representations and warranties for a transaction, the willingness of investors to pursue certain claims, and the outcome of pending litigation. The Federal Reserve will continue to follow closely developments in this market, and will continue to monitor affected firms to ensure they maintain appropriate capital and reserves to protect against future mortgage put-back losses.

We will continue to monitor all of these issues and instruct our supervised institutions accordingly. We appreciate the professionalism of the GAO's review team in conducting this study.

Sincerely,

Appendix V. Comments from the Comptroller of the Currency

Comptroller of the Currency
Administrator of National Banks

Washington, DC 20219

April 15, 2011

Ms. A. Nicole Clowers
Acting Director, Financial Markets and Community Investment
United States Government Accountability Office
Washington, DC 20548

Dear Ms. Clowers:

We have received and reviewed your draft report titled "Mortgage Foreclosures: Documentation Problems Reveal Need for Ongoing Regulatory Oversight." Your report responds to Congressional requests for information concerning various aspects of federal oversight of the residential mortgage foreclosure process.

You found that: (1) federal laws do not specifically address the foreclosure process and past federal oversight of foreclosure activities has been limited and fragmented; (2) federal regulators have conducted reviews in response to foreclosure documentation problems, but the extent and roles in future oversight are unclear; and (3) documentation problems will likely result in delays in the foreclosure process, but the impact on financial institutions and others is less clear.

You recommend that the federal banking regulators and the Consumer Financial Protection Bureau (CFPB) develop plans for overseeing mortgage servicers and include foreclosure practices in any servicing standards that are developed. You also recommend that regulators assess the risks that documentation problems pose for their institutions.

We agree and are pleased to report that development of servicing standards is well underway on an interagency basis. While still a work in progress, the standards, as currently drafted, include provisions covering both foreclosure abeyance and foreclosure governance. The former emphasizes communication with the borrower and the latter emphasizes compliance with legal requirements, documentation, vendor management and other controls.

The OCC will continue to oversee the mortgage servicers under our jurisdiction through regular onsite review and monitoring. In the near term, emphasis will be on assessing compliance with enforcement actions to be sure that those unsafe or unsound practices and other deficiencies in the banks' servicing and foreclosure processes are remedied.

Consistent with the OCC's model of supervision by risk, the servicers are being required by the enforcement actions to assess the risks present in their servicing operations. In turn, these assessments will be evaluated by our examiners together with the banks' plans to mitigate and manage those risks.

We appreciate the opportunity to comment on the draft report.

Sincerely,

John Walsh
Acting Comptroller of the Currency

APPENDIX VI. COMMENTS FROM THE DEPARTMENT OF THE TREASURY

DEPARTMENT OF THE TREASURY
WASHINGTON

UNDER SECRETARY

April 19, 2011

A. Nicole Clowers
Acting Director
Financial Markets and Community Investment
U.S. Government Accountability Office
441 G Street, NW
Washington, DC 20548

Dear Ms. Clowers:

Thank you for providing the Department of the Treasury ("Treasury") an opportunity to review and comment on your draft report on problems in the mortgage foreclosure process, entitled *Mortgage Foreclosures: Documentation Problems Reveal Need for Ongoing Regulatory Oversight ("Draft Report")*.

The Draft Report provides a detailed description of the mortgage servicing and foreclosure processes, including investigations by federal and state agencies into errors made by certain financial institutions in those processes.

Although Treasury does not have regulatory authority over servicers and the recommendations in the Draft Report are not directed at Treasury, we have been closely engaged with the interagency task force seeking to address errors in mortgage servicing and foreclosure processing. As we have said before, servicers that acted improperly must be held accountable and the system must be reformed to prevent these problems from occurring again. To that end, we support a set of national servicing standards to align incentives and provide clarity and consistency to borrowers and investors regarding their treatment by servicers, especially in the event of delinquency.

Thank you again for your work on this important issue.

Sincerely,

Jeffrey A. Goldstein
Under Secretary for Domestic Finance

APPENDIX VII. STAFF ACKNOWLEDGMENTS

Staff Acknowledgments

In addition to the contact named above, Cody Goebel (Assistant Director), Simon Galed, Beth Garcia, Marc Molino, Jill Naamane, Linda Rego, and James Vitarello made key contributions to this report.

End Notes

[1] A home mortgage is an instrument by which the borrower (mortgagor) gives the lender (mortgagee) a lien on residential property as security for the repayment of a loan. A first-lien mortgage creates a primary lien against real property and has priority over subsequent mortgages, which are generally known as junior, or second, mortgages. First liens are the first to be paid when the property is sold.

[2] These challenges question whether the paperwork documenting transfers of loans into securities adequately proves that the trust seeking to foreclose is the actual mortgage holder with the authority to foreclose.

[3] A "holder" "is a person who has legal possession of a negotiable instrument and is entitled to receive payment on it." *Black's Law Dictionary* (9th ed., 2009).

[4] We have previously reported that the servicing fee is usually based on the outstanding unpaid principal balance of the loan and is generally between 25 and 50 basis points. See GAO, *Mortgage Foreclosures: Additional Mortgage Servicer Actions Could Help Reduce the Frequency and Impact of Abandoned Foreclosures*, GAO-11-93 (Washington D.C.: Nov. 15, 2010).

[5] Fannie Mae and Freddie Mac share a primary mission that has been to stabilize and assist the U.S. secondary mortgage market and facilitate the flow of mortgage credit. To accomplish this goal, the enterprises purchase mortgages from primary mortgage lenders. They hold some of the mortgages they purchase in their portfolios, but they package the majority into MBS and sell them to investors in the secondary mortgage market. The enterprises guarantee these investors the timely payment of principal and interest. Fannie Mae and Freddie Mac each have issued servicing guidelines that must be followed by entities servicing loans on behalf of the enterprises. Both enterprises are currently in conservatorship.

[6] "Beneficial interest" refers to the right to occupy or receive rents or other profits from a property or estate, as distinct from the interest of a nonfiduciary legal owner of the entire estate.

[7] Home retention workouts are employed when the borrower has a desire to keep the home and the capacity to carry payments under the workout plan. Home retention workouts can take the following forms: (1) repayment plans, which involve a contracted plan to make up past due amounts; (2) forbearance, which includes a defined period when no or only partial payments are required followed by a repayment plan to make up the arrearage; and (3) loan modifications, which involve a permanent altering of one or more of the loan terms. Other foreclosure alternatives include two types of voluntary home-loss workout, which avoid foreclosure but require the borrower to give up the home. These two types are deed-in-lieu transfers, in which the borrower essentially gives the investor the keys to the property and executes a deed to transfer title to the investor, after the investor agrees to release the debtor from any liability on the outstanding mortgage balance, and short sales, in which the lender agrees to accept proceeds from the sale of the home to a third party even though the sale price is less than the sum of the principal, accrued interest, and other expenses owed.

[8] An "'affidavit' is [a] voluntary declaration of facts written down and sworn to by the declarant before an officer authorized to administer oaths." *Black's Law Dictionary* (9th ed., 2009).

[9] According to HUD, as of July 2008, 25 states used a nonjudicial process as their normal method of foreclosure, 19 states used a judicial process, and 6 states used both.

[10] "Standing" refers to "[a] party's right to make a legal claim or seek judicial enforcement of a duty or right." *Black's Law Dictionary* (9th ed., 2009).

[11] 12 U.S.C. § 1813(q).

[12] OCC will assume oversight responsibility of federal savings associations from OTS in July 2011. Concurrently, FDIC will assume oversight responsibility of state-chartered savings associations from OTS and the Federal Reserve will assume oversight responsibility of savings and loan holding companies and lenders owned by a savings and loan holding company from OTS, according to OTS officials.

[13] The Dodd-Frank Wall Street Reform and Consumer Protection Act (Dodd-Frank Act), enacted on July 21, 2010, established CFPB as an independent bureau within the Federal Reserve System. Section 1066 of the Dodd-Frank Act authorized the Secretary of the Treasury to provide administrative services necessary to support the CFPB before the transfer date and to exercise certain of its powers until the appointment of a CFPB Director. 12 U.S.C. § 5586. "Federal consumer financial law" is a defined term in the Dodd-Frank Act that includes over a dozen existing federal consumer protection laws, including the Truth in Lending Act, the Real Estate Settlement Procedures Act, and the Equal Credit Opportunity Act, as well as title X of the Dodd-Frank Act itself. 12 U.S.C. § 5481(12), (14).

[14] The seven agencies are the Federal Reserve, FDIC, Federal Trade Commission, National Credit Union Administration, OCC, OTS, and HUD.

[15] 12 U.S.C. § 5515.

[16] CFPB's nondepository supervision authorities specifically extend to any covered person that "offers or provides origination, brokerage or servicing of loans secured by real estate for use by consumers primarily for personal, family or household purposes, or loan modification or foreclosure relief services in connection with such loans." 12 U.S.C. § 5514(a)(1)(A).

[17] 12 U.S.C. § 5512. The Federal Trade Commission will retain its current enforcement authority.

[18] On September 6, 2008, FHFA placed Fannie Mae and Freddie Mac in conservatorship out of concern that their deteriorating financial condition and potential default on $5.4 trillion in outstanding financial obligations threatened the stability of financial markets.

[19] The Home Affordable Modification Program is a program designed to help borrowers avoid foreclosure and stay in their homes by providing incentives for servicers to perform loan modifications.

[20] Congressional Research Service, Memorandum, *"Robo-signing" and Related Mortgage Documentation Problems*. (Washington, D.C.: November 15, 2010).

[21] Fair Housing Act, 42 U.S.C. §§ 3601–3619; Equal Credit Opportunity Act, 15 U.S.C. §§ 1691-1691f; Truth in Lending Act, 15 U.S.C. §§ 1601-1667f; Real Estate Settlement Procedures Act of 1974, 12 U.S.C. §§ 2601-2617; Fair Credit Reporting Act, 15 U.S.C. §§ 1681-1681x; SAFE Act, 12 U.S.C. §§ 5101-5116.

[22] Pub. L. No. 111-203, title XIV, §§ 1418, 1420, 124 Stat. 1376, 2154 (2010) (Dodd-Frank Act). Section 1420 also requires that monthly statements be provided to borrowers.

[23] Regulation Z implements TILA. See 12 C.F.R. § 226.36(c)(ii); 73 Fed. Reg. 44522 (July 30, 2008). The regulations also require prompt crediting of mortgage loan payments and the provision of payoff statements within a reasonable time; those requirements were later essentially codified by section 1464 of the Dodd-Frank Act.

[24] 12 U.S.C. § 2605. A "federally related mortgage loan" generally with certain exceptions includes any loan, that is (1) secured by a lien on single family, or up to four-family, residential real property if the proceeds of the loan are used to either purchase the property or to prepay or pay off an existing loan secured by the same property; and (2) is made in whole or in part by any lender the deposits or accounts of which are federally insured, or is made by any federally regulated lender; or (3) is made, or insured, guaranteed, supplemented, or assisted in any way, by the federal government or in connection with a housing or urban development program administered by the federal government; or (4) is intended to be sold by the originating lender to the Federal National Mortgage Association, the Government National Mortgage Association, the Federal Home Loan Mortgage Corporation, or a financial institution from which it is to be purchased by the Federal Home Loan Mortgage Corporation; or (5) is made by certain creditors who make or invest in residential real estate loans aggregating more than $1,000,000 per year. 12 U.S.C. § 2602(1).

[25] 12 U.S.C. §§ 2607, 2609. Section 1463 of the Dodd-Frank Act has expanded some of these requirements and created new requirements. For example, it decreased the timelines applicable to servicer responses to written requests from borrowers and required servicers to respond within 10 days to borrower requests for the identity of the owner of their loan. It also created new restrictions on the force-placement of hazard insurance, requires prompt refund of escrow accounts after loan payoff, and requires timely action by servicers to correct errors.

[26] 12 U.S.C. §§ 5201 note, 5220 note (expires December 31, 2014). 50 App. U.S.C. §§ 501–597b.

[27] 12 U.S.C. § 1831o.

[28] 12 U.S.C. § 1818.

[29] Section 304 of the Federal Deposit Insurance Corporation Improvement Act of 1991 requires the federal banking agencies to prescribe uniform real estate lending standards. 12 U.S.C. § 1828(o). The standards established by the federal banking regulators require every depository institution to establish and maintain comprehensive, written real estate lending policies that are consistent with safe and sound banking practices and appropriate to the size of the institution and nature and scope of its operations. The lending policies must establish loan portfolio diversification standards; prudent underwriting standards; loan administration procedures for the bank's real estate portfolio; and documentation, approval, and reporting requirements to monitor compliance with the bank's real estate lending policies. OCC (12 C.F.R. part 34, subpart D), Federal Reserve System (12 C.F.R. part 208, subpart E), FDIC (12 C.F.R. part 365), OTS (12 C.F.R. § 560.100 and 560.101).

[30] For example, see 12 C.F.R. part 364, App. A(II)(C).

[31] Staff at one of the banking agencies acknowledged that servicers could be subject to significant losses on loans that they are managing that are held in their own portfolios or in the portfolios of their affiliates.

[32] GAO, *Troubled Asset Relief Program: One Year Later, Actions Are Needed to Address Remaining Transparency and Accountability Challenges*, GAO-10-16 (Washington, D.C.: Oct. 8, 2009).

[33] 12 U.S.C. § 1813(q). OTS also has jurisdiction over savings and loan holding companies and their subsidiaries. 12 U.S.C. § 1467a.

[34] 12 U.S.C. § 1844(c)(2). "Functional regulation" refers to the premise that risks within a diversified organization can be managed properly through supervision focused on the individual subsidiaries within the firm. That is, securities activities are supervised by securities regulators, banking activities by banking regulators, and insurance activities by insurance regulators.

[35] GAO, *Consumer Protection: Federal and State Agencies Face Challenges in Combating Predatory Lending*, GAO-04-280 (Washington, D.C.: Jan. 30, 2004). See also GAO, *Alternative Mortgage Products: Impact on Defaults Remains Unclear, but Disclosure of Risks to Borrowers Could Be Improved*, GAO-06-1021 (Washington, D.C.: Sept. 19, 2006), and *Information on Recent Default and Foreclosure Trends for Home Mortgages and Associated Economic and Market Developments*, GAO-08-78R (Washington, D.C.: Oct. 16, 2007).

[36] Statement by Daniel K. Tarullo, Member Board of Governors of the Federal Reserve System before the Committee on Banking, Housing and Urban Affairs, United States Senate, Washington, D.C.: December 1, 2010.

[37] Section 113 of the Dodd-Frank Act provides the Financial Stability Oversight Council the authority to require that a nonbank financial company be supervised by the Board of Governors of the Federal Reserve System and be subject to prudential standards in accordance with title I of the Dodd-Frank Act if the council determines that material financial distress at such a firm, or the nature, scope, size, scale, concentration, interconnectedness, or mix of the activities of the firm, could pose a threat to the financial stability of the United States. 12 U.S.C. § 5323(a). The Council has issued a notice of proposed rulemaking regarding the designation criteria in section 113. 76 Fed. Reg. 7731 (Feb. 11, 2011).

[38] GAO, *Alternative Mortgage Products: Impact on Defaults Remains Unclear, but Disclosure of Risks to Borrowers Could Be Improved*, GAO-06-1021 (Washington, D.C.: Sept. 19, 2006).

[39] GAO, *Financial Regulation: A Framework for Crafting and Assessing Proposals to Modernize the Outdated U.S. Financial Regulatory System*, GAO-09-216 (Washington, D.C.: Jan. 8, 2009).

[40] 24 C.F.R. part 203, subparts B, C.

[41] See, for example, 24 C.F.R. 203.366, concerning conveying marketable title.

[42] 12 U.S.C. § 4513. FHFA oversees the government-sponsored enterprises Fannie Mae, Freddie Mac, and the Federal Home Loan Bank System. The Federal Home Loan Bank System was created by the Federal Home Loan Bank Act as a government-sponsored enterprise to support mortgage lending and related community investment by making loans, called advances, to its member institutions, which in turn lend to home buyers for mortgages. Advances are secured by home mortgage loans and other collateral. 12 U.S.C. §§ 1421-1449. We did not review the Federal Home Loan Bank System for this report.

[43] According to SEC staff, section 943(2) of the Dodd-Frank Act requires new securitization issuances to keep filing certain reports after the first year. See 15 U.S.C. § 78o-7 note; 76 Fed. Reg. 4489 (Jan. 26, 2011).

[44] Under federal securities laws, individuals could be liable for fraud if they made material misstatements or omissions in their SEC filing with intent to deceive or defraud. Criminal penalties may be imposed for willful violations of the federal securities laws or for willfully committing fraud. See, for example, 15 U.S.C. § 77x.

[45] See *FTC v. Countrywide Home Loans, Inc.*, No. CV10-4193 (C.D. Cal. filed June 7, 2010); *FTC v. EMC Mortgage Corp.*, Civil No. 4:08-cv-338 (E.D. Tex. filed Sept. 9, 2008); *U.S. v. Fairbanks Capital Corp.*, Civil No. 03-12219-DPW (D. Mass. filed Nov. 12, 2003). The defendants in each of these cases did not admit to any of the allegations of wrongdoing set forth in the Federal Trade Commission's complaints but agreed to settle to resolve the matters.

[46] According to Justice staff, the primary governing statutes that relate to mortgage servicing for civil and criminal enforcement are the False Claims Act, 31 U.S.C. § 3729, which addresses fraud against the government; Title 18 of the U.S. Code, 18 U.S.C. §§ 1341, 1343, and 1344; and the Financial Institutions Reform, Recovery, and Enforcement Act (FIRREA), 12 U.S.C. 1833a, which provides for civil penalties for bank fraud, mail and wire fraud, illegal participation, embezzlement and other bank fraud-related offenses.

[47] See *US ex rel. Hastings v. Countrywide Home Loans, Inc.*, Case No. 2:07-cv-03897-JFW-PLA (C.D. Ca. filed Oct. 8, 2008); *US ex rel. Pace v. Bank of America NA*, Case No. 2:09-cv-07157-SVW-SS (C.D. Ca. filed Oct. 1, 2010); and *US ex rel. Conrad v. Countrywide Home Loans, Inc.*, Case No. 1:04-cv-01863-RGL (D.D.C. filed Oct. 27, 2004).

[48] OCC led reviews of eight servicers, the Federal Reserve led two reviews, and OTS led the remaining four reviews; FDIC participated in the reviews in a backup role.

[49] See also Office of the Comptroller of the Currency and Office of Thrift Supervision, *OCC and OTS Mortgage Metrics Report, Disclosure of National Bank and Federal Thrift Mortgage Loan Data, Fourth Quarter 2010* (Washington, D.C.: March 2011).

[50] MERS was created in 1995 to streamline the mortgage process and to reduce costs as lenders can buy and sell loans without having to record and pay a fee for each assignment. According to its Web site, MERS serves as the nominal mortgagee of record. LPS, through two subsidiaries, provided document execution activities related to foreclosures. According to regulators, those subsidiaries discontinued their document execution and signing activities in early 2010.

[51] These actions were taken under the agencies' authority in 7(d) of the Bank Service Company Act, 12 U.S.C. § 1867(d), and section 8(b) of the Federal Deposit Insurance Act, 12 U.S.C. § 1818(b).

[52] However, Federal Reserve staff said that examiners checked for evidence that servicers were in contact with borrowers and had considered alternative loss mitigation efforts, including loan modifications.

[53] Regulators noted that they did not review a sufficient number of foreclosure files to reliably estimate the total number of foreclosures that should not have proceeded.

[54] 50 App. U.S.C. §§ 501–597b.

[55] Potential problems arising from loan transfer practices are discussed later in this report.

[56] These actions were taken under the agencies' authority in section 8(b) of the Federal Deposit Insurance Act, 12 U.S.C. § 1818(b).

[57] In addition to the actions against the servicers, the Federal Reserve and OTS have issued formal enforcement actions against 12 parent holding companies to require that they enhance on a consolidated basis their oversight of mortgage servicing activities, including compliance, risk management, and audit. Those actions also were taken under authority of section 8(b) of the Federal Deposit Insurance Act, 12 U.S.C. § 1818(b).

[58] Federal Reserve System, Office of the Comptroller of the Currency, and Office of Thrift Supervision, *Interagency Review of Foreclosure Policies and Practices*, (Washington, D.C.: April 2011).

[59] As OTS will dissolve in July 2011, OTS officials told us that the agency will not effect long-term change as a stand-alone institution but will continue to work with its sister agencies to implement enforcement actions.

[60] See, for example, 12 U.S.C. § 5365.

[61] Testimony of John Walsh, Acting Comptroller of the Currency, Office of the Comptroller of the Currency, before the Committee on Banking, Housing, and Urban Affairs, United States Senate, Washington, D.C.: February 17, 2011.

[62] GAO-09-216.

[63] Statement by Daniel K. Tarullo, Member, Board of Governors of the Federal Reserve System, before the Committee on Banking, Housing and Urban Affairs, United States Senate, Washington, D.C.: December 1, 2010.

[64] Speech delivered by FDIC Chairman Sheila Bair at Mortgage Bankers Association's Summit on Residential Mortgage Servicing for the 21st Century, January 19, 2011. For example, Chairman Bair has suggested that servicers provide borrowers a single point of contact to assist them throughout the loss mitigation and foreclosure process who is authorized to put a hold on any foreclosure proceeding while loss mitigation efforts remain ongoing.

[65] GAO-09-216.

[66] FHA is reviewing foreclosure processes as part of a broader examination that includes evaluation of payment processing and document handling.

[67] Federal Housing Finance Agency, *FHFA Announces Joint Initiative to Consider Alternatives for a New Mortgage Servicing Compensation Structure*, (Washington, D.C.: January 18, 2011).

[68] According to a GSE representative, the GSEs are required to establish appropriate incentives to encourage and support servicer contact with borrowers in the early stages of delinquency, consistent timelines and requirements for communications with borrowers, incentive structures for early engagement, and updated foreclosure process timelines. The representative also noted that the work will include consideration of appropriate penalties to encourage efficient resolution and liquidation of properties in cases where foreclosure is necessary.

[69] MHA is a federal program overseen by Treasury that provides opportunities for struggling homeowners to modify or refinance their mortgages or otherwise avoid foreclosure through a short sale or deed-in-lieu of foreclosure.

[70] MHA-Compliance is a separate division of Freddie Mac contracted to perform compliance activities and to ensure that servicers satisfy obligations under MHA requirements.

[71] *OCC and OTS Mortgage Metrics Report, Disclosure of National Bank and Federal Thrift Mortgage Loan Data, Fourth Quarter 2010* (Washington, D.C.: March 2011). This report provides performance data through December 31, 2010, on first-lien residential mortgages serviced by selected national banks and federally regulated thrifts comprising 63 percent of all mortgages outstanding in the United States.

[72] GAO, *Troubled Asset Relief Program: Treasury's Framework for Deciding to Extend TARP Was Sufficient, but Could Be Strengthened for Future Decisions*, GAO-10-531 (Washington, D.C.: June 30, 2010). While the foreclosure start rate grew 36 percent from the last quarter of 2007 to the last quarter of 2009, the rate for delinquencies of 90 days or more grew by 222 percent over the same period. From the fourth quarter of 2009 to the first quarter of 2010, delinquencies have fallen somewhat, while the foreclosure starts have remained fairly constant.

[73] GAO-11-93.

[74] GAO-11-93.

[75] *In re Foreclosure Cases*, 2007 WL 3232430 (N.D. Ohio 2007) (dismissed without prejudice for failing to file executed assignment demonstrating that the plaintiff seeking foreclosure was the holder and owner of the note and mortgage as of the date the complaint was filed), and *In re Foreclosure Actions*, 2007 WL 4034554 (N.D. Ohio 2007) (case was dismissed without prejudice for failing to produce documentation demonstrating that the plaintiff was the owner and holder of the note and mortgage). See also *In re Foreclosure Cases*, 521 F. Supp. 2d 650 (S.D. Ohio 2007); *DLJ Mtge. Capital, Inc. v. Parsons*, 2008 WL 697400 (Ohio Ct. App. 2008) (reversing summary judgment for lack of evidence that the party seeking foreclosure was the owner of the note and mortgage at the time of summary judgment).

[76] See Katherine Porter, *Misbehavior and Mistake in Bankruptcy Mortgage Claims,* 87 Tex. L. Rev. 121 (2008).

[77] See, for example, *Footbridge Limited Trust v. Countrywide Financial Corp.,* Case No. 1:10-cv-00367-PKC, 95-97 (S.D. N.Y. Jan. 15, 2010) (complaint filed).

[78] These data include Fannie Mae, Freddie Mac, and the Government National Mortgage Association (Ginnie Mae). Ginnie Mae is a wholly owned government corporation that guarantees the timely payment of principal and interest on securities issued by private institutions and backed by pools of federally insured or guaranteed

mortgage loans. Securities guaranteed by Ginnie Mae finance the vast majority of loans backed by the Federal Housing Administration and Department of Veterans Affairs, among other federal agencies.

[79] As will be discussed later, the use of MERS as a foreclosing entity has been challenged in some court cases. According to FHFA, both Fannie Mae and Freddie Mac have eliminated the option for servicers to foreclose in the name of MERS.

[80] According to one academic, the following language is a common provision in Section 2.01 of many pooling and servicing agreements: "the original Mortgage Note bearing all intervening endorsements showing a complete chain of endorsement from the originator to the last endorsee, endorsed 'Pay to the order of________, without recourse' and signed (which may be by facsimile signature) in the name of the last endorsee by an authorized officer."

[81] Statement by Adam J. Levitin, Associate Professor of Law, Georgetown University Law Center, before the Committee on Financial Services, Subcommittee on Insurance, Housing, and Community Opportunity, House of Representatives, Washington, D.C.: November 18, 2010.

[82] The residential mortgage notes in common usage typically are negotiable instruments, similar to a check. As a general matter, under the UCC, a negotiable mortgage note can be transferred from one party to another through an endorsement of the mortgage note and the transfer of possession of the note to the new party or an agent in its behalf. This process is similar to endorsing a check by signing the back and depositing it in a bank. An assignment of the related mortgage is also typically delivered to the transferee or its agent. Such assignments generally are in recordable form, but may not be required to be recorded in local land record offices.

[83] *Kemp v. Countrywide Home Loans, Inc.*, 440 B.R. 624 (Bankr. D. N.J. 2010).

[84] Moody's Investors Service, *Moody's Weekly Credit Outlook:* "Interviews Show Countrywide's Mortgage Processing Did Not Systematically Fail," (New York, NY: January 10, 2011).

[85] *U.S. Bank National Ass'n v. Ibanez,* 941 N.E. 2d 40 (Mass. 2011).

[86] In a recent testimony, a MERS official cited a number of cases where, according to MERS, courts found that MERS had the authority to initiate foreclosure proceedings. Statement by R. K. Arnold, President and CEO of MERSCORP, Inc., before the Committee on Banking, Housing and Urban Affairs, United States Senate, Washington, D.C.: November 16, 2010. However, academics and industry participants have cited cases that seem to come to different conclusions. On March 8, 2011, MERS proposed changes to its procedures that would require an execution of assignment of the mortgage from MERS to the servicer or to another party designated by the beneficial owner of such mortgage loan before initiating foreclosure proceedings.

[87] GAO, *Troubled Asset Relief Program: One Year Later, Actions Are Needed to Address Remaining Transparency and Accountability Challenges*, GAO-10-16 (Washington, D.C.: Oct. 8, 2009).

[88] GAO, *Troubled Asset Relief Program: Status of Efforts to Address Defaults and Foreclosures on Home Mortgages*, GAO-09-231T (Washington, D.C.: Dec. 4, 2008).

In: America's Foreclosure Crisis
Editors: Russell Burns and Roy A. Foster
ISBN: 978-161942- 271-1

Chapter 3

ALTERNATIVE MORTGAGES: CAUSES AND POLICY IMPLICATIONS OF TROUBLED MORTGAGE RESETS IN THE SUBPRIME AND ALT-A MARKETS*

Edward V. Murphy

SUMMARY

Borrowers who used alternative mortgages to finance homes during the housing boom have experienced rising foreclosure rates as housing markets have declined. Some types of alternative mortgages may have exacerbated price declines and damaged the finances of consumers and lenders. The use of mortgages with adjustable rates, zero down payment, interest-only, or negative amortization features raise economic risk compared to traditional mortgages. Because some borrowers and lenders did not adequately evaluate these risks, housing finance markets have been hit with significant losses and financial markets have been in turmoil. Policymakers have responded with a housing rescue package (H.R. 3221 / P.L. 110-289). They have also authorized the Department of Treasury to institute a Troubles Asset Relief Program (TARP) to buy bad debts from banks (H.R. 1424 / P.L. 110-343).

Alternative mortgages offer some combination of adjustable rates, extremely low down payments, negative amortization, and optional monthly payments. The prudent use of alternative mortgages offers benefits. For example, during periods of exceptionally high interest rates, adjustable rates may suit consumers expecting rates to fall. People whose incomes depend on commission or bonuses may be attracted to mortgages with flexible monthly payments.

These benefits come with potential costs for the borrower and for the financial system. Adjustable rates shift the risk of rising interest rates from banks to borrowers. Low down payments increase the risk that borrowers will owe more than their house is worth if prices fall. A borrower owing more than the house is worth may be unable to sell or refinance the house. The use of alternative mortgages in these areas may have contributed to rising defaults

---

* This is an edited, reformatted and augmented version of Congressional Research Services Publication, No. RL33775, dated October 8, 2008.

and more volatile home prices. More than a trillion dollars of mortgages originated during the boom will reset their monthly payments by 2009.

Using its authority under the Truth in Lending Act (TILA) and Regulation Z, the Federal Reserve issued on July 14, 2008, new rules for mortgage origination. These rules apply to banks and to non-bank lenders. These rules would put some restrictions on the use of prepayment penalties for mortgages with introductory periods and requires disclosures for mortgages with adjustable rates. The House of Representatives passed a bill to provide additional rules for underwriting practices of alternative mortgages (H.R. 3221) but a similar bill has not as yet passed the Senate.

This report describes alternative mortgages, summarizes recent regulatory actions, and provides an estimate of the geographic concentration of interest rate risk and negative appreciation risk.

BACKGROUND

More than a trillion dollars of mortgages will have payment resets in 2007-2009.[1] A newspaper account of one resident of Garden Grove, California, illustrates the problem. His monthly mortgage payment doubled and he learned that he owes more than his house is worth because prices of neighboring houses fell by $140,000.[2] It will be a struggle to maintain the higher payments on his resetting mortgage and it is difficult to refinance while he is upside down.[3] The Federal Reserve issued new rules pursuant to the Truth in Lending Act (TILA) to help potential home buyers understand the risks in alternative mortgages and to ensure that lenders follow safe and sound practices. Unlike a regulatory guidance, Regulation Z applies to banks and to non-bank lenders that operate in the subprime and Alt-A mortgage sectors.[4] Mortgage delinquencies and foreclosures are rising and the prospect of coming mortgage resets in declining housing markets suggests that defaults will rise even higher.

Alternative mortgages are sometimes called nontraditional mortgages or exotic mortgages. Alternative mortgages have some combination of variable interest rates, extremely low down payments, interest-only periods, and/or negative amortization. (Amortization refers to the gradual payment of the loan's principal.) In some cases, borrowers intended to refinance these loans or sell the houses relatively quickly. The potential advantages of alternative features for these buyers often depended on the expected path of interest rates and home appreciation. Significant disadvantages became apparent, however, when interest rates and appreciation took what to some was an unexpected turn. The sudden decrease in house price appreciation during 2006-2008 has caused problems for borrowers using alternative mortgages with resets that are expected to occur in coming months.

House prices boomed from 2000 to 2005 in many parts of the country and then suddenly ground to a halt in 2006. Since 2006, house prices have fallen in many markets. Although adjustable rate mortgages are not new, their increased use during the boom was counterintuitive to many economists because mortgage rates were already low by historic standards. Other alternative features were not new but their use by the general public increased during the boom. The increased use of alternative mortgages by unsophisticated borrowers may have been a significant contributor to the rise in mortgage delinquencies and foreclosures.

This report recounts recent events that led to increased foreclosures and the forecast of higher foreclosures, explains salient features of alternative mortgages, summarizes federal agency response, places the potential benefits and risks to consumers and financial systems in the context of economic conditions, and assesses the estimates geographic impact.

EVENTS THAT LED TO UNSUSTAINABLE MORTGAGES

Size and Timing of the Upcoming Mortgage Resets

Mortgage defaults are rising and are expected to increase significantly. Housing prices have slowed or declined in previously booming areas, and it is taking longer to sell homes; troubled borrowers now find it more difficult to sell their property to avoid foreclosure. Many borrowers took out loans with introductory periods that will expire resulting in higher payments even if interest rates are low, and the underwriting of these loans appears to be relatively weak. The combination of mortgage payment resets and weaker housing markets could lead to even higher mortgage defaults in coming years.

There are two periods of higher scheduled resets. *Figure 1* shows that the first period (January 2007 - September 2008) had a high proportion of subprime loans. Month 1 in *Figure 1* represents January of 2007; therefore, month 23 represents November 2008, which has a low number of subprime resets. After November 2008, the number of payment resets in the Alt-A and option ARM categories increases. Alt-A loans are typically loans that would be considered low risk if everything in the loan documentation turns out to be accurate; that is, the loan has an alternative way to meet "A" standards, such as reduced income documentation. Informally, these loans are sometimes referred to as "liar loans" because of the potential for fraud. An option ARM is a loan that allows the borrower several options for any given month's payment, including paying less than the current interest due. If the borrower pays less than current interest due then the loan negatively amortizes — the balance increases and future payments rise.

Resets Are the Result of Decisions Made in 2004-2007

Subprime borrowers often used alternative mortgages with two- or three-year introductory periods, so-called 2-28s and 3-27s. A 2-28 originated in the second half of 2005 resets in the second half of 2007. The 2-28 and 3-27 resets that occurred through summer 2008, therefore, were originated in 2004 through 2006. The state of the housing market and financial markets during 2004 through 2006 may provide clues to the sustainability of these mortgages.

The housing market in many areas appreciated sharply in 2004 and 2005, but then the rate of appreciation slowed in 2006 and has ultimately begun to fall. Rapidly rising house prices build an owner's equity, which improves the borrower's risk-profile and allows refinancing on better terms. Some borrowers and lenders may have agreed to higher-risk loans in rapidly appreciating areas, anticipating that continued house price increases would reduce the chances of default.

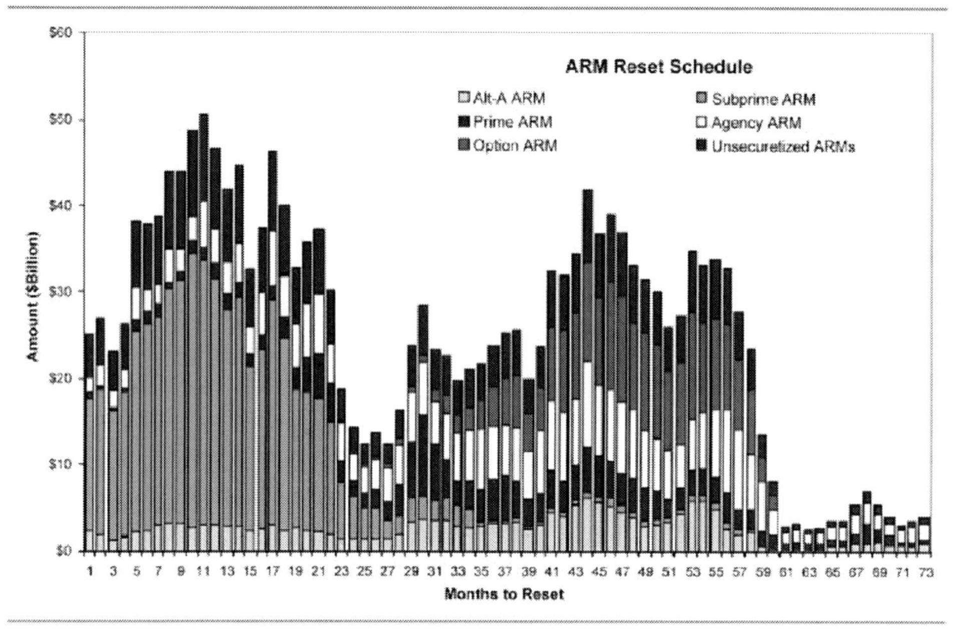

Figure 1. Alternative Mortgage Resets.

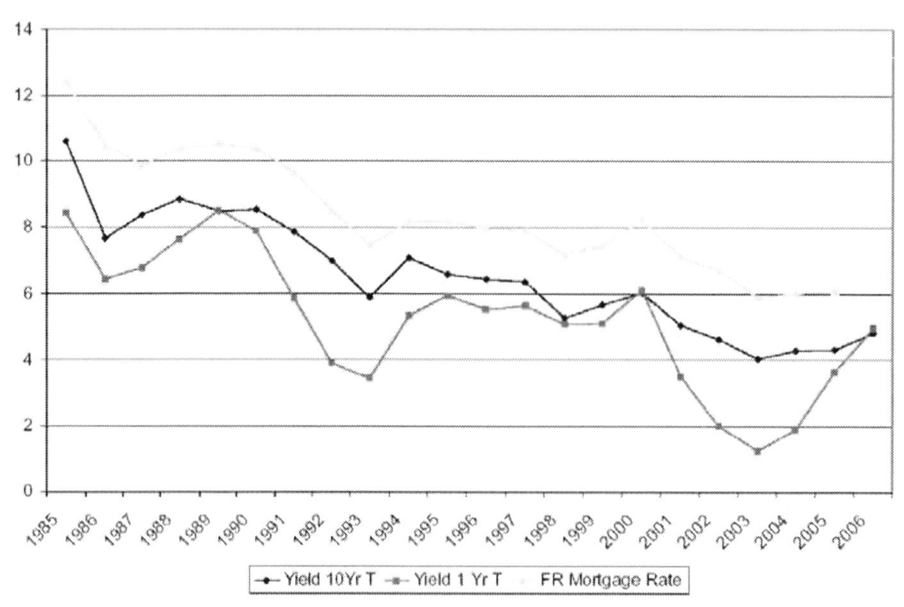

Source: Federal Reserve.

Figure 2. Falling Interest Rates Fueled Housing Markets.

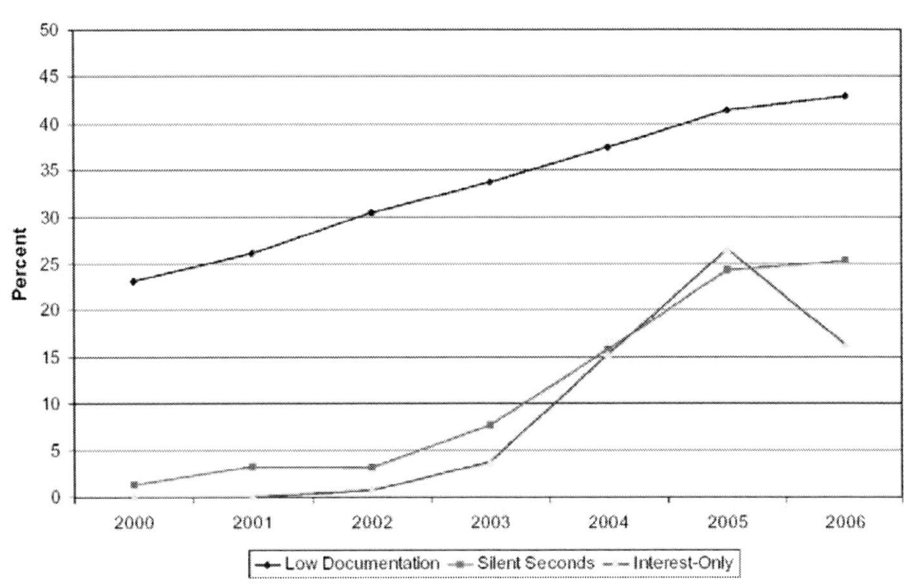

Source: Compile by CRS from UBS data.

Figure 3. Underwriting Standards Weakened.

Interest rates in 2004 through 2006 presented borrowers with conflicting incentives. On the one hand, *Figure 2* shows that rates on 30-year fixed mortgages were generally around 6% during 2004 through 2006, low by historical standards. Borrowers had an incentive to use fixed rate mortgages to lock-in these low rates. On the other hand, *Figure 2* also shows that the gap between short- and long-term rates was relatively large in 2004. The larger this gap, the more a borrower benefits from an adjustable-rate mortgage, which tends to follow short-term rates. Also, the benefit of an adjustable rate mortgage is greater if the borrower intends to quickly sell the house or refinance the loan — which coincides with rapidly appreciating housing markets.

The use of mortgage products with introductory periods and adjustable interest rates arguably was a reasonable response to house price appreciation and interest rates in 2004. By 2005, however, short-term interest rates were rising faster than long-term interest rates. Yet, adjustable rates remained very popular. House price appreciation slowed significantly in 2006, yet introductory periods remained popular. The persistence of nontraditional terms could be evidence that some borrowers intended to sell or refinance quickly — one indicator of speculative behavior.

Credit Quality of Resetting Loans Appears Weak

As the reset dates of billions of dollars of subprime mortgages near, analysts want to know the quality of the underwriting that was used when the loans were originated. For 2-28s and 3-27s, this requires information on the risk-characteristics of loans originated in prior years. Information from industry sources suggests that non-agency subprime loans became more risky as the housing boom progressed. For example, *Figure 3* shows that the percent of subprime loans with low documentation doubled between 2000 and 2005.[5] Similarly, the percent of subprime loans that used silent seconds to avoid private mortgage insurance (PMI) increased from almost none in 2000 to 25% of the subprime market by 2006.[6] *Figure 3* also shows the increased use of subprime loans with interest-only periods, which require higher resets even if interest rates do not rise.

In summary, falling interest rates had two important effects on alternative mortgage markets. First, lower mortgage rates initially helped bid up house prices as households qualified for larger loans, which increased appreciation rates. Second, the incentive to use adjustable rate mortgages increased because short-term rates initially fell faster than long-term rates. House price appreciation and low interest rates, which many expected to continue, encouraged the use of mortgages that reset and have substantially higher future payments. Subsequent increases in interest rates and slowing house prices have resulted in some unsustainable resets and the forecast of more unsustainable resets. Understanding the choice of mortgages containing a reset requires an examination of the features of nontraditional mortgages.

FEATURES OF NONTRADITIONAL MORTGAGES

Discussions of alternative mortgages often focus on some combination of four differences from traditional mortgages. Borrowers increasingly chose one or more of the following features:

- adjustable rates,
- extremely low or zero down payment,
- interest-only payments, and
- negative amortization.

Adjustable Rates

There are many varieties of adjustable rate mortgages (ARMs). One of the simplest forms offers an initial low rate, called a teaser, at the beginning of the loan and then resets after an introductory period. The teaser rate may apply for one year or for as little as one month. The mortgage contract may specify a reset interest rate or may tie the rate to another interest rate by formula. The resulting interest rate may itself be fixed or variable. Teaser rates should be distinguished from fully adjustable rate mortgages. In principle, a 30-year fixed rate mortgage could have a one-month teaser rate without materially affecting the costs and benefits of the mortgage product.

Excluding teaser rates, variable rate mortgages tie the loan to the economy. The future mortgage rate on these loans typically depends on another future interest rate observed in financial markets. The rate might reset each month, each year, or only after several years. The home buyer's mortgage payment would drop if the interest rate dropped but would rise if the interest rate rose. Many adjustable rate mortgages provide for a cap on the amount a rate can rise in any period or over the life of the loan.

Adjustable rate mortgages can be tied to a variety of market interest rates. One common reference rate is the London Interbank Offered Rate (LIBOR). LIBOR rates are determined in the London market for unsecured bank loans. It is a rate that banks charge each other for short term loans (less than 12 months). Typical adjustable rate mortgages will specify a reset date at which time the mortgage rate will adjust to the LIBOR or similar rate plus a predetermined markup.

Extremely Low or Zero Down Payment

Saving enough funds to meet the traditional 20% down payment can be a significant barrier to otherwise credit-worthy potential home buyers. Furthermore, the required down payment grows with the appreciation rate. If home appreciation is growing faster than household income, then it will be difficult for first time home buyers to save sufficiently. Lending programs gradually reduced the required down payment options to 10%, 5%, and eventually 3% of the purchase price. There are mortgages that take this process to its logical conclusion and allow buyers to purchase with no money down. Some programs even roll in closing and other acquisition costs for greater-than-100% financing.

A related practice is using a second mortgage to finance the down payment. Sometimes called piggy back loans or silent seconds, the home buyer uses the second loan to borrow the funds for a 20% down payment. This down payment is enough to improve the interest rate and other terms of the first mortgage. However, the second mortgage carries a higher interest rate and other less desirable features because the first mortgage has prior claim on the collateral. Although the original first-mortgage lender may be aware of the piggy back loan (and may have helped arrange it), subsequent holders of the first mortgage may not be aware of the piggy back loan because lenders often sell the loans they originate to the secondary mortgage market.

Interest Only

An interest-only mortgage allows the home buyer to carry the loan balance for a period of time without having to pay back any principal. The current mortgage payment covers only the monthly interest due on the existing balance. Eventually, the monthly payment must also cover the principal. If the duration of the mortgage is not extended, then the payments will have to amortize the remaining balance over a shorter period of time. Therefore, a homeowner choosing to pay only the interest for a few months increases the monthly payment for later months.

Negative Amortization

Unlike interest-only mortgages which leave the loan balance unchanged, a mortgage with negative amortization allows the borrower to increase the loan's principal by paying less than the current interest due. The remaining interest is added to the loan balance. Future payments are then recalculated based on the increased principal. The homeowner gets lower current payments but at the cost of greater debt and higher future payments.

These four features of alternative mortgages are not mutually exclusive. There are option mortgages which allow borrowers to choose each month to pay a fully amortizing amount, an interest-only amount, or a negatively amortizing amount. Interest-only mortgages that use an adjustable rate when the introductory period ends are also common. The increased use of these mortgages and innovative combination of features has drawn the attention of federal regulators.

FEDERAL AGENCY ACTIONS ON ALTERNATIVE MORTGAGES

Financial Regulatory Institution Guidance

Several federal banking agencies, including the Federal Reserve, the Office of Thrift Supervision (OTS), the National Credit Union Agency (NCUA), the Federal Deposit Insurance Corporation (FDIC), and the Office of the Comptroller of the Currency (OCC), oversee mortgage originations by financial institutions. These agencies are all part of the Federal Financial Institutions Examination Council (FFIEC), and issued a joint guidance statement (the 10/06 Guidance) for alternative mortgages on October 4, 2006.[7] This guidance applies to federally regulated financial institutions but not to many non-bank lenders in the subprime sector. In addition to inter-agency guidance, the Federal Reserve revised Regulation Z under the Truth in Lending Act (TILA) in July 2008. Regulation Z applies to all mortgage lenders.

October 2006 Inter-Agency Guidance

Issues and Comments. The FFIEC agencies are responsible for overseeing both the consumer protection mandates of the Truth in Lending Act (TILA) and the safety and soundness of their regulated institutions. The agencies recognized that alternative mortgages have existed for some time but were concerned that products with possible negative amortization were being offered to a wider spectrum of borrowers by greater numbers of lenders. The 10/06 Guidance addressed three areas of concern: underwriting standards, risk management, and consumer protection. The 10/06 Guidance specified that lenders must tighten underwriting standards to manage risk. Lenders must also provide clear information to consumers to ensure consumer protection, but the guidance explicitly rejected imposing the doctrine of suitability.[8]

The comment period drew a range of views on the proposal that became the 10/06 Guidance. Some depository institutions and industry groups argued against additional restrictions on alternative mortgages. They pointed out that alternatives to the traditional 30-year fixed rate mortgage have been successfully used for many years. Some argued that alternative mortgages contribute to market flexibility in a changing economy. Some also argued that lenders had the incentive and the capability to appropriately manage the risks.

Critics of alternative mortgages encouraged more stringent limitations. Some argued that an agency guidance would not be effective enough because it would not apply to lenders regulated at the state level. These critics argued for new federal legislation. Some consumer groups argued that alternative mortgages were too complex for unsophisticated borrowers to fully understand. Others argued that expanded use of nontraditional mortgages could encourage speculation in real estate and destabilize house prices.

Consumer Disclosure. The 10/06 Guidance addressed some of the commenters' consumer protection concerns. Lenders are to provide full disclosure in plain language. Lenders were already required to give consumers considering adjustable rate mortgages an information booklet published by the Federal Reserve.[9]

The 10/06 Guidance now requires that consumers considering other nontraditional mortgages be given similar information including examples of payment comparisons. As of August 2007, the the FFIEC has not issued a mandatory interest-only or negative-amortization counterpart to the adjustable rate booklet, although the Office of the Comptroller of the Currency has a model booklet.

The Government Accountability Office (GAO) also made recommendations for alternative mortgages. On disclosures, GAO found that "although federal banking regulators have taken a range of proactive steps to address AMP [alternative mortgage product] lending, current federal standards for disclosures do not require information on AMP specific risks."[10] GAO recommended that the Federal Reserve improve its regulations governing disclosures by requiring language that explains the specific risks and features of alternative mortgages.

Prudent Practices. In addition to consumer disclosure, the 10/06 Guidance addresses a number of lending practices that some commenters considered unsafe or unsound. The use of alternative mortgages by less affluent borrowers raised concerns that some home buyers would not be able to sustain payments if housing market conditions changed. The 10/06 Guidance specifically addresses collateral-dependent loans, risk layering, and third-party relationships.

The 10/06 Guidance stated that collateral dependent loans are an unsafe and unsound lending practice. Collateral-dependent loans refers to the practice of lenders to rely solely on the borrower's ability to sell or refinance the property to approve the loan. An example of this practice would be an interest-only loan to a person with no down payment that resets after three or five years. In the first few years of the loan, the borrower is expected to pay a high interest rate. When the loan resets, the buyer is expected to refinance the loan, by which time appreciation could have provided a down payment which would reduce the interest rate the buyer would be expected to pay.

The 10/06 Guidance requires loans to be underwritten for full risk layering. To understand risk layering, consider a mortgage with an optional negative amotization feature. This option is the equivalent of extending the borrower additional credit without additional underwriting. If the borrower chooses to pay less than current interest in the current month, then the remaining interest is added to the loan balance. For example, a borrower may be extended a $200,000 loan that could rise to a $250,000 balance if the borrower pays the minimum each period. The 10/06 Guidance specifies that lenders consider a borrower's ability to repay the maximum loan balance assuming the borrower pays only the minimum monthly payment each period. In the example, the lender would have to qualify the borrower for a $250,000 loan, not a $200,000 loan.

The 10/06 Guidance also addresses third-party relationships and risk management. Banks and financial institutions often do not originate or hold their loans. Mortgage brokers may market the loans to consumers. Once originated, the loans may be sold to investors in the secondary mortgage market. The guidance requires covered institutions to have strong systems and controls for establishing and maintaining third party relationships. While the industry worried that this would require institutions to oversee the marketing practices of third-parties, the agencies responded that an institution's risk management system should address the overall level of risk that third-party relationships create for the institution.

Federal Reserve Revision of Regulation Z

Consumer Protection Hearings. The Federal Reserve administers the consumer protection laws that apply to all lenders, even non-bank lenders that are not subject to agency guidances. The Federal Reserve used the notice and comment rulemaking procedures to modify protections for consumers in mortgage transactions. After a series of hearings had been held on the Truth in Lending Act and the Home Owners Equity Protection Act, which the Federal Reserve implements through Regulation Z, the Federal Reserve revised rules.

The Board heard testimony focusing on four questions regarding its HOEPA authority: (1) should prepayment penalties be restricted to the introductory periods of resetting loans; (2) should escrow accounts for taxes and insurance be mandated for subprime loans (the practice is common in prime markets; (3) should limitations be put on stated income loans, also known as low-doc loans or even liar loans; and (4) should additional limits be placed on underwriting loans based on a borrower's ability to pay out of household income, rather than the value of the collateral?

Final Rule for Regulation Z. The Federal Reserve issued its final rule for Regulation Z on July 14, 2008. Some of the changes made by the Federal Reserve apply only to higher prices loans whereas others apply to all mortgage loans. In addition, the Federal Reserve adjusted its definition of higher priced loans to account for the effect of the gap between short-term and long-term interest rates, as well as lowering the threshold for designation as higher cost.

The Federal Reserve made several significant changes to the rules that apply to the origination of all mortgage loans secured by a principal dwelling. It bans creditors and mortgage brokers from coercing a real estate appraiser to misstate a home's value. It also bans pyramiding late fees and certain other mortgage servicing practices. In addition, lenders and servicers are required to credit borrowers' mortgage payments as of the date of receipt and provide a statement. Borrowers must receive a good faith estimate of the loan costs, including a schedule of payments, within three days after application for all mortgage loans. Consumers cannot be charged any fee until after they receive the early disclosures, except a reasonable fee for obtaining the consumer's credit history.

Some of the changes to Regulation Z apply only to higher priced mortgages. These include prohibiting a lender from making a loan without regard to borrowers' ability to repay the loan from income and assets other than the home's value (so-called collateral dependent lending). For higher price loans, the new rule requires creditors to verify the income and assets they rely upon to determine the borrower's ability to repay the loan. It places a ban on prepayment penalties if the monthly mortgage payment can change in the first four years. For other higher-priced loans, a prepayment penalty period cannot last for more than two years. The rule also requires creditors to establish escrow accounts for property taxes and homeowner's insurance for all first-lien mortgage loans.

FHA's Hope for Homeowners Program

Policymakers enacted the Hope for Homeowners Program in July 2008 (H.R. 3221 / P.L. 110-289). This program allows lenders and borrowers to voluntarily refinance troubled mortgages into an FHA-insured loan. To participate, borrowers must certify that their loan was unaffordable as of March 2008 and lenders must agree to write-down the principal of the loan to a more affordable level. The program allows for up to $300 billion in FHA-insured loans in which the borrower would be responsible for 90% of the new appraised value. The lenders would write-down the loan an additional 4.5% to cover the one time premium and the first annual premium of the FHA insurance. Therefore, the lender must agree to write down the loan to 85.5% of the current appraised value, and in some areas the current appraisal may be significantly below the original loan balance. The FHA loan limit was increased in high cost areas to as much as $625,000. The act also provided for more flexibility for some of FHA's underwriting criteria.[11]

ANALYSIS OF NONTRADITIONAL MORTGAGES

GAO estimates that interest-only and other alternative mortgages approached 30% of the mortgage market by 2005.[12] Payments on these mortgages will reset to higher levels in the next few years. Although such products were sometimes used in the past by sophisticated borrowers as cash management tools, the recent housing boom saw alternative mortgages offered as affordability products to less sophisticated borrowers. Alternative mortgages were used by less wealthy borrowers in areas of high expected appreciation. The concentration of mortgage resets in time and in location can cause concerns for individual borrowers, for local real estate markets, and for financial institutions.

Payment Resets, Affordability Products, and Planned Refinances

The expanded use of alternative mortgages during the housing boom has created a wave of mortgage resets due in the next few years as the introductory periods expire. Not only do adjustable rate mortgages change their payments as interest rates change, but interest-only mortgages increase their payments when the full amortization period begins. Even if interest rates do not increase much further, the increase in monthly payments is substantial for many borrowers.

Table 1. Payment Reset for Interest-Only Mortgages

Interest Only (I/O) Feature and Payment Increases for $200,000 Loan at 6.5% Interest				
	Initial Payments	**Reset Payments**	**Change**	**Percentage Increase**
Traditional 30 Year Fixed	$1,264	$1,264	$0	0%
I/O, Reset Year 5	$1,083	$1,328	$245	23%

Source: Table prepared by the Congressional Research Service (CRS).

Table 2. Payment Reset for Adjustable Rates Mortgages

Interest Rates and Monthly Payments Fully Amortizing $200,000 Loan, 30 Years Rate Resets After 3 Years		
	Interest Rate	**Monthly Payment**
	4%	$971
	5%	$1,082
Base Rate	**6%**	**$1199**
	7%	$1322
	8%	$1449
	9%	$1582
	10%	$1718

Source: Table prepared by the Congressional Research Service (CRS).

Table 3. Payment Driven Loan Qualification

$200,000 Loan Using 28% Qualifying Ratio		
Loan Type	**Payment**	**Qualifying Income**
I/O Years 1-5	$1,083	$46,428
FRM 30 Years	$1,264	$54,177
I/O Years 6-30	$1,328	$56,950

Source: Table prepared by the Congressional Research Service (CRS).

Consider a $200,000 interest-only loan originated at a time when the prevailing mortgage rate is 6.5%. The interest-only period lasts four years then the loan amortizes over the final 26 years at the 6.5 percent rate. The monthly payments during the interest-only period will be $1,083. The monthly payments increase to $1,328 after four years. Even though the borrower will not be affected if interest rates rise above 6.5 percent, monthly payments will still rise $245 per month. *Table 1* compares this hypothetical interest-only loan to a similar fully amortizing fixed rate mortgage. Although the early payments of the interest-only mortgage are lower than the traditional mortgage, the later payments are higher.

Unlike interest-only mortgages, adjustable rate mortgages could have declining payments as well as rising payments. Adjustable rate mortgages were very common in the 1980s when interest rates were high and many people expected mortgage rates to fall. The concern with more-recent adjustable rate mortgages is that their original rate was near historic lows so it is probable that the prevailing interest rate will be higher when they reset.[13] (Interest rate risk will be discussed in greater detail below.) *Table 2* presents sample payment resets after three years for a $200,000 mortgage if interest rates rise or fall by a few percentage points. If the interest rate was originally 6%, then the monthly mortgage payment is $1199. If interest rates rise to 8%, then the monthly mortgage payment rises to $1449. On the other hand, if interest rates fall to 4%, then the monthly payment would drop to $971.

Sophisticated borrowers have used alternative mortgages to manage their cash flow for a long time. Consider a person who can qualify for any type of loan and has plenty of savings for contingencies. If the person must move frequently for work, then the person might not care much about the size of later payments because the loan will not extend that long. If a couple starts in a one-bedroom condominium but expects to move when they have children, then they might not want a traditional mortgage. If the person has other interest-rate-sensitive investments, then the person might use the mortgage as a hedge. For example, the holder of adjustable rate bonds would lose if interest rates fell but could offset part of that loss through an adjustable rate mortgage.

Alternative mortgages were marketed as affordability products to lower income and less sophisticated borrowers during the housing boom. This raises concerns that some home buyers applied for more debt than they could qualify for using traditional underwriting standards. Lenders may have qualified them for the greater debt through these alternative products. In some cases, underwriting standards became more lax even using traditional qualifying ratios because the process was based on the early years of an alternative mortgage product's payments. As a result, underwriters are now qualifying people based on the maximum payment, called the fully indexed rate.

Consider again the $200,000 loan at 6.5% presented in *Table 1.* Traditionally, lenders presumed that there was a cap on the percentage of household income borrowers could devote to housing costs. If that cap was 28%, and the traditional 30-year fixed rate mortgage had monthly payments of $1,264, then a borrower would need an income of $54,177 to qualify for the traditional loan. A borrower with a lower income could not qualify for that loan and presumably could not buy the house.

The interest-only loan presents an interesting qualifying issue. If households can devote 28% of income to housing costs, then an income of $46,428 qualifies for the early years of the loan. However, an income of $56,950 would be required for the later years of the interest-only loan. *Table 3* compares the income required to support the monthly payment assuming that households can devote 28% to housing costs. A borrower with only $46,428 might be tempted to take out a $200,000 loan using the interest-only product and then refinance the house when the payment reset.

A cash-constrained borrower's ability to successfully execute the planned refinancing would depend on the housing market. The borrower is relying on the expected appreciation of the house itself to help pay for the house. This is an example of a collateral-dependent loan which the 10/06 Guidance designates unsafe and unsound. It is not known how many of the loans due to reset in the next two years are collateral-dependent loans. The performance of these loans will depend on the housing market.

REASONS FOR THE RESETS: BOOMING HOUSE PRICES AND THE ATTRACTION OF ALTERNATIVE MORTGAGES

U.S. house prices appreciated rapidly in many regions during 2001 through 2005. Nationally, the Office of Federal Housing Enterprise Oversight (OFHEO) house price index (HPI) rose 51% over the five-year period. *Table 4* compares appreciation during the recent boom to appreciation in other five-year periods. The recent housing boom saw the fastest appreciation since 1980. The boom stands out even more when it is adjusted for inflation. Real house prices rose 34% between 2000 and 2005.

Table 4. U.S. House Price Appreciation, 1980-2005

Nominal and Real Change in OFHEO House Price Index (HPI) 5-Year Increments					
	1980-85	**1985-90**	**1990-95**	**1995-00**	**2000-05**
Nominal HPI	25%	37%	8%	26%	51%
Real HPI	-8%	14%	-9%	12%	34%

Source: Office of Federal Housing Enterprise Oversight (OFHEO)

Table 5. Annual House Price Appreciation, 2000-2006, by Metro Area

	2000	2001	2002	2003	2004	2005	2006	AVG 00-05
US National	**8.1%**	**6.5%**	**7.1%**	**8.2%**	**13.0%**	**12.9%**	**2.1%**	**9.3%**
West Palm Beach	8.7	11.2	13.6	17.0	27.1	28.7	0.2	17.7
Los Angeles	8.9	10.5	14.3	19.3	27.0	23.6	4.4	17.3
Miami	9.1	13.0	14.1	15.2	22.7	28.7	8.4	17.1
Washington	11.7	11.3	10.9	14.0	24.2	22.3	2.7	15.7
San Diego	13.4	11.9	16.6	17.7	25.9	8.7	-0.1	15.7
Las Vegas	6.6	5.9	5.9	18.3	34.9	16.6	1.3	14.7
Orlando	8.7	6.9	7.9	9.1	20.4	32.7	5.5	14.3
Phoenix	6.5	5.4	4.9	6.9	22.2	37.0	3.8	13.8
New York	10.8	10.9	11.3	11.8	16.3	16.6	1.9	13.0
San Francisco	19.2	2.9	6.6	6.3	18.9	15.1	1.2	11.5
Philadelphia	7.1	8.5	9.6	11.3	15.9	14.2	3.0	11.1
Boston	13.6	12.5	12.2	10.3	11.6	5.9	-1.2	11.0
Richmond	5.5	5.3	6.5	8.2	13.6	17.8	4.3	9.5
Minneapolis	11.0	10.2	8.3	8.7	9.5	6.7	0.3	9.1
Portland	5.0	4.0	4.0	6.0	12.7	12.6	7.5	8.9
Chicago	6.7	7.4	6.3	7.7	11.1	10.8	2.9	8.3
New Orleans	5.9	3.8	6.0	6.4	8.3	14.9	5.4	7.6
St. Louis	6.4	6.3	5.2	6.6	8.6	7.6	1.9	6.8
Birmingham	6.4	3.2	4.7	4.7	6.0	8.9	2.3	5.6
Pittsburgh	7.4	4.8	4.5	5.0	5.3	5.6	0.3	5.4
Denver	12.2	6.2	3.3	2.7	3.9	3.5	1.0	5.3
Kansas City	6.5	5.6	4.6	4.0	5.7	5.5	0.5	5.3
Atlanta	8.4	5.0	4.4	3.6	4.9	5.1	1.6	5.2
Buffalo	6.0	3.8	4.2	5.0	6.5	5.4	2.4	5.1

	2000	2001	2002	2003	2004	2005	2006	AVG 00-05
Nashville	5.2	2.8	2.6	3.7	6.2	9.2	4.8	5.0
Houston	7.1	4.0	4.6	3.4	4.7	5.8	2.8	4.9
Cincinnati	5.7	3.8	3.5	3.4	5.2	4.2	0.9	4.3
Detroit	7.4	5.4	3.6	3.4	3.4	1.8	-3.0	4.2
Dallas	7.1	4.1	3.7	2.1	3.1	4.1	1.9	4.0
Charlotte	5.9	2.4	2.9	2.2	4.2	6.1	4.4	3.9
Cleveland	5.6	3.3	3.6	3.8	4.0	2.6	-0.8	3.8

Source: OFHEO HPI, calculated 1st Quarter to 1st Quarter

Table 6. Appreciation, Home Equity, and Loan to Value (LTV)

Appreciation Contribution to Home Equity $200,000 House, Zero Down, I/O Loan Reset Year Appreciation Rate (Annual Percent)										
Beginning Year	0% Equity	LTV	5% Equity	LTV	10% Equity	LTV	15% Equity	LTV	20% Equity	LTV
1	0	1	$0	1.00	$0	1.00	$0	1.00	$0	1.00
2	0	1	10,000	0.95	20,000	0.90	30,000	0.85	40,000	0.80
3	0	1	20,000	0.90	42,000	0.79	64,500	0.68	88,000	0.56
4	0	1	31,525	0.84	66,200	0.67	104,175	0.48	145,600	0.27
5	0	1	43,101	0.78	92,820	0.54	149,801	0.25	214,720	-0.07

Source: CRS Calculations.

The distinction between nominal and real house prices is important. Mortgage contracts are almost always specified in nominal terms. This means that a fall in the real price might not cause a borrower to be upside down on the mortgage if inflation is high enough to counteract the real price decline. This scenario occurred in the early 1980s and the early 1990s. On the other hand, analysts considering the return to housing as an investment often focus on real prices.[14] Although real prices can be important for long term trends in the composition of household savings, nominal prices are more important for determining the stress on borrowers as their payment reset date nears.

Prices rose even more rapidly in some markets. *Table 5* compares the annual appreciation rate of some U.S. cities during 2000 through 2006. The extremely rapid rise in certain markets led to concerns that the 1990s stock bubble had been replaced with a housing bubble.[15] For example, Las Vegas house prices rose 34.9% in a single year, 2004. Orlando's house prices rose 32.7% in 2005. Seven of the cities listed in *Table 5* experienced five consecutive years of appreciation rates exceeding 10% per year. Then in 2006, the housing market slowed dramatically, as shown by the significant decline in the appreciation rate in each of the 31 cities listed in *Table 5.*

Markets with rapid appreciation reduce the ability of first-time buyers to save for down payments. A 20% down payment on a $200,000 house is $40,000. If prices rise 10%, then the 20% down payment rises to $44,000. The down payment becomes a moving target. In areas with rapid home price appreciation, the required down payment may be growing faster than household income. Potential first time buyers may fear being permanently priced out of the market if they do not enter the market as soon as possible.

While rapid home price appreciation may outstrip the savings of renters, an owner's home price appreciation actually increases household savings. Home equity is a form of savings for home owners. Including the growth in home equity, savings rise faster if the household is an owner in a rapidly appreciating market but the household can't become an owner until it has accumulated sufficient savings for a down payment. A mortgage with a low down payment that is designed to be refinanced after a few years could allow the prospective first-time home buyer to get in to the market and take advantage of the house's growing equity.

Rapid appreciation can reduce the time needed for credit enhancement. Lenders typically require some form of credit enhancement if the value of the loan is more than 80% of the value of the property. This loan-to-value ratio (LTV) of 0.8 corresponds with the traditional 20% down payment. One way that buyers with less than 20% down enhanced their credit was through private mortgage insurance (PMI). However, the PMI monthly premium counted towards the funds that underwriters assumed households could devote to housing costs. The more quickly that a household can lower LTV and eliminate the need for PMI, the greater the percentage of the household's total monthly payment can be devoted to paying off the loan.

In rapidly appreciating markets, the effect of growing equity on potential savings and on the need for PMI made alternative mortgages with planned refinances a potential affordability product. If first time buyers could just get into the rising market, then the growing equity would provide sufficient savings to lower LTV and eliminate the need for PMI by the time they had to refinance. Similar logic applies if buyers replace PMI with a piggy back loan at a higher interest rate because the need for the second loan at a higher rate is eliminated when equity rises.

Table 6 presents the growth of equity and reduction in LTV for a $200,000 interest-only loan for various appreciation rates. If appreciation rises 10%, then by the beginning of year three the equity increases to $42,000 and the LTV falls to 0.79. In this case, the buyer who put zero down and paid only interest would be able to refinance into a loan without credit enhancement because the drop in LTV is the equivalent of the 20% down payment. The time required to reduce LTV enough to eliminate credit enhancement decreases as the appreciation rate rises.

The preceding discussion showed two ways that zero down payment and interest-only mortgages could have been used as affordability products. First, if qualification is payment driven, then lower-income borrowers could be qualified based on the payments required during the introductory period of interest-only mortgages. *Table 3* showed that a household with $46,428 income could qualify for the early payments of a $200,000 loan at 6.5% interest, even though that loan would have traditionally required an income of $54,177 to qualify. Second, price appreciation during the introductory period could lower LTV, eliminate the need for credit enhancement, and allow the household to devote more funds to the house payment. *Table 6* showed that 10% annual appreciation can eliminate the need for PMI by the beginning of the third year of payments.

Problems arose when the housing market weakened further. Some of these borrowers are not able to refinance prior to their payment reset dates because their houses failed to appreciate at the expected rate.

Negative Appreciation: Consequences for Resets

Borrowers using alternative mortgages to take advantage of appreciation are exposed to the risk that house prices will fail to appreciate or even decline in price. Recall that *Table 5* showed that the rate of appreciation slowed across the country in 2006. In some formerly hot markets, prices declined in 2006 and the first half of 2007. As payment reset dates approach, many borrowers who used alternative mortgages as affordability products will wish to refinance. Their ability to refinance is obstructed, in many cases, by the failure to achieve home equity through price appreciation.

Local factors usually play a dominant role in determining regional house prices. Because of the role the job market plays in household income, analysts assume the local unemployment rate is important even in the absence of other information. For example, David Lereah, chief economist for the National Association of Realtors, emphasized the labor market in a presentation to residents of Charleston, SC. "Your unemployment situation is very positive ... I really don't know the local industries in Charleston other than tourism, but whatever it is, it's doing a good job."[16] Although Lereah went on to discuss migration patterns and other factors, the stress on labor markets is unmistakable.

Because local economies often play such a crucial role in house prices, one might think that the price risks embodied in low down payment mortgages is only a problem if an area's unemployment rises. While it is true that an increase in local unemployment can help drive down house prices, it is important to note that prices can fall even if the local labor market is healthy. The next sections show how different metro areas can have divergent price trends but that the recent house price slowdown is widespread and independent of local unemployment.

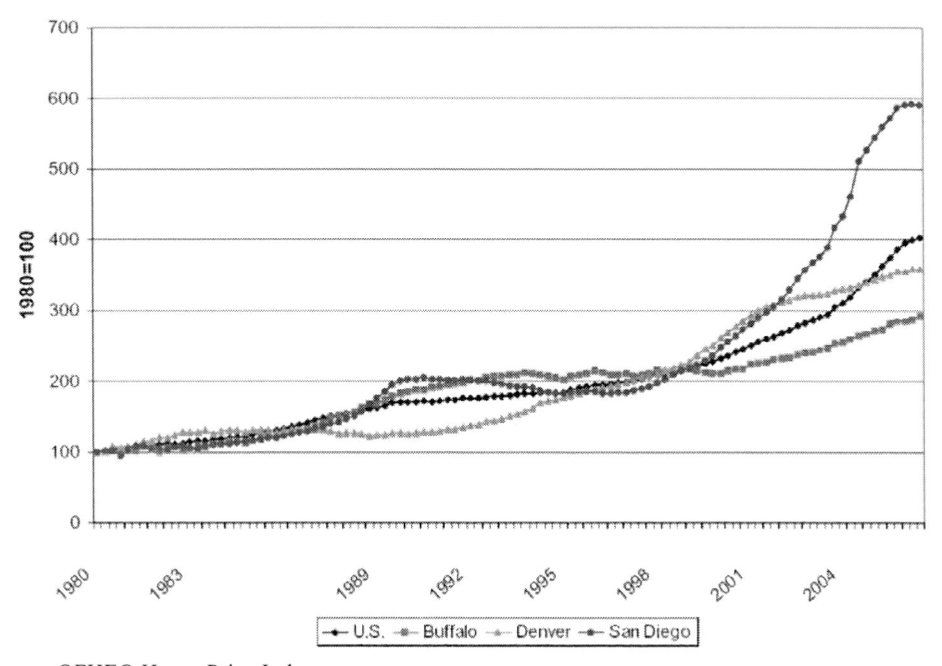

Source: OFHEO House Price Index.

Figure 4. Comparison of Appreciation for 3 Cities, 1980-2005.

Table 7. Local Unemployment and Slowing Appreciation

Local Unemployment and Slowing Appreciation				
Market	**Unemployment**		**Appreciation**	
	10/05	**10/06**	**2005**	**2006**
Phoenix	4.2%	3.4%	37.0%	3.8%
San Diego	4.2	3.6	8.7	-0.1
Los Angeles	4.5	3.9	23.6	4.4
New York	5.8	4.1	16.6	1.9
Miami	3.7	3.5	28.7	8.4
Washington	3.0	2.9	22.3	2.7
Las Vegas	3.7	4.0	16.6	1.3
Orlando	3.1	2.8	32.7	5.5

Source: OFHEO and BLS.

House prices in different metro areas do not always follow the national trend or move in the same direction. Recall again the wide range of appreciation rates for the cities presented in *Table 5*. San Diego's houses appreciated over 15% per year during 2000-2005, but Denver and Buffalo were closer to 5% per year. *Figure 4* tracks house prices for San Diego, Buffalo, and Denver from 1980 to 2005. They do not follow the national average nor do they follow similar patterns. Denver's prices rose more quickly in the early 1980s, when San Diego and Buffalo stagnated. San Diego boomed in the late 1980s but then fell in the 1990s. Buffalo's prices followed a more stable trajectory. Differences in the local economies of the three cities contributed to the divergent paths of home prices.

Many of the biggest house price slowdowns in 2006 cannot be attributed to shocks to local job markets. For example, Boston's appreciation rate dropped during 2004-2006 even though the Massachusetts labor market remained stable. Boston's appreciation rate fell from 11.6% in 2004, to 5.9% in 2005, and finally fell 1.2% in the first three quarters of 2006. Yet the Massachusetts unemployment rate remained close to 5% in all three years.[17] Despite a relatively stable labor market, Boston's house prices stopped appreciating.

The slowdowns in house price appreciation were widespread and occurred in areas with healthy job markets. *Table 7* compares local unemployment rate changes to the slowdown in appreciation for several of the formerly hot housing markets. Notice that the local unemployment rates were relatively unchanged in October 2006 compared to October 2005. Yet the rate of home price appreciation fell precipitously in each market. *Table 7* shows that the rate of appreciation experienced by home buyers while they are choosing their mortgage can decline drastically even if the local economy remains healthy.

Zero or negative appreciation in an otherwise healthy economy is a problem for borrowers who made very low down payments. If they used a piggy back loan to avoid PMI or used an interest-only loan and planned to refinance when they reached an LTV of 0.8, then they may have become upside-down on the mortgage. Borrowers with little savings are finding it difficult to refinance or sell a house before the reset date because their LTV has not improved (i.e., declined). Table 8 shows how declines in house prices affect the LTV of zero-down borrowers for a $200,000 interest-only loan.

If house prices depreciate 3% per year for two years, then the zero-down, interest-only borrower presented in *Table 8* will owe $11,820 more than the house is worth. Recall that one reason a borrower might have been attracted to the interest-only loan was because the borrower did not have the savings for a down payment. When the introductory period ends and the reset date arrives, the borrower's payments will rise. In this hypothetical example of a $200,000 interest-only loan in a period of 6.5% interest rates, *Table 1* shows that the reset payment would rise $245 per month after four years. The borrower must either find an additional $245 per month to maintain the current mortgage or $11,820 to cover the reduction in equity and try to refinance even if interest rates do not rise.

Interest Rate Risk

Although the risk of slowing house price appreciation is already a reality, interest rates are still relatively low. Problems could become more severe for consumers that used adjustable rates if mortgage rates rise despite Federal Reserve attempts to lower short term rates. A common form of alternative mortgage employs adjustable interest rates. Adjustable rate mortgages shift the risk of rising interest rates from the lenders to the borrowers. *Table 2* showed how a rise in interest rates could increase the payment on an adjustable rate mortgage. However, adjustable rate mortgages allow borrowers to benefit when interest rates fall. The availability and popularity of adjustable rate mortgages have changed with changing macroeconomic conditions.

When lenders held most of their loans in their own portfolio, fixed rate mortgages imposed significant costs when interest rates rose. The lenders' own costs of funds depended on the short-term interest rates prevalent as time progressed.[18] However, the lenders' income from their mortgages depended on the interest rates prevalent at the time the mortgages were originated. This is called borrowing short and lending long. Rising interest rates increase the lenders' cost of funds but the lenders' incomes do not rise. In response to strains on the banking sector as interest rates rose in the late 1970s and early 1980s, Congress encouraged wider use of adjustable rate mortgages.[19]

Mortgage rates are affected by conditions in the macroeconomy. Although the Federal Reserve does not directly set long term interest rates such as mortgage rates, Federal Reserve policy can determine short term interest rates and influence inflation. The mortgage rate incorporates expectations of future inflation because mortgages are repaid over long periods. *Figure 5* compares inflation, mortgage rates, and the Federal Reserve discount rate since 1972. The three are related but notice that the steep rise in the discount rate after 2003 has resulted in only a minor rise in mortgage rates during the same period.

Table 8. Negative Appreciation, Equity, and Loan to Value (LTV)

Negative Appreciation and Increasing Debt Burdens $200,000 House, Zero Down, I/O Loan Reset Year 5										
	0%		-1%		-2%		-3%		-4%	
Begin Year	Equity	LTV	Equity	LTV	Equity	LTV	Equity	LTV	Equity	LTV
1	$0	1.00	$0	1.00	$0	1.00	$0	1.00	$0	1.00
2	$0	1.00	$-2,000	1.01	$-4,000	1.02	$-6,000	1.03	$-8,000	1.04
3	$0	1.00	$-3,980	1.02	$-7,920	1.04	$-11,820	1.06	$-15,680	1.08
4	$0	1.00	$-5,940	1.03	$-11,762	1.06	$-17,465	1.09	$-23,053	1.12
5	$0	1.00	$-7,881	1.04	$-15,526	1.08	$-22,941	1.11	$-30,131	1.15

Source: CRS Calculations.

The 1980s exemplify an environment conducive to adjustable rate mortgages. Mortgage rates began to decline as the fear of inflation subsided. Expecting mortgage rates to fall, more people turned to adjustable rates. For example, 61% of the conventional mortgages originated in 1984 were adjustable.[20] Mortgage rates then declined from over 13% in 1984 to under 8% by 1993. Once mortgage rates stabilized, the popularity of adjustable rate mortgages declined. For example, only 12% of mortgages originated in 2001 were adjustable rates. This relatively longstanding response of borrowers to changing macroeconomic conditions distinguishes adjustable rate mortgages from the use of interest-only mortgages as affordability products described earlier.

The pattern of adjustable rate mortgages during the recent boom suggests that borrowers accepted interest rate risk at a time when interest rates were at historic lows. *Figure 5* showed that the mortgage rates prevailing in 2003-2005 represented 30-year lows. Consumers hedging against interest rate changes would be expected to lock in the historic low rates by borrowing at fixed rates. Yet the share of adjustable rates rose from 12% in 2001 to 34% in 2004, perhaps to take advantage of the large gap between short and long term interest rates. Although still well below the 61% share in 1984, the rising number of ARMs during a period of exceptionally low interest rates means that consumers shouldered additional interest rate risk as the boom progressed. There is evidence that this interest rate risk is concentrated in the formerly hot markets.

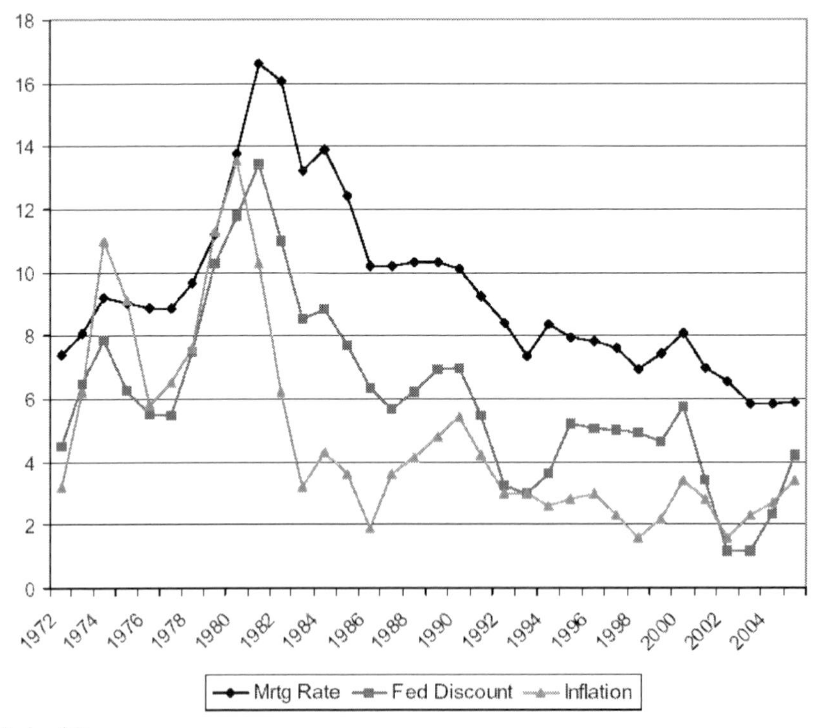

Source: Federal Reserve.

Figure 5. Mortgage Rate, Discount Rate, and Inflation, 1980-2005.

Geographic Correlation of Falling-House-Price Risk and Interest Rate Risk

Which regions are most vulnerable if a shortage of liquidity raises mortgage rates? Concentrated risk is important for cities as well as for financial institutions.

The presence of distressed neighbors affects the price that other sellers can get for their houses. If an area becomes concentrated with borrowers who are unprepared for payment shock and at the same time become upside down on their loans, then downward pressure can be put on housing prices. If this happens, then more homeowners will become upside down on their loans, reinforcing the problem. Exposure to the risk of rising interest rates is geographically concentrated in the areas that may be exposed to the risk of falling house prices.

The Federal Home Finance Board (FHFB) conducts a survey of the use of adjustable rate mortgages. The sample used for the survey excludes many important categories of nontraditional mortgages such as negatively amortizing loans. However, the survey can give some indication of the geographical concentration of some types of alternative mortgages and the exposure of some areas to the risk that inflation and interest rates will increase.

Table 9 uses FHFB data to show the use of adjustable rate mortgages and the recent slowdown in appreciation for 12 metropolitan areas from different parts of the country. The rates reported in *Table 9* are unweighted averages of the five most recent quarters in the FHFB survey.[21] An area is more immediately exposed to rising interest rates if a higher percentage of its loans will reset interest rates in the near future. By this measure, Dallas and Houston are probably less exposed to the risk that interest rates might rise in the near future while California cities appear more exposed to interest rate risk.

In addition to a rise in interest rates for adjustable rate mortgages, regions could suffer if their lenders and home buyers used low down payments and overestimated the rate at which their houses would appreciate. Prior to the issuance of the 10/06 Guidance, some borrowers may have been using expected appreciation to get into larger houses than they could have otherwise afforded. *Table 9* shows the decline in the rate of appreciation from 2005 to the first three quarters of 2006. To the extent that some borrowers counted on the rate of appreciation prevailing at the time they originated their loan to continue, a sudden deceleration in the rate of growth of prices will delay the time that they can achieve an LTV of 0.8 and get better terms when they attempt to refinance. Miami, California, and New York had comparatively large drops in appreciation and could have home buyers who made large mistakes when projecting appreciation rates.

Even though the appreciation rate might still be comparatively rapid, an unexpected drop in appreciation could still foil the plans of a low down payment buyer. For example, Miami's 2006 appreciation rate is still relatively high at 8%. However, if a zero-down Miami buyer in 2005 planned on appreciation of 20% per year and chose a mortgage that reset after one year, the 8% appreciation rate would not achieve the LTV of 0.8 to allow an improved refinance. The buyer wouldn't be upside down but would still pay more than expected costs because the loan might have to be refinanced more than once. Fees are paid each time a loan is refinanced.

Table 9 does not purport to measure the probability that a particular housing market will suffer severe stress. Instead, it is a very simple indication of a region's exposure to interest rate and falling-house-price risk. Industry analysts use more sophisticated methods to predict the probability that housing prices might fall in a particular market. The United States Market Risk index (USMR) is one such measure.[22]

The USMR index takes into account the local job market, recent price acceleration, and the affordability index. Weak job markets and low affordability tend to increase the risk of falling house prices. Stable recent appreciation tends to reduce the risk of falling house prices. *Table 10* presents the market risk index for selected cities. A value of 100 implies a 10% chance that house prices in the area will fall within two years.

Table 9. Adjustable Rate Mortgages and Price Slowdowns

Loan Resets and Price Slowdown by Metro				
	Share of Adjustable Rates '06	Appreciation Rate		Falling
		'05	'06	Appreciation '05-'06
Atlanta	31%	5%	2%	-3%
Boston	29%	6%	-1%	-7%
Chicago	40%	11%	3%	-8%
Dallas-Ft. Worth	11%	4%	2%	-2%
Denver	36%	4%	1%	-3%
Houston	9%	6%	3%	-3%
Kansas City	16%	5%	1%	-4%
Los Angeles	57%	24%	4%	-20%
Miami	36%	29%	8%	-21%
New York	30%	17%	2%	-15%
San Diego	62%	9%	0%	-9%
San Francisco	65%	15%	1%	-14%

Source: FHFB and OFHEO.

Table 10. Adjustable Rate Mortgages and the Market Risk Index

Metropolitan Area	Share of Adjustable Rates 06	PMI Risk Index
San Francisco	65%	587
San Diego	62%	603
Los Angeles	57%	590
Las Vegas	51%	540
Sacramento	48%	601
Phoenix	41%	353
Chicago	40%	147
Seattle	39%	153
Miami	39%	471
Denver	36%	187
Orlando	34%	313
Tampa	34%	404
Portland	32%	158
Atlanta	31%	201

Metropolitan Area	Share of Adjustable Rates 06	PMI Risk Index
Milwaukee	31%	140
New York	30%	543
Boston	30%	596
Virginia Beach	29%	413
Minneapolis	27%	393
Detroit	25%	379
Columbus	24%	74
Washington	22%	540
St. Louis	21%	133
Indianapolis	19%	63
San Antonio	17%	78
Kansas City	16%	109
Philadelphia	13%	179
Dallas	11%	89
Cincinnati	9%	72
Houston	9%	88
Pittsburgh	6%	61
Cleveland	3%	74

Source: FHFB and PMI Group.

Table 10 shows that areas with lower risk of falling house prices as measured by the PMI Group's USMR index tend to have fewer adjustable rate mortgages. The markets with a high percentage of adjustable rate mortgages are correlated with higher risk of falling house prices. Statistical analysis shows that the relationship of the risk of rising interest rates and the risk of falling house prices is positive.[23] There is a geographic concentration of mortgages vulnerable to rising interest rates and risks to any borrowers who made low down payments.

Washington, DC, and Chicago are notable exceptions. Chicago has a relatively high level of interest rate risk as measured by the share of adjustable rate loans but a low level of falling-house-price risk as measured by the USMR. Washington has a high risk of falling house prices but less interest rate risk.

A correlation of ARM share and the risk index does not imply causation. Nor is this a test of a formal model of the determination of regional ARM shares. *Table 10* merely shows that the interest rate risk inherent in adjustable rate mortgages is correlated with the risk of falling house prices identified by PMI's market risk index. The regions using ARMs tend to be the regions most susceptible to changes in macroeconomic conditions such as interest rate changes.

Recent Price Declines

The reversal in housing markets has been more severe than some regulators expected. In late 2006, OFHEO Chief Economist Patrick Lawler, for example, said "house prices continued to rise through the third quarter in most of the country, but generally at only low or moderate rates. The transition from sizzling markets to normal or weak markets has accelerated, and recent drops in interest rates have failed to stem precipitous price changes."[24] Although regulators may have been comforted by a study by the FDIC that reinforced the view that a slowdown in housing does not have to result in collapsing local markets, the result in 2008 has been falling house prices across the nation. Of 46 instances of housing booms in U.S. cities since 1978, 21 experienced a subsequent housing bust. In other words, more than half of the observations of housing booms were not followed by housing busts.[25] The housing busts that did occur were often associated with declines in the local area's predominant industries. In the present circumstances, however, housing markets declined even in areas with relatively healthy economies.

CONCLUSION

Mortgages with adjustable rates and interest-only options have been more widely used in recent years. Once only used by the financially sophisticated, products with significant payment adjustments have been marketed to low-income borrowers as affordable products. The performance of these products among lower-income borrowers in the current stressed environment has been problematic.

The Federal Reserve has issued changes to Regulation Z that may provide improved disclosures for all mortgages, including those with alternative features. In addition, other bank regulatory agencies have issued guidance covering alternative mortgages, but these guidances do not apply to many non-bank lenders in the subprime market. Lenders must disclose adequate information to consumers in plain English. Lenders must take steps to manage the risks of alternative mortgages. These steps include assessing borrowers' capacity to pay the entire potential balance of negative amortization loans and establishing risk management procedures for third party loan partners. Lenders may not rely solely on the ability to sell the property to qualify borrowers for a loan.

By choosing interest-only products, some consumers face the risk of falling house prices as their reset period approaches. Their prospects do not appear good. By choosing adjustable rate mortgages, some consumers have shifted interest rate risk from lenders to themselves. The geographical distribution of alternative mortgages suggests that falling-house-price risk and interest rate risk are concentrated in the same regions. It remains to be seen if interest rates will remain low, but it is clear that some consumers did not adequately prepare for slowing appreciation. Rising numbers of bankruptcies among lenders suggests that many financial institutions also failed to adequately assess relevant risks.

End Notes

[1] "Facing the Fallout from Foreclosures," *Community Banker*, November 2006. p. 40.

[2] "Falling Prices Trap New Home Buyers," *Orange County Register*, December 13, 2006.

[3] When a borrower owes more than the collateral is worth, the borrower is said to be upside down.

[4] Subprime borrowers typically have significantly lower credit scores or other indicators of high risk while Alt-A borrowers have better credit but may have some other defect, such as reduced income documentation.

[5] "The U.S. Subprime Market: An Industry in Turmoil," Thomas Zimmerman, UBS, [http://www.prmia.org/chapter_pages/data/files/1471_2576_zimmerman%20presentation _presentation.pdf].

[6] A silent second is a second loan. It is often used as a substitute for a downpayment so that the first loan receives a lower interest rate. These loans are also sometimes used so that the first loan will be below the conforming

loan limit and eligible for purchase by Fannie Mae and Freddie Mac, but then probably would not be found in this non-agency database.

[7] "Interagency Guidance on Nontraditional Mortgage Product Risks," *Federal Register*, vol. 71, October 4, 2006, p. 58613.

[8] The doctrine of suitability would impose a duty on lenders to ensure that a chosen mortgage product was suitable to the borrower's financial circumstances and goals.

[9] The Federal Reserve publishes the Consumer Handbook for Adjustable Rate Mortgages (CHARM Booklets). Regulation Z requires that consumers be given CHARM booklets in the shopping phase if they ask for, or are offered, adjustable rate mortgages.

[10] U.S. Government Accountability Office, *Alternative Mortgage Products: Impact on Defaults Remains Unclear, But Disclosure of Risks to Borrowers Could be Improved*, GAO-06-1112T, September 20, 2006. p. 2.

[11] For a discussion of FHA and related reform proposals, see CRS Report RS20530, *FHA Loan Insurance Program: An Overview*, by Bruce E. Foote and Meredith Peterson, and CRS Report RS22662, *H.R. 1852 and Revisiting the FHA Premium Pricing Structure: Proposed Legislation in the 110th Congress*, by Darryl E. Getter.

[12] *Alternative Mortgage Products*, September 20, 2006.

[13] Some adjustable rates are tied to short-term interest rates while traditional mortgages are long term. Some sophisticated borrowers choose adjustable or fixed rate mortgages based on the difference between short- and long-term rates, called the yield curve. For these borrowers, the steepness of the yield curve, not the relation of current mortgage rates to their long-term trend, would be the important consideration.

[14] Robert Schiller's critique of the housing market uses real prices and attempts to adjust for changes in housing quality. See "Be Warned: Mr. Bubble is Worried Again," *New York Times*, August 21, 2005.

[15] When asked about a national housing bubble, former Federal Reserve Chairman Alan Greenspan replied that there was no national bubble but that some markets showed signs of froth. *Testimony before the Joint Economic Committee*, June 9, 2005.

[16] "Realtors' economist rates area 'very healthy'" *The Post and Courier*, July 18, 2005, p. F8.

[17] Bureau of Labor Statistics, Series ID LASST25000003.

[18] Many lenders now sell their mortgages to investors in the secondary market reducing exposure to rising interest rates.

[19] Alternative Mortgages Parity Act, 1982. 12 U.S.C. sec. 3801.

[20] Federal Housing Finance Board, *2006 Mortgage Market Statistical Annual - Volume 1*, p. 17.

[21] The FHFB combines some MSAs for reporting purposes so there is not an exact match with the OFHEO price index.

[22] *Economic Real Estate Trends*, Fall 2006 p. 7. The index is published by the PMI Group which sells private mortgage insurance.

[23] Statistical analysis of the share of ARMs and the risk index shows a positive and significant correlation. [coefficient =9.2, t-stat =5.7, R-Squared = 0.72, df=30].

[24] OFHEO News Release, November 30, 2006.

[25] *U.S. Home Prices: Does Bust Always Follow Boom?*, FDIC, February 10, 2005.

In: America's Foreclosure Crisis
Editors: Russell Burns and Roy A. Foster
ISBN: 978-161942- 271-1

Chapter 4

THE PROCESS, DATA, AND COSTS OF MORTGAGE FORECLOSURE*

Darryl E. Getter, N. Eric Weiss,
Oscar R. Gonzales and David H. Carpenter

SUMMARY

The introduction of legislation such as H.R. 1106, the Helping Families Save Their Homes Act of 2009 (Representative John Conyers Jr. et. al.) serve as evidence of the concern in the 111th Congress over recent foreclosure activity. This report describes and analyzes foreclosure and related issues generated by the behavior of U.S. housing and mortgage markets.

Specifically, this report explains the foreclosure process, both from the point of view of a traditional financial lending institution, and from the viewpoint of securitization when loans are sold in secondary markets. The decision by the servicer to foreclose is also discussed, as are foreclosure data sources and recent foreclosure trends. Finally, this report examines estimates of average foreclosure costs and relevant computational issues.

INTRODUCTION

This report provides an analysis of the process, activity, and policy issues related to mortgage foreclosures. A description of the foreclosure process is presented, first in a traditional banking context, and then under securitization, when the loan originator no longer owns the distressed mortgage. A brief discussion is also included concerning what guides the decisions to foreclose. Next, the various foreclosure data sources are summarized. Lastly, some estimates of foreclosure costs are presented.

---

* This is an edited, reformatted and augmented version of Congressional Research Services Publication, No. RL34232, from www.crs.gov, dated September 23, 2009.

THE GENERAL FORECLOSURE PROCESS

The foreclosure process is governed by state law and varies widely by state. The description of the foreclosure process provided in this report is in general terms, first assuming a traditional lending framework, followed by a brief explanation of how the process works when the mortgage has been securitized.

Foreclosure under a Traditional Lending Framework

Foreclosure can begin after a borrower defaults on the mortgage loan.[1] Default is generally defined as being 90 days (or more) delinquent, although some lenders may use other definitions. Once in default, the lender must decide whether a loss mitigation or workout option would suffice, or whether to proceed with foreclosure (the process of recovering losses by repossessing and selling the property).[2] A financially motivated lender will try to select the option that minimizes losses.

Depending upon the state, a foreclosure process may take from several months to almost two years to complete. To ensure a valid transfer of title, the lender must prove that the borrower is in default, and follow various legal procedures prior to the authorization of a foreclosure auction. In states that follow a *judicial foreclosure* process, a foreclosure petition must be heard and ruled upon by a judge who examines all of the evidence in the case. In *power-of-sale* states, the lender holds a deed of trust with a clause that allows foreclosure without court action. Because of the additional legal work, foreclosure generally takes longer and is more costly to complete in judicial foreclosure states.

After proper notification requirements and other legal procedures have been completed, a foreclosure auction process begins. States typically require that the property owner be given advance notice regarding when the foreclosure auction will take place. In addition, a legal advertisement must appear in local news media announcing the time and place of the auction, a legal description of the property, and the sale terms and conditions. At the auction, the auctioneer may begin with a reading of the legal advertisement and then set a minimum bid. The highest bidder at the conclusion of the bidding period assumes title of (and responsibility for) the property.

If no one purchases the property above the minimum bid, the lender receives title; the property becomes *real estate owned* (REO), a term used for foreclosed houses that lenders carry until they can be resold by conventional means. Like any seller, the lender may need to incur expenses for deferred maintenance or outright damage before putting the property on the market. Lenders may hire the services of realty brokers, who are paid commissions, to sell REO properties. Meanwhile, the lender still incurs costs such as forgone interest, property taxes, and any other delinquent liabilities assumed from the previous borrower. Consequently, even if the property were sold at market value, the lender may incur losses. The stigma of being a REO property, however, may have the effect of reducing the list price below current market value. Furthermore, the lender may pay some or all of the closing costs to entice new buyers, just as any seller might do in any ordinary real estate transaction. Once title has been transferred to a new owner, the tabulation of the lender's total foreclosure costs, from borrower default to final property disposition, may begin.

The foreclosure process does not necessarily end after title of the property is transferred. Some states provide borrowers with a *statutory right of redemption*, which allows the borrower a period of time, perhaps longer than a full year, to repurchase the property after the foreclosure auction. Hence, the foreclosure sale is not final in these states until the end of the redemption period.[3] The length of time from initiation to completion of the foreclosure process, therefore, depends on whether the foreclosure must go to court and whether a right of redemption exists.

The discussion so far has focused upon a single lender foreclosing on a single mortgage. If the borrower used two loans to acquire the property, however, then two lenders would be affected. Suppose a borrower whose property has been foreclosed obtained a primary loan for 80% of the total needed amount and a "piggy-back" or secondary loan for the remaining 20%. After subtraction of legal and administrative costs, the proceeds of the foreclosure or REO sale go to pay off the primary lender first, and the lender of the secondary loan gets whatever is left over. Given that foreclosure costs can be substantial, the second lender risks not recouping anything on the unpaid secondary loan balance.

Foreclosure under a Structured Financing Framework

The term *lender* has so far been used in the traditional context in which a bank that originates a mortgage also holds it in portfolio. In modern financial markets, however, originators do not necessarily keep loans in their own portfolios. Loans originated in the primary market, where the home purchaser and the loan originator conduct business, are often sold in a secondary market, where the loan originator and an investor conduct business. The process of structured financing in the mortgage market involves the following steps.

First, a home buyer goes to an originator, which can be a financial institution or a mortgage broker, who approves and issues a mortgage loan. Second, the originator sells the loan to a securitizer. A securitizer can be a government-sponsored enterprise (GSE), such as Fannie Mae or Freddie Mac, or a private securitization trust. Third, the securitizer bundles the individual mortgages together and creates a new financial product, the mortgage-backed securities (MBS). Finally, the securitizer may sell MBS payment streams to investors, who become the ultimate "lenders." Investors may be hedge funds, pension funds, sovereign wealth funds, or other financial institutions. (If the securitizer decides not to sell the securities to third party investors and instead holds them in its own portfolio, then the securitizer becomes the investor.) MBS payment streams, which are called *tranches*, have specific risk or return requirements that meet various investor needs. For example, a securitizer may create a senior-junior tranching structure in which the senior tranche investors receive payment first, but their yield is lower than for the junior tranche investors. The senior tranche would appeal to investors who prefer lower risk investments, and the junior tranche would appeal to investors who prefer to take higher risks for the possibility of earning a higher yield. The senior-junior tranching structure is only one of the numerous disbursement structures securitizers can use to attract investors. This particular tranching structure, however, is used throughout this report for the sake of illustration.[4]

The key difference between the foreclosure process under traditional banking versus structured financing frameworks has to do with the amount of flexibility that the mortgage holder has to make important financial decisions if default occurs. Suppose the securitizer either acts as or appoints a *servicer*, who collects mortgage payments from borrowers and disburses these to the tranches. The investor and servicer negotiate rules that the servicer will follow while acting on the investor's behalf. If default occurs, servicer contract provisions (along with state law) determine (1) whether the servicer can offer loss mitigation solutions, and if so, of what types and with what limitations; (2) when the servicer can initiate foreclosure; (3) if the servicer may act as an agent at the foreclosure auction; and (4) any bidding rules the servicer must follow. For example, if a servicer can initiate foreclosure, the rules are likely to state how much can be bid (e.g., up to a certain percentage or the full amount of a borrower's unpaid balance) at a foreclosure auction. Given that the costs associated with foreclosure will be borne by the ultimate investors, the rules are designed to minimize those expenses.[5]

Any foreclosure costs generated from defaulted mortgages in a pool of MBS must be subtracted from the proceeds paid to the securitization trust. Suppose the securitizer is currently using the senior-junior tranching structure described above. If the senior tranche gets paid first, then the junior tranche will initially suffer the revenue loss. The investors in the senior tranche would be adversely affected should the number of foreclosures be greater than expected, and associated costs exceed the stream of revenues that would have been paid out to the junior tranche. Of course, fewer foreclosures can translate into the junior tranche holders being rewarded with higher yield than senior holders, which compensates them for assuming more default risk.[6]

More on Foreclosure Incentives

Lenders may try a loss mitigation solution with defaulted borrowers. While a workout may result in a reduction of revenues compared with the original mortgage agreement, the revenue loss may still be a less costly alternative to foreclosure. Of course, if a loan falls into default a second time after a loss mitigation option has been applied, the additional forgone interest expenses are also added to the overall foreclosure costs. Hence, loss mitigation may be a less costly alternative to foreclosure if it is successful in getting the mortgage loan to perform again. For this reason, lenders may be cautious and adopt different policies regarding the frequency of loss mitigation usage based upon their individual experiences.

Another consideration regarding the decision to foreclose is whether the mortgage loan carries mortgage insurance. Foreclosure costs can be reduced if some or all of the delinquent mortgage loss is covered by private or government mortgage insurance. Private mortgage insurance (PMI) is typically required by lenders when the borrower puts down less than 20% of the appraised value of the home. PMI pays the lender based on the outstanding balance of the loan, foreclosure costs, property maintenance costs, taxes, and hazard insurance. Federally insured mortgages, which are typically guaranteed up to 100% of the statutory maximums for eligible borrowers, are provided by the Federal Housing Administration (FHA) and the Veterans Administration (VA). When lenders file insurance claims, mortgage providers may either pay just a fraction of the loss (allowing lenders to retain title) or pay the full amount of the mortgage balance and take title to the property (and then decide whether to proceed with foreclosure). Consequently, a lender incurring a loss from a defaulted mortgage, in particular one with private insurance, may decide to initiate foreclosure and pass on some of the loss to the mortgage insurance provider.[7]

As stated earlier in this report, however, the foreclosure decision is usually guided by the contracts negotiated by the lender or investor and the servicer. For example, the contracts typically specify how servicers will get paid and reimbursed for expenses. Suppose a servicer collects fees in the form of a commission, which may be calculated as a percentage of the interest (or mortgage coupon) paid by the borrower. Under this arrangement, payment occurs as long as the mortgage loan is performing, so a foreclosure would translate into a lost income stream. There may even be additional financial penalties associated with the inability to get delinquent loans to re-perform. Some servicing firms have incentive compensation plans that *deduct* money from employees unable to avoid completing foreclosure.[8] Servicers who acquire a reputation for not being able to get a sufficient number of loans to re-perform may risk being unable to obtain future servicing rights for other types of loans (e.g., for automobiles or credit cards). Hence, some payment structures provide servicers the incentive to avoid foreclosure.

Some servicing agreements may not allow servicers to have much discretion. For example, for mortgages that Fannie Mae holds in its portfolio, servicers must follow guidance on how to proceed with loss mitigation solutions.[9] The servicer must first get written permission from Fannie Mae before implementing a loss mitigation solution as well as follow guidances on how to implement the solution. Given that it is subject to various capital requirements, accounting, and tax rules, Fannie Mae must purchase a delinquent mortgage from its MBS pool before a loss mitigation solution can be applied. As a result, Fannie Mae monitors and approves all decisions concerning troubled loans in its portfolio. Similarly, FHA servicers must follow FHA guidelines for troubled loans. FHA servicers, however, have more discretion over how to get troubled loans to re-perform. FHA, a federal mortgage insurance company, does not face the capital requirements and tax consequences of a private mortgage securitizer. Hence, FHA *requires* its servicers to participate in the FHA Loss Mitigation Program and avoid foreclosure if at all possible.[10] Servicers cannot simply file a claim on a troubled mortgage and convey title of the property to FHA without permission from the Department of Housing and Urban Development (HUD). FHA servicers will not be reimbursed unless they show evidence of adherence to FHA policies and procedures regarding troubled loans.

Because of the various contractual arrangements that loan servicers are obligated to follow, borrowers cannot necessarily avoid foreclosure by contacting their servicers. In some cases, present and future compensation for servicers depends on the number of loans they can get to perform, which encourages servicers to try solutions to avoid completing foreclosure; in other cases, servicers may have limited authority and options.[11] Consequently, understanding why servicers may or may not complete the foreclosure process requires an understanding of the servicing contractual agreements or guidelines attached to the various mortgage loans.

MEASURING U.S. FORECLOSURES

The federal government does not collect mortgage foreclosure data; various private data sources are therefore used to measure foreclosure developments. Different sources employ different approaches to measuring foreclosures. One approach is to look at the number of foreclosures as a percentage of mortgages outstanding. Another approach is to count the number of foreclosure filings or starts. The selected measurement approach may affect whether changes in foreclosure activity are viewed as being more or less severe. This section examines some key differences in the various data sources as well as interpretation caveats.

Foreclosure Data Sources

The National Delinquency Survey

The Mortgage Bankers Association (MBA) reports on the percentage of delinquencies and foreclosure filings in its quarterly National Delinquency Survey (NDS).[12] The NDS sample consists of more than 40 million loans serviced by mortgage companies, commercial banks, thrifts, credit unions, and other servicing institutions.[13] This measurement approach counts foreclosures as a percentage of outstanding mortgage loans. The NDS data include delinquency and foreclosure information about primary or first-lien mortgage loans at the state, regional and national levels. Homes that have *completed* the foreclosure process and are currently sitting in REO inventory are no longer included in the foreclosure data. The NDS dates back to 1979.

RealtyTrac

RealtyTrac, an on-line real estate marketplace designed to facilitate real estate transactions, reports monthly on the total number of properties with at least one foreclosure filing.[14] The foreclosure data are compiled from approximately 2500 counties, using data from courthouses and newspapers. Data are obtained at the address level and can be aggregated to zip code, county, metropolitan, and state levels. RealtyTrac counts properties in the default or pre-foreclosure period, the auction period, and those properties sitting in REO. RealtyTrac data have been collected since 1996.

Loan Performance Securitized Subprime Loans

Loan Performance provides information on mortgage financing, servicing, and securitization.[15] A Loan Performance data subscriber or client may access its database and receive delinquency, bankruptcy and REO information for more than 75% of U.S. prime first-lien mortgages, including the portfolios of Fannie Mae and Freddie Mac. Loan Performance also provides this information for its repository of subprime mortgage loans, home equity lines of credit and secondary mortgage loans, and jumbo (mortgages exceeding the GSE purchase limits) loans.[16] Loan Performance data are collected monthly at the zip code, core based statistical area, county, and state levels. Loan Performance has been in business for over 20 years.

Credit Bureau Data

Experian, Equifax, and TransUnion are three national U.S. credit reporting agencies that collect data on consumer payment activity, which can be used to capture trends in borrowing and payment behavior.[17] These data contain useful borrower credit usage and repayment information pertaining to all types of credit—automobile, credit card, other installment debt, as well as mortgage debt. Taking on additional amounts of debt or being 90 days or more delinquent on a mortgage payment can signal higher mortgage foreclosure risk. If a consumer has experienced a pre-foreclosure sale or a completed foreclosure, this information also appears on the credit report.[18] Individual credit report information can be aggregated to local, state, or regional levels to identify geographic areas with neighborhood traits more prone to foreclosure risk.[19]

Measurement Issues

Given that not all properties that begin a foreclosure process will complete it, foreclosure starts represents an "upper-limit" of completed foreclosures. Foreclosure starts or filings refer to the filing of legal documents during various stages of the foreclosure process. As previously described, many states require lenders to file a notice of foreclosure to begin the process. A borrower and servicer can nonetheless resolve a repayment problem and avoid completing foreclosure. Some states require a lender or servicer to file an initial notice of foreclosure intent followed by another filing when the foreclosure sale takes place. Consequently, if every filing is counted as a new foreclosure, then multiple counting will inflate or severely overstate foreclosure activity.[20] This report uses the NDS data, which provide an upper-limit measure of completed foreclosures, to track foreclosure activity.

Tracking Foreclosure Activity

The data on foreclosure rates used in *Figure 1* and *Figure 2* come from the NDS. The figures include data on foreclosure filing rates for prime loans, FHA insured loans, subprime loans, and a composite rate for all foreclosed loans. The foreclosure rate for each loan category is computed as the total number of foreclosures filed at the end of the quarter divided by the total number of loans in that particular category. The loan categories are defined as follows:

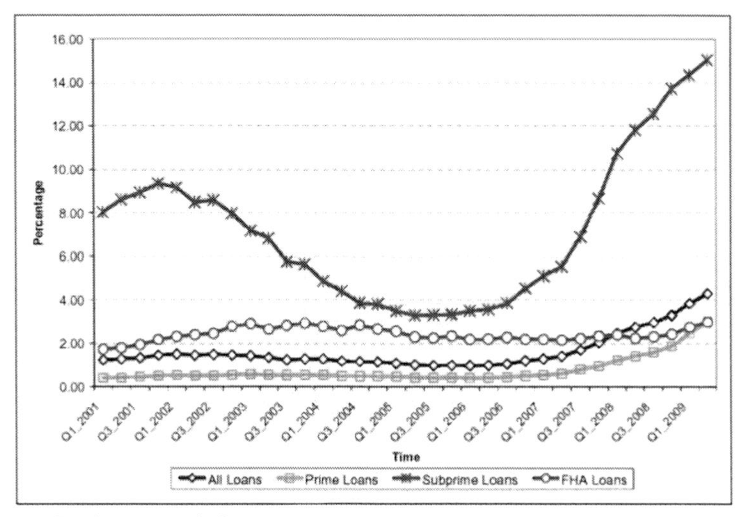

Source: Mortgage Bankers Association.

Figure 1. Percentage of Foreclosures by Aggregate Category.

- Prime loans, typically made to creditworthy borrowers who meet the standards set by the GSEs.[21]
- Alternative or "Alt-A" loans, which typically meet the GSE credit score requirements; they do not meet the standard requirements for documentation, property type, debt (or qualifying) ratios, or loan-to-value (LTV) ratios. FHA targets Alt-A borrowers, although it does insure loans for borrowers with lower credit scores. FHA also allows more flexibility with respect to debt and LTV ratios than prime lenders, and FHA borrowers must comply with standard documentation requirements.
- Subprime loans are primarily made to borrowers with impaired or limited credit. Subprime loans do not have to meet the GSE credit score requirements, and other standard underwriting requirements may also be waived, including standard documentation requirements.

Figure 1 indicates that subprime foreclosure rates since 2001 have consistently been greater than prime and FHA foreclosure rates. When housing prices were rising and interest rates were falling between 2002 and 2005, the overall foreclosure rate for prime loans was steady, while subprime foreclosure rates declined markedly.[22] Foreclosures began to rise in early 2006, and have continued rising.

The average foreclosure rate for all subprime loans from 2006 to the first quarter of 2009 was 8.56%, whereas the average foreclosure rate for all FHA loans was 2.35%. The foreclosure rate for all prime loans averaged 1.16%. Given a low prime foreclosure rate relative to the other loan type categories and the fact that prime loans make up a larger share of the mortgage market, the overall foreclosure rate for all loans in the survey averaged 2.16%. The maximum foreclosure rate over the entire period for all loans in the survey was 4.30%, which occurred during the second quarter of 2009. The rise in the overall foreclosure rate since 2006, therefore, reflects the large increase in subprime foreclosure rates.

In *Figure 2*, the composite categories have been further separated into fixed rate mortgage (FRM) foreclosures and adjustable rate mortgage (ARM) foreclosures. From 2006 to the first quarter of 2009, subprime foreclosure rates were again the highest, followed by FHA, and then prime loans. Foreclosure rates averaged 4.37% for subprime FRM loans, 13.09% for subprime ARM loans, 2.12% for FHA FRM loans, 3.42% for FHA ARM loans, 0.71% for prime FRM loans, and 3.20% for prime ARM loans. The NDS does not report composite foreclosure rates for all FRM loans or all ARM loans. Based upon the information provided here, however, the overall FRM and ARM composite foreclosure rates are likely to be much lower than the equivalent rates computed for the subprime and FHA categories. Furthermore, the composite series of FRM loan foreclosure rates is likely to be lower than the composite series of foreclosure rates for ARM loans.[23] The descriptive data in *Figure 2* indicate that many foreclosures were associated with ARMs and particularly subprime ARMs.

Microeconomic factors that help explain foreclosures include unanticipated changes in economic or personal circumstances. Examples of unanticipated changes in personal circumstances include divorce, sudden changes in health, and job loss. Given no abnormal rise in national divorce rates or debilitating medical injuries, those reasons do not fully explain the recent rise in foreclosures. Foreclosures could potentially be attributed to local labor market conditions. For example, foreclosures in Ohio rose when its unemployment rate rose to approximately one percentage point higher than the annual U.S. national unemployment rate (5.5% compared with 4.6% in 2006). Rising job losses, however, still cannot entirely account for aggregate developments. Florida, for instance, had unemployment rates at or below the U.S. national average during 2006, yet the state still experienced a marked rise in foreclosures. Hence, unanticipated changes in personal circumstances do not entirely explain the recent rise in foreclosures.

Regional and more widespread macroeconomic factors that can translate into a rise in foreclosures include a slowdown in sales activity and the rate of house price appreciation. Declining sales activity increases the difficulty of borrowers with cash flow problems to avoid foreclosure because they cannot quickly sell their homes and reduce expensive mortgage payments. Falling house prices affects the ability to refinance a mortgage and may even encourage some borrowers to stop making mortgage payments altogether.[24] Homeowners with substantial equity in their homes arguably have a greater incentive to cooperate with the lender and renegotiate an arrangement to avoid foreclosure. Foreclosures are, however, more likely to occur when homeowners have little (10% or less) equity in their homes. If the market value of a house falls sufficiently below the value of the mortgage, or if very little or no downpayment was used to purchase the home, the borrower may have a financial incentive to walk away and not attempt steps to avoid foreclosure.[25]

According to national U.S. Census Bureau data, new home prices fell by 4.11% between June 2006 and June 2007, and new home sales were down by 22.18% during the same period. According to the National Association of Realtors, median existing home prices fell by 0.04% during the same period, and existing home sales declined by 11.25%.[26] Hence, selling a home or refinancing a mortgage, perhaps prior to an interest rate adjustment on an ARM loan that would result in a substantial increase in the monthly payment, would appear to be a less feasible option. Consequently, a rise in foreclosures would not be considered unusual given the recent decline in housing market activity. Housing market activity and foreclosure rates are cyclical and typically move in opposite directions.[27]

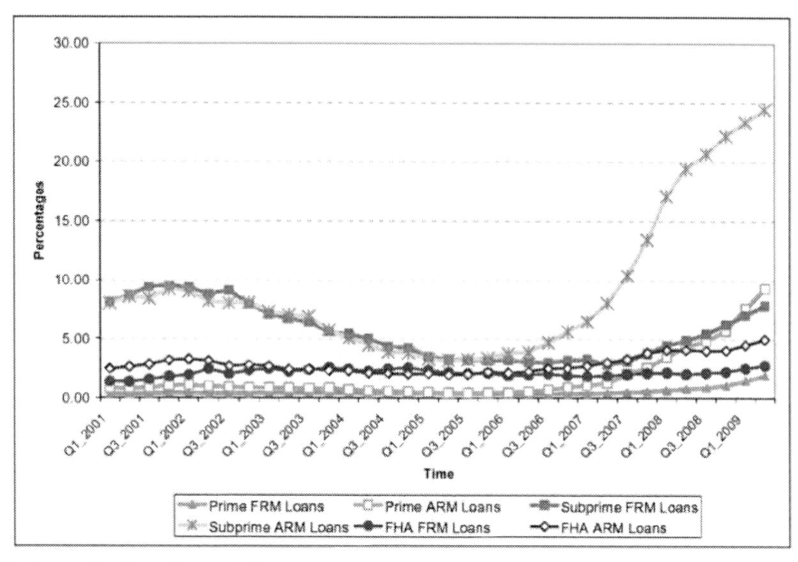

Source: Mortgage Bankers Association.

Figure 2. Percentage of Foreclosures, FRM versus ARM.

In addition to unanticipated housing market changes, the mortgage market also experienced structural changes, including the expansion of the subprime market. Prior to this expansion, people with impaired credit were unable to obtain home equity or cash-out refinance loans from prime market lenders. Furthermore, when home prices began to exceed the maximum FHA loan limits in various regions, credit impaired borrowers looked for alternative credit sources. Hence, the growth in subprime lending during the late 1990s and early to mid-2000s enabled people evaluated as having lesser credit quality to gain access to mortgage credit. By 2005, subprime loans accounted for an estimated 20% of all mortgage originations.[28] The recent housing market slowdown has revealed that subprime borrowers appear to be more susceptible than prime borrowers to changing housing market conditions, and perhaps also more susceptible than those who satisfy current FHA requirements for mortgage insurance.

ESTIMATES OF FORECLOSURE COSTS

Foreclosures are rarely profitable for lenders.[29] The legal fees, lost interest, property taxes, other delinquent obligations incurred by the former homeowners (e.g., association fees), and selling expenses make foreclosures costly to lenders.[30]

Although many studies provide dollar value estimates of foreclosure costs, it is difficult to know how cost estimates were obtained without access to proprietary data.[31] A study cited in a Freddie Mac working paper estimated the total costs of foreclosure for a sample of loans at approximately $58,759 per loan.[32] Those costs include the interest lost during the delinquency period, foreclosure costs, and disposition of the property—costs that the lender would be likely to incur. The working paper does not state explicitly if these costs were paid by the lender, nor whether the $58,759 was an average or median amount per foreclosure, but it did say the foreclosure process took an average of 18 months to resolve. Hence, this reported dollar amount may be fairly representative of the actual costs incurred only by a single lender, presumably in 2002.[33]

Foreclosure costs are far-reaching. In addition to losing their homes, borrowers are likely to find it difficult to obtain credit in the future, even at high interest rates. Lenders suffer the losses associated with acquiring the property from the borrower, settling outstanding claims, repairing any damages, and selling the property. Local governments may face the problem of vacant units in neighborhoods and loss of tax revenues. Foreclosure may reduce the value of neighboring homes. As a result, foreclosure is something that parties directly and indirectly involved with the property would want to avoid.[34]

End Notes

[1] For a primer on delinquency, default, foreclosure, and loan workouts, see Charles A. Capone, "Research Into Mortgage Default and Affordable Housing: A Primer," prepared for the Local Initiatives Support Corporation for Home Ownership Summit 2001, November 8, 2001, available at http://www.lisc.org/files/906_file_asset_upload_file755_793.pdf.

[2] Loss mitigation or 'workouts' refer to a menu of possible options to avoid foreclosure. Lenders may choose from various options such as forebearance, rescheduling payments, or restructuring the loan, which may help distressed borrowers become current and continue to stay current in the payments. After forebearance or loan

modification, a borrower can become delinquent again. If borrower circumstances will not allow for a loan to re-perform, agreement to a pre-foreclosure sale or deed-in-lieu of foreclosure may also be viable options to mitigate losses.

[3] If a property sells for less than the current mortgage, there will be a remaining unpaid balance. The tax consequences on the unpaid mortgage debt vary according to state law. For more information, see CRS Report RL34212, *Analysis of the Tax Exclusion for Canceled Mortgage Debt Income*, by Mark P. Keightley and Erika K. Lunder.

[4] For more information on the securitization process, See CRS Report RS22722, *Securitization and Federal Regulation of Mortgages for Safety and Soundness*, by Edward V. Murphy.

[5] See CRS Report RL33775, *Alternative Mortgages: Causes and Policy Implications of Troubled Mortgage Resets in the Subprime and Alt-A Markets*, by Edward V. Murphy.

[6] The liquidity problem of August 2007 was triggered by senior tranche holders reassessing the riskiness of their exposure to financial problems. See CRS Report RL34182, *Financial Crisis? The Liquidity Crunch of August 2007*, by Darryl E. Getter et al.

[7] FHA typically assumes all of the borrower's default risk by insuring 100% of the mortgage loan. After a default, the agency pays an insurance claim filed by the lender. FHA can then decide whether to initiate foreclosure and dispose of the property.

[8] See http://www.ocwenbusiness.com/documents/pdf/Congressional_Testimony.pdf.

[9] See https://www.efanniemae.com/sf/guides/ssg/annltrs/pdf/2006/0627.pdf.

[10] See http://www.hud.gov/offices/adm/hudclips/letters/mortgagee/files/00-05.doc.

[11] See CRS Report RL34386, *Could Securitization Obstruct Voluntary Loan Modifications and Payment Freezes?*, by Edward V. Murphy and CRS Report RL34372, *The HOPE NOW Alliance/American Securitization Forum (ASF) Plan to Freeze Certain Mortgage Interest Rates*, by David H. Carpenter and Edward V. Murphy.

[12] See http://www.mbaa.org/ResearchandForecasts/ProductsandSurveys/National Delinquency Survey.htm.

[13] For more information about the Mortgage Bankers Association and the National Delinquency Survey, please go to http://www.mbaa.org.

[14] See http://www.realtytrac.com/.

[15] See http://www.loanperformance.com/.

[16] The Federal Reserve Bank of New York has currently made county-level subprime data from the Loan Performance database available on its website at http://www.newyorkfed.org/regional/subprime.html.

[17] See http://www.experian.com, http://www.equifax.com/home, http://www.transunion.com/, and http://findarticles.com/p/articles/mi_m1094/is_1_35/ai_59964463.

[18] According to one report, a homeowner's credit score may drop by 200 to 300 points after a pre-foreclosure sale, deed-in-lieu of foreclosure, or an actual foreclosure. See http://homebuying.about.com/od/4closureshortsales/qt/ 060907SScredit.htm. When this report was written, no information could be found directly on the websites of the credit bureau agencies to verify the numerical score deductions reported on the cited blogsite.

[19] For empirical academic discussions on the use of credit history data as a predictor of foreclosure, see Michael Grover, Laura Smith, and Richard M. Todd, "Targeting Foreclosure Interventions: An Analysis of Neighborhood Characteristics Associated with High Foreclosure Rates in Two Minnesota Counties," *Federal Reserve Bank of Minneapolis Community Affairs Report No. 2006-1* (Revised June 2007) at http://www.minneapolisfed.org/community/ pubs/foreclosureinterventions.pdf; and Robert B. Avery, Raphael W. Bostic, Paul S. Calem, and Glenn B. Canner, "Credit Risk, Credit Scoring, and the Performance of Home Mortgages", *Federal Reserve Bulletin* (July 1996) at http://www.federalreserve.gov/pubs/bulletin/1996/796lead.pdf.

[20] See discussions pertaining to the reporting of overstated foreclosure numbers at http://www.msnbc.msn.com/id/22011114/, http://www.inman.com/news/2007/05/3/foreclosure-activity-62-last-year, and http://www.businessandmedia. org/printer/2007/20070907071643.aspx.

[21] For background and other information about GSEs, see CRS Report RS21724, *GSE Regulatory Reform: Frequently Asked Questions*, by N. Eric Weiss.

[22] FHA foreclosures saw an increase arguably because some of its more creditworthy borrowers were refinancing out of FHA. These borrowers were either obtaining prime loans and no longer paying FHA mortgage insurance premiums or they wanted to obtain cash-out refinances that exceeded the FHA loan limits, since house prices were rapidly appreciating. Hence, the rise in the FHA foreclosure rate might reflect a decrease in the denominator of total mortgage loans, rather than an increase in the numerator of total foreclosures.

[23] See CRS Report RL33775, *Alternative Mortgages: Causes and Policy Implications of Troubled Mortgage Resets in the Subprime and Alt-A Markets*, by Edward V. Murphy.

[24] In some cases, rising mortgage rates may have the same financial impact as falling house prices.

[25] See http://news.bbc.co.uk/1/hi/business/7529277.stm. Although a borrower with little home equity may not suffer a major financial loss after foreclosure, the subsequent ability to obtain loans may be severely affected for several years.

[26] The January 2006 to June 2007 time frame would have best coincided with the period that foreclosures began to rise (as reported by the NDS). Some of the housing price and sales data, however, are not seasonally adjusted, making it necessary to use the June 2006 to June 2007 period for computing annual rates.

[27] See Jan Hatzius, "Beyond Leverate Losses: The Balance Sheet Effects of the Home Price Downturn,"*Brookings Papers on Economic Activity*, (Fall 2008) Conference Draft, p. 20 at http://www.brookings.edu/economics/bpea/~/ media/Files/Programs/ES/BPEA/2008_fall_bpea_papers/2008_fall_bpea_hatzius.pdf; and John B. Taylor, "Housing and Monetary Policy," presentation at the *Policy Panel at the Symposium on Housing, Housing Finance, and Monetary Policy* sponsored by the Federal Reserve Bank of Kansas City (September 2007), p. 6, Figure 4 at http://www.stanford.edu/~johntayl/ Housing%20and%20Monetary%20Policy—Taylor—Jackson% 20Hole% 202007.pdf.

[28] See Robert B. Avery, Kenneth P. Brevoort, and Glenn B. Canner, "Higher-Priced Home Lending and the 2005 HMDA Data," *Federal Reserve Bulletin* (September 2008), p. A125.

[29] Fraudulent sellers, as opposed to lenders, may profit by successfully selling overvalued properties. Damaged properties may be sold at inflated prices using fraudulent appraisals or making shoddy repairs that pass inspections. Should home buyers suspect they may be victims of fraud and perhaps have loans higher than the actual property values, they may simply choose to walk away and allow the property to be foreclosed upon. Under these circumstances, the lender, who is likely to be saddled with an over-valued property that must be repaired and resold, may also be considered a victim of fraud.

[30] Although the generic 'lender' term is being used, this discussion is still applicable to investors who have servicers acting on their behalf.

[31] See Desiree Hatcher, *Foreclosure Alternatives: A Case for Preserving Homeownership,* Profitwise News and Views, published by the Federal Reserve Bank of Chicago (February 2006). The article mentions that GMAC-RFC (Residential Funding Corporation) reported losing $50,000 per foreclosed home.

[32] See Amy Crews Cutts and Richard K. Green, *Innovative Servicing Technology: Smart Enough to Keep People in Their Houses?,* Freddie Mac Working Paper #04-03 (July 2004). The authors cite Craig Focardi, *Servicing Default Management: An Overview of the Process and Underlying Technology,* TowerGroup Research Note, No. 033-13C (November 15, 2002). The $58,759 cited in the Freddie Mac report comes from Focardi's study.

[33] It is not clear whether the final sales price was subtracted from the gross costs in order to obtain the net cost of foreclosures to lenders. If this figure is net costs, then estimated foreclosure costs reflect current market conditions at the time the estimates were computed. Foreclosure costs are likely to be higher during 2006 and 2007 when housing market activity has slowed. Lenders would be unable to turn over foreclosed properties as quickly and market prices have declined in many areas over this period.

[34] The Joint Economic Committee estimates that foreclosures on average may cost as much as $80,000. This estimate includes costs to homeowners, loan servicers, lenders, neighbors, and local governments. See U.S. Congress, Senate Joint Economic Committee, *Sheltering Neighborhoods from the Subprime Foreclosure Storm*, Special Report by the Joint Economic Committee, 110th Cong., 1st sess. (Washington: GPO 2007) at http://jec.senate.gov/Documents/Reports/ subprime11apr2007revised.pdf.

INDEX

A

B

C

D

E

F

J

L

M

N

O

P

Q

R

S

T

U

V

W

Y

Z